French Feminisms

French Feminisms
Gender and violence in contemporary theory

Gill Allwood

Nottingham Trent University

UCL PRESS
UCL
PRESS
Taylor & Francis Group

© Gill Allwood 1998

Published in the UK in 1998 by UCL Press

UCL Press Limited
1 Gunpowder Square
London
EC4A 3DE

and

1900 Frost Road, Suite 101
Bristol
Pennsylvania 19007–1598
USA

The name of University College London (UCL) is a registered trade mark used by
UCL Press with the consent of the owner.

British Library Cataloguing-in-Publication Data
A catalogue record for this book is available from the British Library.

Library of Congress Cataloging-in-Publication Data are available

ISBN: 1–85728–802–5 HB
        1–85728–803–3 PB

Typeset by Graphicraft Typesetters Ltd., Hong Kong
Printed and bound by T.J. International Ltd, Padstow, UK

Contents

Series editor's preface   vii

Acknowledgements   ix

List of acronyms   xi

Introduction   1

1   French feminism: movement, theory and representation   25

2   French theories of masculinity   45

3   Difference   63

4   Gender   77

5   Feminism and male violence   99

6   Gender and violence   119

Conclusion   135

Notes   149

References   153

Index   165

Series editor's preface

This volume is a particularly apt illustration of the aims of this series, *Gender, Change and Society*. As the title suggests, this book clearly deals with issues of gender but is especially significant here in that it deals with gender as concerning both men and women, masculinity and femininity. Further, through concentrating on the topic of violence, these terms are seen in interaction rather than as topics standing in isolation from each other.

This contribution is also clearly and directly dealing with issues of change. It is, of course, the wider process of social and political change that have put issues of men's violence against women on to the agenda and Gill Allwood's book both reflects and contributes to these changes in perspective. However there are also more specific processes of change under consideration here, namely changes taking place within feminism partly as a result of the tensions and shifts between theory and practice and the ways in which a focus upon issues to do with men's violence inevitably, if unevenly, led to a critical examination of issues of men and masculinity themselves. Further, the book also points to issues of individual change as men come to look critically at their own practices and women shift from seeing themselves as victims of violence to more positive understandings around notions of "survivors".

The society in question here is French society. More specifically, in fact the book is dealing with constructions of French society, and French feminisms, both from outside and from within. One of the most valuable contributions of this text is the way in which it enables us to look past some conventional Anglophone constructions of French feminism (concentrating on three "big names") and to explore some of the complexities of feminism as an active movement, engaging with immediate individual and societal problems, rather than simply a body of rather complex theorizing. This is not to reject the role and significance of theory but to recognize that it can look rather different when seen through the prism of this particular issue of men's violence against women.

However, this is not simply a comparative study of a highly specific period of French history. While some of the issues considered and debated here can only be understood in their historical and political contexts, there is much here that will be recognized as relevant to the experiences of women and men in English speaking countries. In this careful exploration of debates around violence and masculinity, Gill Allwood constantly reminds the reader of commonalities of experience as well as of differences. This is the value of detailed comparative work of this kind.

David H.J. Morgan
University of Manchester

Acknowledgements

Many people have contributed to this project. The original research was funded by a British Academy Major State Studentship, and completion of the book was made possible by support from Nottingham Trent University and from my editor, Caroline Wintersgill. I am grateful to the Bibliothèque Marguerite Durand; the Collectif féministe contre le viol; the Association contre les violences faites aux femmes au travail; the Ligue du droit des femmes; and all those who agreed to be interviewed and who provided contacts, bibliographies and suggestions. In particular, I wish to thank Christine Delphy, Claire Duchen, Di Holmes, Marie-Victoire Louis, Joni Lovenduski, Ailbhe Smyth and the anonymous readers for their comments on various versions of parts, or all, of this book. Finally, I must thank Dave Berry for both intellectual and emotional support at all stages of the research and writing.

   Although I wish to thank all of these people for their help, it must be stressed that I take full responsibility for the interpretation of their comments and for any mistakes which remain in the text. All translations are mine, unless it is otherwise stated.

List of acronyms

ANEF   Association nationale des études féministes
APRE   Atelier production/reproduction
AVFT   Association européenne contre les violences faites aux femmes au travail
CEFUP   Centre d'études féminines de l'université de Provence
CNRS   Centre nationale de la recherche scientifique
MLF   Mouvement de libération de la femme/des femmes
NQF   *Nouvelles questions féministes*
QF   *Questions féministes*
RIME   Recherches et interventions masculines

Introduction

The aim of this book is to demonstrate how and why some French feminists have become interested in the study of masculinity and what they have contributed to the debate around it. This can be expected to enable us to draw certain conclusions about French feminism and its representation in and outside France; the production and reception of theories of masculinity; the relationship between feminist and non-feminist theory; and the continuities and discontinuities between Anglo-American and French theory.

Firstly, this book aims to show which French feminists are interested in masculinity and how they are situated in relation to other French feminists. Secondly, it aims to show how they became interested in this area of thought, by tracing the developments in their other areas of concern which led to a realization of the necessity of theorizing masculinity. Thirdly, it aims to establish what French feminists have contributed to an understanding of masculinity. Fourthly, it aims to discover the current state of feminist theories of masculinity and how they might develop in the future. And finally, it aims to describe the relation between feminist and non-feminist theories of masculinity.

The purpose of this introduction is to explain how these objectives will be achieved, why they are important, how the research was carried out and how its findings are to be presented. It begins with an attempt to explain the relevance of this research by situating it in relation to the current literature on French feminism and masculinity.

The study of French feminism

French feminism seems to have held a certain fascination for many non-French observers and has consequently been the subject of numerous publications. British and American interest was stimulated by a special issue of *Yale French studies* which appeared in 1981, and by *New French feminisms*, a collection of articles by French feminists edited by two Americans, Elaine Marks and Isabelle de Courtivron (1981), published in the same year. The representation of feminism in these two publications was distorted by an over-emphasis on a certain type of theory produced by a small number of French intellectuals heavily influenced by psychoanalysis and semiology. As a result, French feminism acquired a reputation for being more theoretical than its British or American counterparts, and its "exoticism" attracted the attention of many social and literary theorists and critics, particularly in literature departments in American universities.[1]

Of course, this interpretation was not entirely unfounded. As Claire Duchen (1986: 68–9) explains in *Feminism in France*, the intellectual context in which French feminist theory has developed differs from the British in its greater interest in psychoanalysis, linguistics and philosophy, in the greater respect accorded to intellectuals in France than in Britain, and in the anti-hierarchical and anti-authoritarian ideals highlighted by the events of May 1968, and present in left-wing and feminist thought. French feminist theory may therefore have a more intellectual appearance than its British or American counterparts. However, this is a broad generalization and one could argue that it does not justify the unbalanced selection of texts which many British and American academics have chosen to call "French feminism". This is an argument which will be expanded on and supported in more detail in Chapter 1. What is necessary here is simply to explain that this is one of the reasons why the English-language literature on French feminism concentrates mainly on just one aspect: theories produced by a relatively small number of French women intellectuals, who may or may not describe themselves as feminist. Examples of English-language critiques of these theories abound, including well-known publications by Toril Moi (1985, 1987) and Elizabeth Grosz (1989). The effect of this selectivity is that it obscures any other type of French feminism. Publications on poststructuralism, psychoanalysis, Lacan and Foucault far outnumber those which concentrate on the French women's movement and the ideas produced within it.

The most comprehensive and accessible English-language account of the history of the French women's movement between 1968 and 1981 is Claire Duchen's *Feminism in France* (1986). As well as explaining the relationship between the different groups and the main events and achievements of the movement, Duchen discusses some of the major theoretical debates which dominated the movement during the 1970s. Jane Jenson (1989, 1990) has also written clear and informative articles on the French women's movement, concentrating on its diversity and the splits between the different groups. The collection of writings by French feminists edited by Claire Duchen, *French connections* (1987), aimed to correct the overemphasis on psychoanalysis and semiotics which was found in *New French feminisms*, to stress the similarities between French and British feminisms, and to publish feminist thought which emerged directly from the women's movement. It was only in 1996 that other authors began to focus their work on the theoretical production of French materialist feminists (Adkins & Leonard, 1996; Jackson, 1996).

In French, two histories of the movement have been published: Monique Remy's *De l'utopie à l'intégration: histoire des mouvements de femmes* (1990) and Françoise Picq's *Libération des femmes: les années-mouvement* (1993). Although comparable in subject matter, the books by Remy and Picq have different emphases. Remy concentrates entirely on written sources and consequently pays more attention to those debates which took place in print. Picq, on the other hand, a feminist activist from the very beginning of the movement, concentrates more on the history of the movement as she and her sister activists knew it.

Like Duchen's *Feminism in France*, both of these books concentrate more or less exclusively on the period between 1968 and 1981, the period referred to by Picq as "the movement years". Some of the reasons why little attention has been paid to the movement of the 1980s and its theoretical products are immediately obvious: the feminist dynamic slowed down in France from about 1978 and especially when the Socialists came to power in 1981; institutional support and funding for feminist research has always been limited in France; publishers have not responded to feminism in France as they have in Britain and the United States; and many feminists who entered academic institutions became reluctant to advertise their feminism.

To summarize, then: although much has been published on French feminism, a review of the literature shows that most of it considers only the period 1968–81 and that the Anglo-American literature concentrates heavily on a particular variety of French feminism. This book extends the period under consideration to the present day; focuses on an aspect of French feminism which has received less attention in Britain and the United States than the "French feminists" Luce Irigaray, Hélène Cixous and Julia Kristeva; and examines examples of the production of ideas from the movement and from feminist research, highlighting the relationship between them.

The study of masculinity

It is unnecessary here to undertake a critical review of the Anglo-American literature on men and masculinity, since such reviews are already plentiful (Connell, 1995; Hearn & Morgan, 1990; Edley & Wetherell, 1995). However, it is useful to point out the wide variety of perspectives on masculinity and the consequent heterogeneity of meanings attributed to the term, since this helps identify what I am looking for when I say that I will be examining French feminist theories of masculinity. It needs to be stated at the outset that masculinity cannot be defined in a straightforward way. While each study of masculinity attempts to define its object of study, these definitions vary widely. For some theorists, masculinity is an essence or a quality, whereas for others it is something men do or practise. Masculinity may originate in biology, society or the psyche. It may be fixed or in a process of constant change. For many contemporary theorists, masculinity cannot be seen simply as an aspect of individual personality. Its construction or expression is intertwined with institutions, the state and collective expressions of gender. For example, many theorists will point to the existence of non-violent societies to support their arguments that violence cannot be seen as an expression of the inherent masculinity of an individual, but is rather an expression of cultural expectations. Thus, an exploration of the links between patriarchy and gender, between masculinity and institutions or the state, becomes essential to an understanding of masculinity. Lynne Segal (1990: 123), for example, writes:

> masculinity is not some type of single essence, innate or acquired. As it is represented in our culture, "masculinity" is a quality of being which is always incomplete, and which is equally based on a social as on a psychic reality. It exists in the various forms of power men ideally possess: the power to assert control over women, over other men, over their own bodies, over machines and technology.

In their synthesis of the main approaches towards the theorization of masculinity, Nigel Edley and Margaret Wetherell (1995) divide them into the following categories: those based on biology, psychoanalysis, sex roles, social relations, cultural constructions and feminism. Arguing that these competing discourses are ultimately irreconcilable, they examine the answers offered by each perspective to a set of key questions: what is it which binds men together as a social group? Why does masculinity take a particular form? How do men acquire their masculinity? And how can we account for deviations from the dominant model of masculinity?

The main research question here is whether and how these questions have been addressed in France, and this is the subject of the three sections of the book, which concentrate on difference, violence and gender. This enables us to consider whether there is any coherence to French feminist studies of masculinity or whether they arise for different reasons and to different ends. It also enables us to consider whether the study of masculinity makes a positive contribution to the French feminist critique.

The main focus of this book is the relation of French feminists to the theorization of masculinity and the theories which they have produced. The starting-point was what appeared to be a relatively sudden growth in interest in this subject on the part of Anglo-American feminists in the late 1980s and early 1990s (Segal, 1990; Hanmer, 1990; Canaan, 1991). The explicit theorization of masculinity by feminists is often portrayed as a response to the burgeoning literature produced by men, which was consolidated, particularly in the United States, into "men's studies". However, feminists such as Jalna Hanmer (1990) are suspicious of this chronology and insist that men's studies should not be allowed to claim the study of men and masculinity as its own. Feminism had been engaged in a critique of men and masculinity through analyses of male violence, sexual difference and patriarchy before the emergence of men's studies. Hanmer writes (1990: 26), "The Women's Liberation Movement began with a critique of men. They were always present, explicitly and implicitly. To reduce women's studies to the study of women and the differences between us is to deny our origins."

She sees a danger in men's critiques of masculinity, particularly those which ignore the effects of masculinity on women and on gendered power relations. In order to avoid the monopolization of the field by men, Hanmer states that feminists must insist on their contributions to the debate, to which gendered power relations have always been central. This is endorsed by Liz Stanley and Sue Wise (1984: 2), who write:

> Any feminist concerned with understanding the nature of women's oppression is necessarily concerned with *men*. It's all very well to examine pre-history, the formation of the unconscious, constructions of gender, and so on in explaining "why" women are oppressed; but the "how" of the situations involved is that it's males who do it – they articulate, through their "thought, word and deed" the "how" we're concerned to describe and analyse. So, for those of us concerned with this "how", there's no escape from turning our attention towards actual male behaviours, actual male sexisms, rather than abstracting these into discussions of "structures" and "systems" and their operations. Until we know how it is that men do sexual politics, we can't stop them; and we know for sure that they won't stop themselves, for they've far too much invested in the successful continuation of patriarchy.

The study of masculinity is important to the larger feminist project of understanding and challenging male power, and it is only through understanding masculinity that feminists can devise strategies for challenging male dominance. As Lynne Segal (1990) writes, ". . . feminist interest in men and masculinity is readily intelligible. It is part of the search for an explanation of men's power over women." Similarly, Caroline Ramazanoglu (1992) states that the feminist interest in men and masculinity lies in the possibility of changing gendered power relations: whether they can be changed and if so, how. In a lengthy critique of the "men's studies" literature, she argues that in order for studies of men and masculinity to be of use to feminism, they need to be incorporated into theories of gender relations and power, areas which, she claims, are underdeveloped in "men's studies". Ramazanoglu (1992: 346) writes:

> Reconstructing masculinity, recognising social divisions between men and acknowledging men's pain is only part of the process of making men less powerful in relation to women and to each other. Changing masculinity for the better, in feminist terms, implies reconstructing gender relations as explicit, shared or complementary, rather than as naturally unequal, or hidden power relations. Understanding the social character of men's power is then central to any reappraisal of masculinity, but it is this area which is first, underdeveloped in the literature, and second, developed in isolation from feminist work on power.

For feminists, what is important about masculinity is its role in the apparently universal subordination of women by men. While recognizing that masculinity is not an invariable essence present in men all over the world, feminists ask what it is about men as a group which means that they benefit from a power relation between the sexes.

Recently, some of the leading theorists of masculinity have begun to question the usefulness of this area of research and even the validity of the concept itself. Jeff Hearn (1996), for example, lists his concerns, which include the wide variety of meanings attributed to the term "masculinity"; the imprecision with which it is used in many cases; and its tendency to focus attention on men, thus rendering women invisible yet again. He claims that much of the work on masculinity fails to relate it to men's practices and does not contribute to a materialist analysis of gendered power relations. He also expresses doubts about the widely held assumption that masculinity, while varying culturally and historically, exists everywhere and at all times.

Hearn's criticisms of the way in which some studies of masculinity have shifted the focus from an analysis of gendered power relations to an analysis of masculine identities are valid. However, this does not mean that feminists should abandon the attempt to understand what it is about men which means that, despite individual variations, they dominate women universally. If the reason is not simply that it is because they are biologically male, then there must be some other explanation, and if the power relation between men and women is to be changed, then this explanation needs to be found.

A central question for feminists undertaking a critical study of masculinity is the relationship between individual men and the structure of gender relations. In order to avoid theorizing male power on an individual level, theories of patriarchy were developed specifically to explain the systemic nature of male power. Patriarchy refers to the powers and privileges men enjoy as a group in relation to women, and within patriarchy relations between gendered individuals can take a multitude of forms. While early theories of patriarchy were (rightly) criticized for representing the interests of white Western heterosexual feminists as though they were universally relevant to all women, contemporary theories of patriarchy incorporate differences between women. The theorization of patriarchy has caused many problems and conflicts. One of the main problems has been that as feminist research has revealed more and more areas in which supposedly gender-neutral institutions and processes have been built on men's experiences, so the breadth of the term has had to expand.[2] There is still no agreement among feminists on the usefulness and meaning of the term "patriarchy". Major problems exist when it comes to explaining the interaction between patriarchy and other systems of domination and exploitation, including most obviously capitalism. In Anglo-American theory it seems that dissatisfaction with the apparent inability of theories of patriarchy to explain the gendered aspects of social relations of class has led to the development of gender theories. Joan Acker (1989: 238) defines gender as "structural, relational, and symbolic differentiations between women and men". Acker writes:

> From asking about how the subordination of women is produced, maintained, and changed we move to questions about how gender is involved in processes and structures that previously have been conceived as having

nothing to do with gender. This includes attention to men and masculinities not only in relation to the subordination of women, but also in relation to other types of institutionalised power and the domination of men over other men. Making the assumption that all social relations are gendered, we ask questions about gender and science, gender and the military, gender and organisations. The claim, finally, is that society, including class structure, the state, and the political economies of late capitalism, contemporary socialism, and recently industrialising countries, cannot be understood without a consideration of gender.

Acker suggests that what is needed, and in fact what is already taking place in much contemporary theorizing of gender, is to see social relations as constituted through processes which are already linked. This is in preference to looking at separate structures and then trying to explain how they are linked. So gender and class relations may already be present in the same social processes. The danger with abandoning the concept of patriarchy, however, as Acker points out herself at the end of her article, is that political force can be lost. Gender can be more easily assimilated and co-opted than patriarchy, as can be seen in the struggles around institutional support and funding for women's studies and gender studies.

In an attempt to explain the wide variations between the positions of individual men on the axis of gender relations, Anglo-American theories of masculinity have concentrated on diversity and difference. They have examined the way that gender interacts with other social relations such as sexuality, class and ethnicity. They have examined "gay masculinities", "black masculinities" and "working-class masculinities" and the relations between them. The concept of "hegemonic masculinity" has been used to explain how certain groups of men can define what masculinity should be. This is often done in terms of what masculinity is not; for example, masculinity is "not-femininity", but it is also "not-gay". The creation of "hegemonic masculinity" enables certain groups of men to enjoy power in relation to other subordinate groups of men, but it also allows all men to enjoy power in relation to women. While the concept of hegemonic masculinity has been criticized by feminists who see it as a way for men to excuse their own less harmful types of masculinity, the emphasis on the differences between men has provided a means of explaining variations on an individual level at the same time as accounting for the overall structure of male dominance.

Defining terms

Before attempting to define the key terms used in this study, it is important to stress that definitions are not fixed, but are historically and culturally specific. The power to define is the subject of conflicting claims and constant struggles and is a central issue for feminist politics. This does not mean that all definitions are equally valid, however. Many form part of a specific political project; for example, theories of masculinity constructed by feminists form part of their project of removing the power relation between men and women.

This book does not aim to produce a fixed definition of gender and masculinity, but rather to examine the competing discourses surrounding these concepts and ask not only what they each tell us about masculinity, but also which discourses are dominant and what are the implications of each particular discourse or set of discourses for men, women and the relations between them. To this extent, then, the definitions proposed by various groups of theorists or practitioners are the substance of the book, and will emerge as the arguments progress.

"Feminism" and "feminist thought" are terms which are already difficult to define; "French feminism" is even more so. In *Feminism and the contradictions of oppression*, Caroline Ramazanoglu (1989: 6–8) explains that attempts to define feminism have been confused by the diversity of women's struggles. The definition of feminism also depends largely on who is defining it, she argues. For example, while liberal feminists and some male commentators who see feminism as a social movement describe it as either American 1970s radical feminism or nineteenth-century bourgeois feminism, many feminist writers employ a broad definition which attempts to encompass all types of feminism. Ramazánoglu argues that both these approaches have their disadvantages. The former narrow definition excludes many political practices and schools of thought which are widely regarded as feminist; the latter fails to convey the contradictions in feminist thought. As a solution, therefore, some feminists have used the term "feminism" loosely to refer to different conceptions of the relations between women and men and how they might be improved. Ramazanoglu's book is an attempt to explain some of the problems involved in defining feminism and its visions of the future, but in order to begin this task she too needs at least a working definition. The one she adopts is relatively general and includes a list of characteristics which the different varieties of feminism share. She claims that, for all versions of feminism, the existing relations between the sexes in which women are subordinated to men are unsatisfactory and should be changed; that feminism questions much that is considered natural or desirable in society; that feminism challenges the whole of human history and the course it will take in the future; that since feminism's aim is to change the relations between women and men, it has a political practice as well as a set of ideas; that feminist political practice is varied, provocative and always encounters resistance; and that feminism raises questions about knowledge and science, because all feminist thought depends on a subjective engagement, a belief that the relations between women and men are unjust and should be changed.

While some of these points are less pertinent than others for this particular study, and while this list of characteristics would not be accepted by all feminists, Ramazanoglu's guidelines seem a useful starting-point for a definition of feminism. It is unnecessary to offer a more precise set of criteria here. In fact, to try to do so could present further problems, since the more exacting the definition, the easier it becomes to exclude types of feminism which do not meet the criteria, thus creating "right" and "wrong" feminisms. Here, I use the term "feminism" to refer to any theory or political practice which is based on the belief that women are subordinated by men and that these unequal relations between the sexes should be changed, in favour of women.

The difficulty of defining what is meant by "French feminism" has already been raised, but some further points need to be added. Firstly, to talk of national feminisms in this way runs the risk of implying that they are homogenous. In an attempt to minimize this risk, Chapter 1 will introduce the variety of French feminisms and some of the conflicts and debates which have split the movement throughout its history. The decision to concentrate only on French feminist theories also enables their diversity to be emphasized, whereas, as Alice Jardine (1985: 15) argues in *Gynesis*, an attempt to undertake a more direct comparison between French and, for example, Anglo-American theories could introduce more of a tendency to reduce each set to its lowest common denominator, thus concealing important differences.

There is the further complication that, although it is vital to situate these theories within their originating context, as well as to remain aware of the fact that they are being observed from within another cultural context, it is clear that it is impossible to be certain of the dividing line between the two. Although there are (even taking into account the dangers of cultural stereotypes) identifiable differences between Anglo-American and French theory, there are also continuities, and there has inevitably been an exchange between the two. The cross-fertilization between national feminisms operates to varying extents and is dependent on a number of factors. As was mentioned above and will be examined in more detail in Chapter 1, the selection of French texts imported and translated into English has been unrepresentative. Moreover, there is nothing to suggest that the English-language feminist texts which are translated into French are representative of the variety of publications available in Britain and the United States.[3] Theoretical exchange does not occur only because of translated texts, however, and there are clear differences between the publications of French feminist theorists who read and refer to English-language publications and those who do not.

Finally, I use the term "Anglo-American feminism" with great reservation. The term "Anglo-American" probably became widespread in this context as a translation of the French "anglosaxon", which is used loosely, often to mean American, but sometimes American and British. Here, I use it as a convenient shorthand for British, American and Australian feminisms, which, although wildly divergent in many respects, have together produced a corpus of theory. This is often referred to as "feminist theory", despite the fact that it is as culturally specific as any other form of feminist theory. While recognizing that "Anglo-American" is a problematic term, I find it useful in the context of this book, which is, after all, primarily about French feminist theory, as a means of referring to the broadest of trends in British, American and Australian feminisms. I do not intend to suggest in any way that these are homogeneous.

Investigating French feminism and masculinity

During the 1980s and early 1990s, the masculinity debate evolved within Anglo-American feminism and men's studies with a certain amount of inter-action between the two. This debate was the starting-point for this research, which began by asking whether a similar debate was taking place in France. Was the need expressed by Anglo-American feminists to understand masculinity in order to bring about changes in the power relations between women and men also felt by French feminists? Are there any factors specific to French feminism which mean that the debate is taking place in different terms? The French historian Michèle Sarde (1983) addresses the question of the specificity of French women and French feminisms, arguing that the notion of national "mentalités" is not a myth. There are differences, she states, between the way American and British women (and men) behave and relate to each other. Criticizing feminists who present their analyses as universally valid, instead of considering what is cultur-ally specific about them, Sarde devotes the rest of the book to exposing these differences. The question of what is specifically French about the theories exam-ined here is clearly by no means straightforward, and conflicting views are held by many of the authors whose work is discussed. This is therefore a question which will recur throughout the book.

It is clear that there are dangers involved in talking of national feminisms. There is a constant fear of falling into the trap of stereotyping and xenophobia. There is also the danger of representing each national feminism as homogen-eous, hiding its internal debates and divisions. However, there is also a danger in *not* recognizing the differences between, and specificities of, national feminisms. And that danger is that we generalize from our own position, claiming (impli-citly or explicitly) to speak for all women, denying or obscuring the experience of women who inhabit different cultures from our own and have different priorities and preoccupations, even if we also have much in common. It is as a reaction to being spoken for, ignored or misrepresented by Anglophone feminists that French feminists joined together with other non-Anglophones to hold a conference in Rio in 1995 (*Cahiers du CEDREF*, 4/5: 1995). This was an attempt to reclaim a space, from which dialogue would then be possible with Anglophone feminists, but without the dominance of the English language and the theoretical assump-tions which go with it. So how can we talk of French feminism without falling into these traps? It is in an attempt to do this that I have placed the discussion of French feminist theories of masculinity within the context of the women's move-ment and other sites of feminist theoretical production. I have also tried to point out areas of commonalities and difference.

Although this is not, and was never intended to be, a comparative study, one of the motivations for doing it was to discover whether feminists in France shared an interest in masculinity, and if so, whether their analyses differed from their Anglo-American counterparts. As the research progressed, it became increasingly clear that a comparative study, in the sense of a balanced or parallel consideration of theories from France, the United States, Australia and Britain, would be beyond the scope of this study. The main reasons for this are, firstly, that the subject has been given far more specific attention in Anglo-American than in French theory, producing a situation where the sheer amount and detail of the literature available is not comparable, and where any attempt at comparison would entail repetition of well-documented areas. Secondly, the way in which feminist thought on masculinity developed in these countries differs to such an extent that it was felt that too much space would be devoted to the differences to do justice to the French theories themselves. Therefore, this study concentrates on French thought, and only the most striking similarities and differences between it and Anglo-American thought will be pointed out.

The first important task of this book is to identify what is meant by French feminism, and, more specifically, which types of French feminism are to be examined. In order to do this, it is necessary to describe the diversity of French feminism and to examine the various ways in which it has been represented by feminists, non-French observers and non-feminist writers in France, including intellectuals, journalists and members of men's groups. Focusing on specific types of feminism, in particular radical feminist theory and practice and a certain type of academic research, yet situating them in relation to other aspects of feminism and to various interpretations of it, this book facilitates a discussion of the meanings of "French feminism" and "postfeminism", both in and outside France. In particular, it considers the construction of a certain type of French feminism by Anglo-American academics, the declaration of a postfeminist era by French journalists, and the repeated attempts by feminists in France to redefine their purpose and raison d'être. It discovers a great number of inconsistencies and conflicts in the way feminism is represented.

The analysis of French feminism is followed by an investigation of various aspects of the masculinity debate in France. Before concentrating on the contributions made by feminists, it discusses those made by men's groups, journalists and intellectuals. The debate on masculinity in France emerged in the 1970s from newly created men's groups. As in Britain and the United States, men's groups began to appear in France in the early 1970s as a response to feminism. The form this response took varied from anti-feminist reaction to pro-feminist searches for ways to respond positively to the questions raised by feminism, and these variations were reflected in the diversity of men's groups. Many feminists at this time insisted that, although masculinity was a problem which needed to be investigated, it was men, not feminists, who should be doing this. However, a few began to respond critically to early publications and conference papers by men involved in men's groups, and it was these critical responses which were the first attempts by feminists to address the subject of masculinity explicitly. An examination of these publications and debates enables us to consider the relationship between feminist and men's groups' analyses of masculinity. We find an initial hostility and suspicion on the part of feminists towards men's attempts to explain masculinity, followed in recent years by evidence of a certain, if limited, amount of co-operation between them (CEFUP, 1992).

During the 1980s and 1990s, masculinity also became an increasingly popular subject for journalists and authors of books which were expected to reach a wide audience. These include Evelyne Sullerot's *Quels pères? Quels fils?* (1992), Elisabeth Badinter's *XY: de l'identité masculine* (1992) and collections of articles in *Le nouvel observateur*, *L'événement du jeudi* and *L'express*. Some of the characteristics of the popular manifestations of the debate will be examined and, in particular, the representation of feminism which underlies many of the arguments in these publications. It is demonstrated that feminism is portrayed by the authors of these books and articles as something which was relevant in the 1970s, but which, having achieved its aims, no longer has a role. Moreover, feminism is said to have caused many changes, including the destabilizing of masculine identity. Many of the popular interpretations of masculinity are concerned with how men have coped with this and with their loss of power and rights. It is interesting to contrast this assessment of the impact of feminism with the way in which it is perceived by feminists themselves.

These popular interpretations of masculinity also often contain implicit or explicit comparisons with Anglo-American feminism. American feminists in particular are represented as ridiculously extreme. French women are told by the authors of these books and articles that this is dangerous for national gender relations and fortunately unnecessary in France, where, it is alleged, men and women understand each other better. The effect of this opposition between French and American feminism is that many problems are hidden by it. For example, Elisabeth Badinter (1992) implies in *XY: de l'identité masculine* that male violence is not a problem in France, as it is in the United States, thus denying the experiences of many French women and silencing those who are trying to raise public awareness of its existence.

In the chapters that follow, feminist contributions to the masculinity debate are examined in detail. Two areas of feminist concern in which a particular interest in masculinity can be identified are taken as examples, and the way in which the interest developed, the importance of the theories produced and the contributions made to an understanding of masculinity are discussed.

The first area of feminist concern which is examined in detail is the "difference debate" and the production of theories of gender which have risen out of it. The question of difference is central to feminism, and feminists in France as elsewhere have been divided over it. At its simplest, the term "difference debate" refers to conflicting views over the origins and nature of the differences between men and women. While all feminists agree that there is a power relation between men and women which operates in men's favour, they do not agree about how this relation should be changed. "Difference feminists" argue that women should have the space necessary to develop their femininity, attaining equality while remaining different. "Sameness feminists" argue that the differences between men and women are socially constructed and should be removed, along with the relation of oppression between the sexes. Since the debate is concerned with the acquisition, construction and reproduction of gender, it seems a fruitful place to begin a search for feminist theories of masculinity. An examination of the debate reveals that there has been a growing interest in masculinity, but mainly at the social constructionist end of the difference spectrum. "Difference feminists" have been concerned mainly with femininity and, while they have produced a detailed critique of masculine discursive structures, they have not developed theories of masculine identity and how this relates to the lives of men and women.

Social constructionist theorists, especially those involved in the radical feminist theory journal *Questions féministes* (*QF*) in the 1970s and the research group APRE (Atelier production/reproduction) since the 1980s, have been particularly concerned with producing theories of gender. A growing interest in masculinity can be traced through the development of these theories. It is shown that, as the emphasis on the inequality and hierarchy of the gender relation increases, so does the necessity of examining the dominant and subordinate terms of the relation and the maintenance and reproduction of both terms. Thus it is necessary to study masculinity as well as femininity, but also the relation between them.

By examining the changing use of key concepts in feminist theory, such as gender, we can discover some of the similarities and differences between the development of French and Anglo-American feminist thought. There is great diversity in the meanings attributed to the term "gender" and, even within feminist theory, its meaning is contentious. French feminists are as divided over the term "gender" as are their British and American counterparts, and the debate within French feminism has been constructed in opposition to Anglophone theory, thus adding further complications.

The second set of feminist ideas on masculinity examined here are those produced by grassroots feminists involved in the struggle against male violence. At first they concentrated their efforts on helping women victims of male violence, as well as attempting to raise public consciousness and campaigning for legislative reform. However, as they slowly made progress in these areas, they also began to extend their interests in the direction of violent men and the construction of masculine identity around violence. Ideas about the reasons for male violence developed, and with them, a growing interest in the examination of masculinity. Changes in feminist understanding of this violence and their strategies for fighting against it are traced, revealing a growing tendency to consider the causes of male violence and the links between violence and masculine identity. This illustrates the changing priorities in this area of feminist activism, both in its practice and the ideas which have emerged out of this practice.

The selection of one example of theories produced almost entirely by academic feminists having little contact with the women's movement, and another example from feminist activists whose theories are directly linked to their action, enables us to identify where their ideas meet and where they part and to try to explain why they should be similar or different by looking at the conditions of their production. Observing these two areas of development reveals continuities in the ideas that are being produced in both areas, but also a major debilitating split between theorists and activists and a lack of contact and exchange which might be acting as an obstacle to further developments. It makes possible the discussion of whether this split is inevitable; whether a change in the present situation is possible and desirable; and, if so, under what conditions it might take place.

Having examined theories of gender and the problem of male violence separately, Chapter 6 considers the work which is taking place on the border-line between the two. This facilitates a discussion not only of what it contributes to an understanding of masculinity, but also what it can tell us about changes in feminist action and theory in France; about continuities and discontinuities between studies of masculinity in French and Anglo-American feminism; and about the possibilities for future developments, both theoretical and practical, including more work with men, greater contact between the movement and research, and greater exchange between Anglo-American and French thought. For example, it is argued that there is currently little exchange between Anglo-American and French feminist theory on this subject. It is suggested that some of the reasons for this might be the Anglo-American portrayal of French feminism as exotic and therefore the refusal to acknowledge the similarities between them; and the insistence among certain French feminists that the Anglo-American concept of gender is incapable of expressing the meaning of "rapports sociaux de sexe" (social relations of sex), despite striking similarities in their uses.

The split between the movement and research and the relatively undeveloped state of the masculinity debate make it impossible to offer a coherent and satisfying conclusion to the arguments presented here. However, certain elements of a conclusion can be drawn about the links and continuities between the different aspects of the debate, and suggestions can be made as to whether the debate might become more coherent in the future and under what circumstances this might occur.

Sources

Given the theoretical nature of much of the material discussed in this research, the most important source was publications by French feminists. These can be split into movement and research publications, although some fall on the dividing line between these two categories. The literature from the women's movement was essential to this research, most importantly in the construction of a history of the elements of French feminism which are of most relevance to the study of the development of theories of masculinity. It was also vital to the investigation of the specific issue of feminist action around male violence. It includes journals, reviews, newsletters, pamphlets, conference papers and interviews. Of the movement publications consulted, some are still produced today, but most of the numerous feminist reviews and journals which were around in the 1970s have now disappeared, including, for example, *La revue d'en face: revue de politique féministe du mouvement de libération des femmes* (1977–84) and *Pénélope*, a feminist history journal which disappeared in 1986. Most of those that are left are theoretical rather than movement journals, although some try to span the gap between theory and practice. One of the most practical publications as far as feminist activism is concerned is *Paris féministe* published by the Maison des Femmes.[4] It functions as a newsletter where events in Paris, in the rest of France, and to a lesser extent internationally, are listed. It also contains short articles about topical items. The other long-running review which has existed since 1977 is *Les cahiers du féminisme*[5], published by the Trotskyist Ligue communiste révolutionnaire.

In addition to the reviews, the most important sources for information on feminist action around male violence are annual reports of the information gained from helplines, for example, those of the Collectif féministe contre le viol[6]; pamphlets and articles by feminists who work in refuges for women victims of male violence, for example Geneviève Devèze; and newsletters from small feminist organizations, such as the Maison des femmes at Cergy-St-Christophe.[7]

More theoretical feminist publications were also a major resource. An important source for early contributions to theories of gender relations is *QF*, which (with its successor *Nouvelles questions féministes*, *NQF*) is one of the longest-running feminist journals in France.[8] It is the only French feminist theory journal[9] and the only one to attempt to act as a bridge between the movement and theory, with the intention of establishing an exchange between the two (*NQF*, 1981: 3–14). It first appeared in November 1977, describing itself as "a theoretical radical feminist journal" (*QF*, 1977: 5). In 1980, having published eight issues, the collective split around the question of political lesbianism, and the journal disappeared (Beauvoir, 1982). Simone de Beauvoir and Christine Delphy, the original founders of *QF*, then created *NQF*, of which the first issue appeared in March 1981. Although there was a break between 1986 and 1991, it has appeared more or less regularly since then.

Journals published by academic feminist research groups were also used, including *BIEF* (*Bulletin d'information des études féminines*), a thematically organized publication which has existed since 1979 (with a gap between 1986 and 1989) and which was launched with the self-professed aim of providing a link between universities and women's experiences. Publications by the Association européenne contre les violences faites aux femmes au travail (AVFT) are an important source of theoretical feminist articles on male violence as well as accounts of specific cases and campaigns. They published *Cette violence dont nous ne voulons plus* from 1985 until 1992, when it became *Projets féministes*. The journal began as a newsletter, then became a thematic review on sexual harassment. It gradually extended its interest to cover all sorts of violence towards women, and *Projets féministes* has an even broader aim of linking all these types of violence within a framework of theories of gender.

Academic feminist theories of gender relations were obtained from the feminist journals mentioned above; conference proceedings, for example, the 1982 Toulouse conference on Femmes, féminisme et recherches; the publications of research papers by APRE; and non-feminist journals, for example *Les temps modernes* and *L'homme*.

Due to the relatively undeveloped state of feminist publishing in France compared with Britain and the United States, there are few feminist books on this subject.[10] The exceptions include histories of the movement, for example, Françoise Picq's *Libération des femmes: les années-mouvement* (1993), and a series of collections of theoretical articles by individual authors, published by a feminist publishing house, Côté-femmes[11], which has since been taken over by L'Harmattan.

In order to establish the contours of a broader non-feminist debate on masculinity and to assess the role that a certain portrayal of feminism plays in the construction of these ideas on masculinity, the following were examined: men's groups' publications, including books, for example Guido de Ridder's *Du côté des hommes: à la recherche de nouveaux rapports avec les femmes* (1982), and reviews, for example, *Types – paroles d'hommes*; articles from news magazines, for example *Le nouvel observateur* and *L'événement du jeudi*; and best-selling books on masculinity, for example, Evelyne Sullerot's *Quels pères? Quels fils?* (1992) and Elisabeth Badinter's *XY: de l'identité masculine* (1992).

Structure

The first three chapters present the contexts in which feminist theories of masculinity need to be situated. The first context is French feminism as a whole. This identifies the areas of feminist theory and practice in which an interest in masculinity has developed. It considers how these areas relate to the rest of the women's movement and feminist research. The second context is the debate on masculinity which is taking place in men's groups, popular books, newspapers and magazines. The aim is to demonstrate how the feminist involvement in the debate relates to these other aspects of it. The third context is the "difference debate", which has played a central role in French feminist theory and practice and has influenced the areas in which theories of masculinity could develop.

There follows a detailed examination of feminist theories of masculinity, which focuses on two specific areas of feminist interest in which these theories have developed. The first is theories of gender which has been of particular interest to feminist intellectuals. The second is male violence towards women, which has been a focus of grassroots activism since the 1970s and which is at the heart of questions of masculinity, gender and power. The point at which these two areas of French feminism meet, and the implications of work taking place on this borderline for future developments in the understanding of men, male violence and masculinity is discussed at the end of this section. Theory and practice are brought together in a limited number of nonetheless significant initiatives which are also discussed.

The arguments and evidence are organized into the six substantive chapters which follow.

The aim of Chapter 1 is to explain which French feminists are interested in masculinity, why they are interested, and where masculinity fits into their broader concerns. It discusses the changes that have taken place in French feminism since the mouvement de libération des femmes (MLF) of the 1970s, beginning with the origins and history of the movement, the currents and conflicts, the early debates and campaigns. It examines the "institutionalization" of feminism, for example, through the introduction of a Ministry for Women's Rights and the recognition of feminist studies in French universities. It examines claims by French feminists that there is a debilitating split between activists and researchers, which seems especially apparent in activities aimed at bringing an end to male violence towards women. It discusses feminism in the 1980s and 1990s, countering suggestions that France has entered a postfeminist era, and examining current issues and debates. It discusses the impact of feminism in France and the way in which this impact is perceived differently depending on the position of the observer. Finally, it examines the representation of French feminism by Anglo-American academics and the problems that this has posed.

One of the important functions of Chapter 1 is to establish what is understood by the term "French feminism" in this research. It discusses how the term is used by Anglo-American feminist academics, by French journalists and by French feminists. So, for example, Anglo-American academics might consider French feminism to be the work of Luce Irigaray, Hélène Cixous and Julia Kristeva; French journalists might represent feminism as an excess of the past or as something which was necessary but has now achieved its aims and consequently disappeared; and French feminists might think of it as a heterogeneous mix of activism, research, political pressure, a diffusion of ideas and involvement in academic and political institutions.

Chapter 1 shows that, not only are there numerous varieties of French feminism, but that it is also represented in a variety of ways, and that this has implications for the way in which issues related to feminism are interpreted, including masculinity and male violence. This is further complicated by the fact that feminism in France has undergone many changes since 1970, related to the social and political climate of the time, broader reactions to feminism, and the extent to which feminist ideas have been incorporated into institutions, political party programmes and legislative reforms.

This chapter also identifies the specific aspects of French feminism which are examined more closely later in the book. These are shown to have their roots mainly in radical feminism. Radical feminists produced the feminist journal *QF*, in which much of the early development of feminist theories of gender appeared. Radical feminists were involved in the various campaigns against male violence towards women, and organizations continuing this work, such as the Ligue du droit des femmes and the AVFT, come from the radical feminist tradition. This chapter explains the relation between this feminist tendency, and its offspring, and the rest of the women's movement.

The relationship between activists and theorists is also examined in Chapter 1. The split between movement and research appears pronounced, at least in certain areas, and it is suggested that this has its roots in the suspicions of grassroots activists towards feminists who entered the institutions, whether these were academic or political, a situation which was aggravated by the arrival of the Socialist government in 1981, forcing feminists to adopt new strategies in response to a certain number of reforms. The split is maintained and even widened by an increasing reluctance on the part of feminist academics to exhibit their feminism.

The implications of the gap between activism and research become more evident in Chapters 4, 5 and 6, when the contrast between practice and theory in relation to male violence towards women is revealed, and the minimal amount of work which attempts to draw together the two areas is discussed. A major argument which emerges from this is that this split between movement and theory limits the insights into male violence and masculine identity, and that each area would benefit from exchange with the other.

The examination in Chapter 2 of a variety of perspectives on masculinity which have developed since the eruption of the second wave of feminism is revealing in several respects. It is argued that the assessment of the impact of feminism varies according to the standpoint of the observer, and that this has implications for the way in which the debate around masculinity has developed. For example, men's groups formed as a reaction to feminism, and the way in which they perceived feminism and its impact on society affected their attitude towards the study of masculinity. Some men's groups aimed to prevent the changes brought about by feminism having harmful effects on them, such as the reduction of their power or the limitation of their rights as fathers or husbands. Others wanted to join feminists in their attempts to bring about change. Whereas the former tended to ignore the study of masculinity or to consider only its disadvantages for men, the latter were more likely to consider masculinity in the context of gender relations.

The media portrayal of feminism has affected the popular interpretation of masculinity. Journalists portrayed feminism as excessively radical and therefore to be ridiculed and marginalized or as having achieved its aims and therefore having lost its relevance. In this context, masculinity was said to have been seriously damaged by feminism, and men were portrayed as having suffered considerably and made an effort to respond. The construction of postfeminism means that men are represented either as victims of excessive feminist demands or as having lost a considerable amount of power as a result of the changes brought about by a successful feminism. They are forced to change and search for a new identity. This interpretation ignores feminist issues and obscures the questioning of men's continuing domination of women.

In a consideration of the relation between feminist and non-feminist analyses of masculinity, it is argued that, for several reasons, feminists were late to enter the debate, but that they *did* enter it. The reasons why they entered it late are, firstly, that they had other priorities. For example, in the case of feminists involved in action around the problem of male violence, the initial priority was the provision of refuges for the women victims, and they began a critical analysis of violent men only much later. Secondly, many feminists wanted men to deal with their own problems and felt that women should devote their time and energy to themselves and other women. Thirdly, there was a certain uneasiness around the question of men in a movement split around the question of sexuality. However, feminists later began to show more of an interest in masculinity, partly as a reaction to men's groups, but also because some of feminism's own concerns had reached a point at which the question of men and masculinity needed to be raised. And it is the developments in certain feminist debates which facilitated or necessitated an increase in interest in men and masculinity which will be discussed in detail in Chapters 4–6.

The focus of Chapter 3 is the debate on sexual difference. This is central to feminism, since it determines its raison d'être and the strategies it will employ. It is also central to an understanding of masculinity. Attempts to account for the seemingly universal occurrence of gender difference include the sociological, anthropological, biological and psychoanalytic. These theories are assessed, along with a consideration of their contribution to an understanding of masculinity and its links with male violence and the power relations between women and men. A central question for feminist politics is whether these power relations can be changed, and it is in the context of this question that the nature-versus-culture debate is discussed. Important differences in the development of the difference debate within French and Anglo-American feminism are examined. While the Anglo-American debate has been cut through by poststructuralism and identity politics so that the either/or dichotomy has been replaced to a large extent by notions of multiplicity and plurality, this is not the case in France. This has implications for the development of theories of gender, which are far less concerned with the differences *within* each sex category than with the differences between them. It is suggested that part of the reason for this is the influence of the universalist tradition in French thought, in which the recognition of differences is seen as a threat to equality.

The question of sexual difference and its relation to other differences is at the centre of the debate around the political representation of women. Since 1992, a feminist-led campaign demanding a law which would impose the equal representation of men and women in political institutions has been gathering momentum. The campaign for parity, as it is known, is supported both by "difference" feminists, on the grounds that women do politics differently from men and should therefore be present in sites of political power, and by "sameness" feminists, on the grounds that women are as competent as men and are unjustly excluded from male-dominated institutions. Critics argue that the opposition between sameness and difference is imposed on feminists. They demand a fundamental examination of concepts such as democracy and representation which can move beyond the sterile difference debate. It is suggested, therefore, that the debate which has been stimulated by the campaign for parity may offer a way of moving beyond sameness versus difference.

This chapter then examines the contributions of difference theorists to theories of masculinity. It considers in particular the work of Luce Irigaray, concluding that the theorization of femininity plays a more important role than that of masculinity, although she offers an influential critique of phallocentric discourses. However, concentrating on a male sexuality which is constructed through discourse, Irigaray is unable to provide a convincing analysis of material manifestations of male sexuality such as sexual violence.

Chapters 4–6 examine two complementary examples of areas of growing feminist interest in the study of men and masculinity. The first, the development of theories of gender which led to the construction of men and masculinity as explicit objects of research, concentrates on the production of academic feminist theory. The second, the emergence of theories of masculinity out of movement activities against male violence towards women, illustrates how practical feminist action led to the production of certain ideas about men and masculinity. The contrast between the two enables questions to be asked about the production and exchange of feminist theory, and the lack of contact between theorists and activists, which, it will be argued, is one of the salient characteristics of feminism in France.

Chapter 4 asks how the development of theories of gender by social constructionist, or sameness feminists contributes to a growing interest in masculinity, and looks at a number of examples of theorists working in this area who insist that the theorization of masculinity as well as femininity is necessary in order to explain the power relations between them. Early theories of the social construction of gender which were developed in the radical feminist journal *QF* demonstrated firstly that difference, masculinity and femininity are socially constructed. Secondly, they attempted to show that the social construction of difference, masculinity and femininity is responsible for women's oppression and male power. Finally, they argued that this social construction was historically and culturally variable and could therefore be changed. The first two of these findings have contributed greatly to the way in which ideas about gender and masculinity have continued to develop. The third has been more recently brought into question by some feminists in France, as in Britain and the United States. The idea that something which has been shown to be socially constructed rather than natural can be changed is politically important. It functions as a theoretical support for action to bring about this change. However, as the revolutionary fervour and political optimism of the 1970s MLF turned into the more downbeat and disparate pockets of feminist activity in the 1980s, this idea began to be questioned. The debate around whether masculinity is natural or socially constructed has been cut through by attempts by feminist biologists to demonstrate that biology is itself socially constructed. Their claims that there is little scientific proof of a natural division of humanity into two clear-cut sex categories have implications for the theorization of male violence, since they contribute to the arguments refuting the notion that aggression occurs naturally in men and has biological and sex-specific causes.

Chapter 4 raises from another angle the question which will be addressed in Chapter 6: how male violence can be explained in a way that goes beyond the essentialist view that men are naturally more aggressive than women. Underlying this belief, which is still held by many people, are certain assumptions about what is natural. It is these assumptions that have been challenged by feminists, including those involved in the production of theories of gender. This chapter, then, also needs to demonstrate how feminist arguments against naturalism produced theories of the social construction of gender and of sexual difference, and later of gender as a power relation, which, they argue, can be expressed in the form of male violence.

In the light of the theoretical developments described in this chapter, two observations can be made. Firstly, the QF generation of theorists developed theories of gender as a relation and began to examine the construction of femininity, and, to a lesser extent, masculinity. Secondly, it can be seen that it was the development of theories of gender which highlighted the importance of constructing masculinity as a gendered research object and no longer viewing it as a gender-neutral norm. Thus, research into the behaviour of men was presented as just that, and no longer as representative of "human" behaviour.

Chapter 5 introduces the attention which has been paid by the French women's movement to male violence towards women. It shows how it was a major concern for feminists from the early 1970s, when they first began to expose the seriousness of the problem and its massive occurrence, and how the initial concerns were raising public consciousness, campaigning for legislative reform and providing aid for the women victims. It then argues that the theories that have developed out of this action over the last two decades have changed considerably, and there has been a development from an almost exclusive concern with women victims of male violence to a growing interest in its perpetrators. Since the main reason for feminist interest in violence against women is that they want to put an end to it, the emphasis on prevention has grown. Some French feminists have recently begun to argue that the way to prevent male violence is to concentrate on the men who do it. This chapter, then, looks at how feminist action (public consciousness-raising, refuges, campaigns) led to feminist ideas about male violence; how what they really wanted to know was why men are violent towards women and how it can be stopped; how these ideas changed until some (although few) feminists began to consider the importance of thinking about men; and the analyses that this has produced.

Chapter 5 shows that grassroots feminists have been actively engaging with the problem of male violence towards women since the early 1970s, and that there has been a growth in interest in explaining why certain men are violent and how it can be prevented. It tries to identify the links between the practical work done in refuges and on helplines, and the ideas which have developed out of this experience. It discovers that this link is difficult to pin down, that ideas sometimes emerge directly out of the practice, but that they also sometimes precede it, contradict it, and develop far more slowly than, or independently of, feminist activism.

It identifies an increase in attempts to explain the reasons why men are violent towards women, rather than why women are the victims of male violence. It finds that this interest began with the realization that violent men are ordinary, "normal" men, and that assailants are not always strangers; and the links between male violence and problems associated with masculinity such as frustration, unfulfilled sexual needs and inability to control sexual urges in the face of provocation were attacked on the grounds that they were socially constructed by a patriarchal society, and not natural.

The aim of examining the changes and developments in the way that feminists approached the problem of male violence, the priorities they drew up, the campaigns they organized, the action they took, and the ideas they wrote about was to see if any trends could be identified. It was discovered that feminists gradually identified different kinds of violence, made connections between them, and began to theorize them as part of a whole. It was also found that there was an increasing concern with violent men, associated with an increasing concern with prevention rather than dealing with the effects.

The aim of Chapters 4 and 5 is to demonstrate firstly that the development of theories of gender has contributed to a growing interest in masculinity, and secondly, that feminist work on male violence has begun to examine the perpetrators in an attempt to explain and prevent violence towards women. These chapters argue that both of these developments have contributed to the establishment of masculinity as a legitimate object of study. However, it is at the point where these two areas of feminist theory and practice meet that some of the most interesting and important questions about masculinity – and about French feminism – can be posed. The problem of male violence towards women is central to an understanding of masculinity, raising questions such as how male identity is constructed around violence, how male violence functions within a system of male dominance, and how individual acts of male violence fit into this broader system.

Chapter 6 looks at the small amount of work which is situated at this point of convergence. It examines attempts to explain male violence within the framework of gender or social relations of sex. It considers what this tells us about masculinity and power and about how an end could be brought to the connections between masculinity and violence. It also looks at what this tells us about French feminism. The work on male violence has taken place almost exclusively within the movement, while theories of gender or social relations of sex have been elaborated mostly by researchers in the Centre nationale de la recherche scientifique (CNRS) and feminist theorists, who have little contact with the movement. This split between theory and practice highlights the gulf between the two, even though both of them are providing crucial insights into masculinity and male power.

Finally, the conclusion considers how feminist ideas about masculinity relate to the more general debate which is taking place around it, and assesses the contribution that feminists have made to an understanding of masculinity and its links with power and violence. It also discusses, in the light of the previous chapters, the state of French feminism today and the relation between it and Anglo-American feminism. It asks whether the representation of French feminism from the outside has masked similarities between it and Anglo-American feminism and attempts to identify what is specific to French feminism. It considers in particular the fact that, while in Britain and the United States challenges to the concept of sisterhood by black, lesbian and working-class women led to a broadening of the difference debate to incorporate differences between women, in France sexual difference remains at the centre of the debate.

1 French feminism: movement, theory and representation

The theories of masculinity discussed in this book have their origins in the French feminist movement. Their reception, however, is influenced not only by the characteristics of French feminist activism and research, but also by its representation in France and abroad. This chapter examines the production of French feminist theory and its relation to the movement. It then examines cultural representations of feminism, in particular the media construction of postfeminism. Finally, it examines the construction by Anglo-American academics of "French feminism", a term which is applied to a group of theorists unrepresentative of feminism in France.

Le mouvement de libération des femmes (MLF)

This account of the development of feminism in France since 1968 pays particular attention to the production of theory and the relation between activism and research. In the early days of the MLF, the relation between theory and practice was intimate and direct. Theory emerged from women's experiences, and the personal was political. However, when feminist research in the universities began to grow in the 1970s and received official recognition in the early 1980s, activists criticized the gap between the movement and research. Feminist researchers, for their part, were sometimes reluctant to advertise their feminism or pursue obviously feminist research. The relation between activism and theory has had an important effect in particular areas of feminist interest, including violence against women, which is examined in detail in Chapter 5.

A view which represents the movement in terms only of sites of theoretical production is, however, necessarily distorted. This chapter does not aim to provide a comprehensive or representative account of the history of the French women's movement, a history which has been told in various ways elsewhere (Tristan & Pisan, 1977; Delphy, 1980; Picq, 1981; Duchen, 1986; Jenson, 1989, 1990; Remy, 1990; Picq, 1993). Instead, it focuses on some groups and developments more than others, pays more attention to written texts than events and discussions, and smoothes over many of the inconsistencies and contradictions of practical feminist politics. It concentrates, for example, more on the debates

25

within the movement about the role of the institutions in feminism; whether feminists can work in academia and, if they do, what relationship exists between their research and activism; the "institutionalization" of feminism and the division between movement and theory, than on other questions central to the women's movement such as the relative importance of struggles against patriarchy and capitalism; political lesbianism; and the role of separatism.

Although I am concentrating here on the women's movement since 1968, it must not be forgotten that this was not the birth of feminism in France. Maïté Albistur and Daniel Armogathe's history of French feminism (1977) devotes only one of its 25 chapters to the post-1968 period, the rest of the book covering feminism in the Middle Ages, during the Revolution, and numerous examples of individual feminists and feminist movements in the last 200 years. And when Simone de Beauvoir (1972: 13) wrote the introductory sentences to *The second sex* in 1949, she felt that "The subject . . . is not new. Enough ink has been spilt in quarrelling over feminism, and perhaps we should say no more about it."

The student and workers' revolt of May 1968 is often seen as the origin of French feminism. While feminist history has now gathered together a body of evidence which suggests that the MLF was a historically specific manifestation of a feminism which can take many forms, the spirit of the time was concerned more with revolution than with continuity. To the women involved in the emergence of the movement in the 1970s, it seemed that they were beginning something new. One of the reasons for this was the ignorance surrounding the struggles of the past. Women's history was yet to be written. In fact, this became one of the projects of the second wave. In addition, the events of May 1968 were to have a profound effect on the evolution of the women's movement, and played a vital role in the creation of the "new feminism". The emerging women's movement was closely linked with other new political movements of the time, and it shared with them an opposition to hierarchy, to the authoritarianism of de Gaulle's France, and to party politics. The exciting new ideas of this period stimulated women into action, but at the same time they began to realize their lack of status in the events, and it was the anger at their treatment by male activists which led to the creation of an autonomous women's movement. Many of them broke away from mixed organizations and organized separately around issues which had not previously been discussed.

During the 1970s, many women's groups were created, and feminist publications began to appear. Most of this activity went unnoticed by the general public and the media, but what they did notice was a series of highly visible actions. For example, a group of women laid a wreath at the Tomb of the Unknown Soldier at the Arc de Triomphe in memory of one more unknown than him: his wife. In 1971, the "Manifeste des 343" was published in the centre-left intellectual weekly, *Le nouvel observateur*. This was a statement signed by 343 women, many of them public figures, to say that they had had illegal abortions. Reporting these events, the press, borrowing from the American, coined the phrase "mouvement de libération de la femme" (the women's liberation movement).[12]

The press also began to describe the movement as divided into tendencies, and these divisions are usually used in analyses of the movement, especially as it was in the 1970s.

However, even among activists involved from the very beginning, opinions vary on the extent to which a description of the movement in terms of tendencies is an accurate representation of it. For example, Françoise Picq (1981), in an account of how she experienced the early women's movement in Paris, argues that, although activists disagreed and formed separate groups depending on their interests and priorities, between 1970 and 1972 the women's movement could not be described as being divided into tendencies. According to Picq, women drifted in and out of groups at different times, or were involved in activities organized by different groups, and the notion of sisterhood was still strong enough to give them a sense of identity as "feminists". Christine Delphy, another feminist activist since the beginning of the second wave, does not share this view (Delphy, personal correspondence). She sees the fluidity and exchange described by Picq as existing only within the confines of a "central" feminism, which was unaware of other feminist activity and therefore of divisions which might be visible from another standpoint. For example, Delphy claims that from as early as 1970 there was a clear split between "revolutionary" and "class struggle" feminists.

To write of tendencies, then, should not imply that these divisions were well-defined and fixed, or that all feminists and feminist groups could be categorized in this way.[13] Many feminists were active in trade unions and political parties and involved in campaigns which did not fit into these categories. They campaigned on specific issues for specific groups of women, for example women workers or mothers. This type of feminism increased towards the end of the 1970s. However, there were splits within the movement and conflict between certain groups which should not be underestimated. The categories most often used in analyses of the movement are class struggle feminists, revolutionary feminists, and Psychanalyse et politique (Jenson, 1990; Duchen, 1986; Remy, 1990).[14]

Class struggle tendency

One of the major divisions within the movement was the relative importance accorded to the struggle against capitalism and against patriarchy. For the class struggle tendency, the destruction of capitalism was the priority. Many women in the MLF had come from the extreme left, and brought with them its theoretical frameworks and its conflicts. The "class struggle tendency" was heavily influenced by the Ligue communiste révolutionnaire (LCR), the French section of the Fourth International, and the Organisation communiste des travailleurs. Heated arguments took place between the class struggle and revolutionary feminists, and the conflict between them began to die down only in about 1980, when the ideological divisions between them were weakened as a result of increasing feminist involvement in mainstream politics.

Conflicts between class struggle and revolutionary feminists also concerned the organization of the movement. Whereas the former demanded a structured organization, the latter were opposed to vertical power structures and traditional forms of political organization. They were proud of the movement's informal and flexible structure and objected to any attempts to make it more rigid. But there were also problems on an individual level. The women who entered the MLF from the extreme left often experienced intense conflict between their activities within the movement and those within their political organizations, a conflict which, for many women, became debilitating. Neither trusted nor fully recognized by either, they were fighting a difficult battle. By 1976, the pull of these divided loyalties had forced many of them to make a decision to go one way or the other, and the tendency as such disappeared (Duchen, 1986: 28–30). However, the feminists in the LCR are probably the most active today and the review which they publish, *Les cahiers du féminisme*, has appeared regularly without a break since 1977.

Féministes révolutionnaires

Revolutionary, or radical, feminists, as they would probably be called today (Duchen, 1987: 22n), constituted the most active tendency of the MLF in the early 1970s, and were responsible for the highly visible actions which brought feminism into the public eye. However, they are also the most difficult to define. Françoise Picq (1993: 198) writes, "Strictly speaking, there is no revolutionary feminist 'tendency'. There is not even a group which meets regularly. It is rather a collection of ideas, whose boundaries are variable and difficult to define." The first revolutionary feminist group, Les petites marguerites, formed in November 1970, but lasted only three months. After that, groups formed, split and re-formed with some of the same women and some new ones, especially during important campaigns, such as the one against rape, when it appeared necessary to present a radical feminist position represented by a specific group (Delphy, personal correspondence).

Revolutionary feminism was influenced by American radical feminism, and had much in common with it. It saw gender as the primary dividing factor in society; women were seen to constitute a sex class; patriarchy, not capitalism, was the main enemy; and separatism was seen as the only effective political strategy (Jenson, 1990: 131). The revolutionary feminists were in constant conflict with the class struggle tendency. Les petites marguerites formed as a means of escaping the "incessant quarrels" with the women who held the "capitalism first" position, who were, at the time, grouped around Antoinette Fouque (see below) (Delphy, personal correspondence). However, they were divided on many questions, including the issue of sexual difference: whereas some revolutionary feminists wanted sexual difference eliminated, others wanted to accentuate it. They were also divided on the question of sexuality, with lesbian feminists accusing heterosexual feminists of collaborating with the enemy.[15]

Revolutionary feminists produced many publications, reflecting the plurality of the tendency. *QF* (1977–80), which, with its successor, *NQF* (1981–), will be examined in detail in Chapter 4, was among these. In contrast to British radical feminists, French "revolutionary feminists" have been good at theorizing, although relatively incapable of organizing and sustaining campaigns. However, there are exceptions, and a variety of groups and projects have emerged from this tendency. These include the Ligue du droit des femmes, which, among other activities, formed women's aid collectives, including SOS femmes-alternatives (offering support to battered women) and SOS femmes violées (Remy, 1990: 43–3). The AVFT is in the same radical feminist tradition, as are the women who are currently organizing the campaign for parity between men and women in political institutions.

Psychanalyse et politique

One of the first feminist groups to form in Paris, Psychanalyse et politique, also known as Psych et po, maintained a high profile throughout the 1970s. Part of its influence was due to its creation of a publishing house, magazine and bookshops (all called des femmes). Another reason for its influence was its charismatic founder and leader, psychoanalyst Antoinette Fouque.

Psych et po was intellectually influential. Luce Irigaray, Hélène Cixous and Julia Kristeva all passed through the group, although Cixous was the only one to maintain any long-term relations with them, publishing all her work with des femmes between 1976 and 1982 (Moi, 1987: 4). However, the group was attacked by other feminists for being politically divisive. It was criticized for using inaccessible language which excluded the majority of women. Other feminists also objected to Psych et po's repeated public claims to be representative of the women's movement, the MLF, claims which culminated in 1979 when Psych et po registered the name Mouvement de libération des femmes and the initials MLF as company trademarks, thus preventing anyone else from using them.[16] Naturally, this enraged the women in the movement. They joined together to denounce this behaviour, writing to the press and subtitling all their reviews "du mouvement de libération des femmes", thus challenging Fouque to take them all to court (Delphy, 1991a: 145).

Their anger was aggravated by the fact that at the same time as writing in the name of the MLF, Psych et po considered themselves "anti-feminist", and their review *Des femmes en mouvements – hebdo* constantly attacked the rest of the movement (Kandel, 1980). According to Fouque, feminism was a reformist compromise with the patriarchy. What she advocated was a complete overthrow of "phallogocentrism", the entire masculine tradition of thought. A couple of years later, the media were talking of the "MLF-déposé" (the registered or official MLF) and the "MLF-non-déposé" (the unofficial MLF), and the issue died down for a while (Delphy, 1991a: 145).

1978–81: A period of change

The period around 1978–81 was one of change, uncertainty and reflection for the women's movement in France. The Left was on the decline and had suffered defeat in the legislative elections in March 1978; the effects of the economic crisis were worsening and this brought a move from collective struggle to individualism, a search for security and a rising anti-feminism. Although many women remained active within the parties and the unions, many feminist groups disappeared, and there was a move from radical activism to feminist research (Remy, 1990: 103–4). In 1979 Psych et po appropriated the name of the movement and, with the name, its actions and visibility. In 1980 a number of articles appeared reflecting on the ten years of feminism which had passed (Delphy, 1980; Picq, 1981). The arrival in power of the Left in 1981 posed further problems for the women's movement, with regards to its relationship to institutions and strategies for achieving short-term reforms (*NQF*, 2, 1981, 5). The women who had been involved in the movement from the beginning also began to worry about the new generation of young women who, they felt, were taking the gains of ten years of hard struggle for granted (Delphy, 1980; Picq, 1981).

While denying that feminism was dead, feminists were nevertheless aware of the changes taking place in the movement. A frequent declaration by feminists was that feminism had been "institutionalized". For many, the most potent symbol of this institutionalization was the creation of the Ministry for Women's Rights when the Socialists came to power in 1981. Françoise Picq (1993: 332) goes so far as to write that "the Ministry for Women's Rights has replaced the women's movement". During its short period of existence (1981–6), the ministry achieved a number of reforms. Abortions were reimbursed by social security; women's centres were established with ministry funding; projects were set up; and feminist research was introduced into the CNRS. However, it is clear that these would not have happened had it not been for the preceding decade of feminist struggle, and feminist criticisms of the ministry continued.

The existence of the ministry, the (very limited) insertion of women's studies into universities, the success of some reforms and the ways in which political parties and trade unions took on a number of feminist ideas all contributed to the changes that took place in the movement. Feminists remained active, but the revolutionary fervour of the 1970s was replaced by longer-term projects, such as setting up refuges for women and children and doing feminist research. As these long-term, low-profile projects began to replace the highly visible actions of the early years, media attention waned (Remy, 1990: 117).

The term "postfeminism" was increasingly used by the media to refer to the social climate in which these changes took place. The meaning of "postfeminism" varies according to the author and the context. Two of the most common meanings are that feminism has achieved its aims and is no longer necessary, or that it has given up and is no longer relevant. Although feminism in France had been accompanied almost from the beginning by media suggestions that it was already over, this opinion was reinforced in 1978 when Maria Antoinetta Macciochi, an Italian politician and writer who lived and taught in Paris, published a book entitled *Les femmes et leurs maîtres*, in which she declared that feminism was dead. This was echoed by the media over the next few years (Duchen, 1987: 44n).[17] An example of the cultural expression of the notion of "postfeminism" was the launch of *F Magazine*, a women's magazine appearing for the first time in January 1978. It was aimed at the "new woman", the intelligent, successful career woman, who can juggle the demands of home and the office while still maintaining a smart professional, yet unerringly sexy, appearance.

Feminist research

One of the major changes which took place in French feminism in the 1980s was its introduction into academic institutions. Student demand and the commitment of individual lecturers had led to the creation of some feminist courses in the early 1970s, especially in the universities Paris VIII Vincennes, Paris VII Jussieu and Aix-en-Provence. By the end of the 1970s, courses were being offered in other universities at all levels, but often in a low-profile or underground way. Informal feminist groups also began to meet in universities in the mid-1970s, one of the first being the Centre d'études féminines de l'université de Provence (CEFUP), formed in 1972, and recognized by the university in 1976, when it received funding for its educational activities. It organized the first conference Les femmes et les sciences humaines in 1975. In Paris, the Groupe d'études féministes was created at Paris VII in 1975, and the Centre lyonnais d'études féministes has organized and run a library, resource centre and interdisciplinary seminars since 1976. Feminist research groups such as the Centre de recherches d'études féministes at Paris VII and the Groupe interdisciplinaire d'études des femmes at Toulouse also appeared. Other groups, including the interdisciplinary seminar group Limites-frontières, organized on the borderline between the universities and the movement (ANEF, 1995). However, the form of this research changed considerably with the official recognition by academic institutions, following the first national conference on feminist research in 1982. This conference, Femmes, féminisme et recherche, was held in Toulouse, and was supported by the Ministry of Research, the Ministry for Women's Rights and the CNRS (CNRS, 1989: 2). Following the conference, the CNRS launched a research programme that financed 70 Actions thématiques programmées (ATPs) called Recherches féministes et recherches sur les femmes.

Within the women's movement, a certain amount of conflict arose between feminists in the institutions and those outside. The conference at Toulouse was criticized on the grounds that it marked the institutionalization of French feminism, which had, at least in its early days, prided itself on its opposition to, and independence from, the institutions. According to some critics, the fact that the conference was funded by the Ministry of Research and the Ministry for Women's

Rights explained why so many of the feminists who spoke came from within the institutions, whether the universities or the CNRS (Basch, 1983). Although one of the questions which was addressed at Toulouse was how to increase contact between the movement and the institutions (Picq, 1984; Zelensky, 1984), some commentators have expressed scepticism about the sincerity of this concern. For example, the group Ruptures . . . et féminisme en devenir (Brun et al., 1984) criticized the way in which "theory" was becoming the reserve of a small number of women, while others went unheard. They saw a widening gap between theory and practice which they feared could destroy the movement. A controversial criticism of the direction which was being taken by feminist studies in France was offered by Rose-Marie Lagrave (1990), who argues that the advent of women's studies marked the death of the movement.

According to the ATP (CNRS, 1989: 2), the links between research within the institutions, research outside the institutions, and the women's movement were strong, for example:

> This development of research "within the institution" was linked to its rapid expansion "outside the institution", as we used to say in those days, and to which the "Limites-frontières" [Limits and Boundaries] seminar programme, which has been held in Paris since 1980, bears witness. Between the two, there are numerous connections and openings, even if this is only on an individual level. Both types of research have sought to respond to the women's movement in the largest sense, to all the questions and issues that it has raised.

During the early days of feminist research, the small number of women's studies courses on offer in the universities were marginalized, both in terms of the programmes in which they appeared and the buildings in which they took place. At the same time, feminists had to adopt a certain number of institutionally acceptable practices, and conform to the rules of academic writing (Lagrave, 1990: 30). A constant cause for complaint from feminists involved in women's studies was the extent to which the exchange between feminism and traditional institutional knowledge was one-way. Whereas some academic feminists had to abandon certain values in favour of those of academic research (replacing anonymous and collective projects with individually authored books and articles, for example), other disciplines did not take any notice of contributions by feminist theorists, marginalizing women's studies, and perceiving it as "unscientific", "subjective" and "politically biased". Feminists were in conflict about the extent to which male academic values and conventions should be accepted, especially among feminists who were involved in the teaching of women's studies, "thereby attempting to reconcile activism and research, or to continue their activism through their research" (Lagrave, 1990: 28). For feminists in the movement this represented a betrayal, and women who might have been tempted to make a career in "male" institutions experienced both pressure and guilt (Picq, 1984: 916).

The ATP was confronted with the same problems. Should the successful research projects employ conventional methodology and demonstrate that feminist research is "scientific" and "objective", or should they challenge conventional methodologies and demonstrate the radical nature of feminist research, which exists only in relation to the women's movement?

The debate over the role of the institutions in feminism has lost some of its impetus now that feminism has once again almost completely disappeared from academic circles. There are currently five university lectureships in "women's studies", although they are all part of another department. There are no feminist studies in the sense of fixed courses and syllabuses that remain after the original holder of the post has left; it is individuals who take responsibility for teaching feminist studies within the context of their discipline. Not only that, but some individuals have chosen not to call their work "feminist", believing that to do so could jeopardize their careers (Delphy, interview). Although there are feminist researchers in the CNRS, there are currently few research teams which call themselves feminist. In fact, there is only one clearly feminist research team, the Groupe d'études sur la division sexuelle et sociale du travail. However, feminist research in the CNRS (which for a long time concentrated on work and the family) now explores a broader range of subjects and there has been some diffusion of feminist methodologies, despite the resistance on the part of a very conservative university sector. While the number of university posts in women's studies is limited, a growing number of courses are offered, and research continues to take place, even though funding is rarely available (ANEF, 1995: 701). Outside the universities and research institutes, feminist research takes place within various organizations, including the AVFT, which publishes *Projets féministes*; the Archives, recherches et cultures lesbiennes, which publishes a directory of feminist activities and runs a resource centre; and the collective Femmes sous lois musulmanes.

Toulouse stands out now as an exception rather than the precedent which it was thought to be at the time. The research programme which emerged from the conference lasted only four years, and was not replaced with any new initiatives at the end of this period. This was despite the fact that at the time women's studies was receiving an increasing amount of support in other European countries. The institutionalization of feminist studies in France was thus very short-lived.

French feminism today

It is difficult to establish what exactly French feminism is today. Many feminists will admit the existence of feminist groups involved in specific projects, but not of a movement as such (Sert, 1989: 141). Françoise Collin (1989: 165) claims that while French feminism is currently suffering a lack of visibility, this is not to say that it is dead. A latent period in which the feminism of the 1970s disappeared is being followed by a redefinition. Feminism no longer consists of spectacular struggles, but of a gradual spread of ideas:

It is striking to consider the extent to which a consciousness and practice has developed among young women which is feminist, but is not
always recognised as such and which does not lead to the creation of
active groups, which have gradually disappeared. (Collin, 1989: 165)

Françoise Picq (1991: 265) concluded the 1988 conference Crises de la
société: féminisme et changement with the words, "Feminism is not dead. It
carries on in different, historically specific forms. The forms it took in the 1970s
belong to that period." And similarly, Françoise Thébaud (1992: 21) writes in
the introduction to *L'histoire des femmes en occident: le vingtième siècle*,

What may appear to be the decline of feminism – some talk of postfeminism – is as much a transformation as a disappearance. Its history
continues as a non-stop process of change which is unpredictable, but
at the same time contained in the past.

Many feminists argue that part of the reason why feminism is now seen
as outmoded is its relative success on a social and cultural level (Delphy, 1980;
Collin, 1992; Lesselier, 1992). This does not mean that feminism has achieved
all of its aims; feminists are perfectly aware that even the legislative changes
that they have forced could be retracted at any time. For example, despite the
fact that the right to free contraception is now taken for granted by many French
women, 13 of the 27 types of contraceptive pill currently available in France are
not reimbursed by social security, and others are under threat (Halimi, 1992:
XLII). Violent attacks on abortion clinics are increasing.[18] But feminism has had
an effect. By 1979, when they were already having to respond to claims that
they no longer existed, feminists were offering explanations such as the following for the decreased visibility of the movement:

The movement is spreading and affecting even the most everyday
behaviour, as was its aim. This is happening to such an extent that it
can pass unnoticed. The feminist tendencies which have appeared within
the parties . . . and the diffusion by the media of feminist ideas demonstrate the strength of the movement. . . . The "co-option" of feminist
ideas (for example, the creation of the Secretariat for Women's Affairs)
still serves as a pretext for talking of feminism's failure, for which we
are held responsible. Historically, however, co-option is in fact indica-
tive of the vitality of the movement: by trying to co-opt feminism, the
establishment is in fact recognizing its existence, even as it tries to
neutralize it. (Des féministes de Collectif féministe contre le viol et
Elles voient rouges, 1979: 103)

This gradual spread of feminist ideas throughout society was initially criticised by many feminists for whom it represented a "watering-down" of feminist

ideas and their co-option by, for example, political parties. Monique Remy's main thesis in her history of the movement, *De l'utopie à l'intégration: histoire des mouvements de femmes* (1990), is that feminism in France lost its strength as a result of the move from "revolution to reform". However, Françoise Picq (1993: 349) states succinctly that "Reform is not simply the antithesis of revolution, as we believed in the heat of the struggle; it is just as much its consequence." And in an article published in 1980, Christine Delphy (1980: 5–6) suggests that "reformism" should not necessarily be seen as negative. She writes:

> While we rejoice when a sister, a mother or a friend begins to respond to feminism, we paradoxically condemn the collective expression of this nascent consciousness. How often do we describe the first, timid adoption of feminist positions as the "watering-down", the "betrayal", or even the "co-option" of "our" ideas? This is to misunderstand not only the way in which we achieve a greater consciousness, a process we have nevertheless all been through, and ought therefore to know about, but also of the way in which ideas are spread; it also suggests a desire, which is both unrealistic and politically suspect, to keep control of the ideas which we produce.

A quick survey of feminist activity in France today would reveal small groups of project-orientated feminists working in specific areas, whether this is solidarity with the women of the former Yugoslavia[19], the campaign for parity (Gaspard et al., 1992), or women and Aids.[20] Other issue-specific feminist groups are active around male violence towards women (Association contre les violences faites aux femmes au travail, Collectif féministe contre le viol); the defence of the right to abortion and contraception (Mouvement français pour le planning familial); the problems faced by immigrant women (Collectif des femmes immigrées); and solidarity with the women of Algeria.[21]

Some recent campaigns seem to be acting as a remobilizing force for feminists in France. The right to free and legal abortion, which is increasingly under threat, is still high on the feminist agenda. A demonstration organized by the Coordination nationale des associations pour le droit à l'avortement et à la contraception brought 40,000 supporters onto the streets of Paris on 25 November 1995. Commentators have remarked not only on the size of the demonstration, but on the breadth of support which it attracted for a wide range of demands in addition to reproductive rights. These included the right to work and sexual equality at work. It is significant that the demonstration was supported by much of the left, which had previously withheld its support from feminist demands (Picq, 1996). This is being presented as a positive opportunity for feminism, and the organization of a national conference on women's rights in 1997 was a direct result of the demonstration (Forest, 1996: 39).

Psych et po

Psych et po no longer exists as such, but Antoinette Fouque continues to exert a strong influence on the representation of the women's movement and of feminist ideas in France. Fouque's ability to use the media to her advantage, coupled with the reluctance of the rest of the movement to do this, have meant that she has generated much of the publicity for feminist actions in France and has consequently been represented as the spokesperson for the movement (Visser, 1993). Since 1989, when Fouque created the Alliance des femmes pour la démocratie, it has become more difficult to discern her underlying ideology (Trat, 1996). The Alliance des femmes continues to demand the recognition of women's specificity, a position which has been a source of conflict with other feminists since the 1970s. *QF*, in particular, has always opposed the idea of women's difference (*QF*, 1997). However, Fouque seems to have revoked her total opposition to equality, which she used to perceive as women striving to be like men, instead of discovering ways to realize their own femininity. Far from the total rejection of male power structures which she advocated in the 1970s, Fouque now seems happy to join in. In the 1994 European elections she supported Bernard Tapie and was herself elected MEP. She also seems to have revoked her anti-feminism. Josette Trat (1996: 28), in an article in *Cahiers du féminisme*, quotes Fouque from 1990 in a surprising about-turn in her attitude towards feminism:

> As for feminism, I did not know what it was and now I could say that I regret it. It was a sign of my ignorance of women's struggles throughout history. . . At the time, I was fighting to prevent the women's movement becoming the "feminist movement". I thought, maybe wrongly, that with the word "women" we had the chance to speak, if not to all women, at least to the largest possible number.

Josette Trat, argues, perhaps surprisingly, that Antoinette Fouque should not be condemned outright and excluded from all feminist actions. Trat urges us to see the Alliance des femmes not simply as the successor of Psych et po, but as an association with a feminist agenda. The Alliance des femmes supports the struggle of women against fundamentalism in Algeria. It opposes the subordination of women, the rape of women in the former Yugoslavia and the proposed *salaire maternel* (an allowance for women who stay at home to look after their children). The solution, argues Trat, is not to exclude them, but to bring them into feminist discussions, while insisting that they respect the rules of the "movement". However, this is not the position taken by *NQF* (Delphy, 1995: 6) and ANEF, who are refusing to co-operate with Fouque and her supporters in the organization of feminist actions.

Feminist research continues to take place in universities and in the CNRS, although the funding and institutional recognition it receives are minimal. In some areas of feminist activity the gap between the movement and research is striking, and contact between activists and theorists limited. For example, talking about feminist work on male violence towards women, Marie-Victoire Louis (interview, 1993) of the AVFT commented, "There is all this work by activists, but it has nevertheless been completely divorced from the theoretical work of intellectuals." On the question of violence, there are, she adds, better relations between activists and feminist lawyers than between activists and researchers. Françoise Collin (1989: 163–4) also describes feminism as split in two:

> French feminism today seems to have fallen back onto just two of its many areas of activity: on the one hand, "feminist research", which was established at the Toulouse conference, and on the other hand, social services, in which I would include help-groups for battered women or women immigrants. Between the two, despite certain initiatives, there is an absence of thought and political action, which is nevertheless no worse than that which affects the traditional political scene of the parties. . . . Feminism is no longer, or has not become, the common ground of intellectuals and non-intellectuals, of theory and practice, which it dreamt of becoming. The absence I am describing is hardly ever analyzed by researchers, either because they have abandoned their hopes of changing the world or because they believe that the fundamental change in knowledge, which they are attempting to bring about, will of itself change the world.

To summarize, then, feminism in France has undergone a dramatic transformation since 1968. The turning-point can probably be identified as 1978–81, and this period usually marks the cut-off point in accounts of "the movement years". Since then, feminist activity has been more localized and issue-centred. Important reforms have been gained through feminist pressure. Some feminist ideas have been taken up by political parties, the media and large sections of society, producing the phenomenon known as "everyday feminism". This is subject to less criticism now than in the late 1970s, when the debate around revolution and reform was at its height, and it is seen more as a sign of feminism's success than its failures. Research has continued to take place, although in the face of strong resistance from the universities and a distinct lack of interest on the part of publishers. The gap between movement and research seems to differ according to the specific issue or campaign. Thus, while activists and theorists seem to be in contact around reproductive rights, those involved in male violence are very critical of the distance between the two aspects of feminist activity.

There are signs, however, that the gap between movement and theory could be bridged. This is most likely to happen around specific campaigns, for example the campaign for the equal representation of men and women in politics. This is an issue which is showing signs of remobilizing feminists across theory and practice. As a campaign focused on a single concrete demand, it attracts support from a wide range of feminists. At the same time, it raises numerous theoretical questions which cannot be ignored.

Representations of feminism

The way in which feminism is represented in France and abroad has an effect on the reception of the theories of masculinity which it has produced. The representation of feminism in the media provides some clues about the impact of feminism on French society and about the climate in which theories of masculinity are being produced and received. The fact that so much attention is being paid to masculinity is an indication that feminism has had some impact. An examination of the representation of feminism in the media shows that it is, as far as possible, presented as a thing of the past. The weekly news magazine *L'événement du jeudi* (Domenach, 1992: 52) has declared that feminism is dead: "The feminist revolt which shook the 1970s is over. The war of the sexes is finished." This assertion is also found in *L'express* (Remy et al., 1993: 29), another weekly news magazine. Both talk of feminism only in the past tense. Women who are challenging gender relations today are referred to as "postfeminists". There is no definition of either term and no attempt to justify the distinction between the two. The assumption is that feminism is over and that we are now in a postfeminist era.

Although anti-feminism is not new in France, some commentators are currently talking of a backlash, following the success in French bookshops of Susan Faludi's (1991) book of the same name, which charted incidences of American anti-feminism in the 1980s. The term "backlash" is not universally accepted, however. As Sylvia Walby (1993) argues, it implies a straightforward reaction to feminism, and this is probably too simplistic. Given the radical nature of the feminist project, resistance should be expected. Opposition to feminism is inevitable; it is the expression of men's attempts to hold on to their power, which is currently under threat. At the same time, however, patriarchy continues to exert itself in many ways and there are numerous examples of anti-feminist practices which were not planned as a reaction to feminism. For example, cuts in welfare spending are anti-feminist in that they are, on the whole, much more damaging for women than for men, but they are motivated not by opposition to feminism, but by liberal economic policy. In other words, policies which are introduced for other political reasons may have a particularly damaging effect on women, but it is far more complicated than a simple backlash.

A study by psychologists Marie-Claire Hurtig and Marie-France Pichevin (1995) traces changes in the popular representation of sexual difference, demonstrating, they claim, a rising anti-feminism. Hurtig and Pichevin claim that scientific evidence is selectively used to support the idea that the sexes are biologically different. This evidence is unrepresentative of the heterogeneity of theories from the scientific community. Hurtig and Pichevin conclude that this revival of biologism is part of a backlash against feminism, whose other manifestations include attacks on abortion clinics and attempts to encourage women back into the home.

Anti-feminism in the media is often accompanied by expressions of anti-Americanism. Feminism is portrayed as something which was indulged in briefly by some French women in the 1970s, but is essentially American. This has the effect of removing discussions of feminism from the French experience and instead portraying France as "postfeminist" or no longer in need of feminism. There are two variations on this theme. According to the first, feminism has achieved its aims and is now no longer necessary. According to the second, feminists have realized the errors of their ways and are now happy to forget it all and re-embrace the French way of being a woman.

This is often bound up with the idea that men and women relate to each other differently in France; that there is a complementarity between the sexes and a different attitude towards seduction and sexuality. "Feminism" is often presented as a brief aberration from this French national characteristic. In opposition to this, and representing a danger to it, is American feminism, which is radical, man-hating and powerful. Here we see the idea of the nation joining together against imported American ideas which could contaminate the idealism of French sexual relations. The message is that all French citizens, men and women, have an interest in joining together to resist this external threat. This is evident in the debate around sexual harassment, sexual violence and political correctness.

Political correctness is ridiculed in France not only on the right, as is the case in Britain and the United States, but also on the left. This is probably due to the fact that the main source of information about political correctness has been the largely conservative American popular press (Ezekiel, 1995). The debate around political correctness, which in the United States is highly politicized and deeply rooted in a specific cultural and historical context, has been removed from this context to become nothing more than a joke and an example of American extremism. Ridicule is used to undermine the recognition of difference, which is at the base of political correctness. The rejection of political correctness in France has to a large extent ignored racism, which is much higher on the political agenda in the United States than in France; the impact of the women's movement, which has been far greater than in France; the strength of the Moral Majority, or the conservative religious right; and the problem of sexual violence on American university campuses (Lévy-Willard, 1995).

One of the main reasons for the French rejection of political correctness is the republican tradition of universalism. Within the logic of universalism, according to which all citizens are the same and equal, there is no room for the recognition of difference, for to recognize differences between citizens would provide reasons for inequality. Feminists have criticized the notion of universalism, arguing that what is supposed to be universal is in practice masculine. While there is theoretically no difference between a male and a female citizen, the state has a very different impact on the life of an individual depending on whether or not that individual may want an abortion, may not be able to enter politics because of widespread inequality in the sharing of domestic chores, or may be limited in career choices and earning power because of the feminization of low-paid sectors of the labour market. What French feminists have not done, however, is to concentrate on the multiple differences among women themselves, and a particularly noticeable difference between French and Anglophone feminism is the level of theorization of multiple identities.

The effect of the opposition between French and American feminism is that many problems are hidden by it. For example, Elisabeth Badinter (1992), a very well-known intellectual who has written a best-selling book on men and masculinity, implies that male violence is not a problem in France, as it is in the United States, thus denying the experiences of many French women and silencing those who are trying to raise public awareness of its existence. The debate on sexual harassment which surrounded the introduction of legislation against it was also conducted in opposition to what is represented as the ridiculously extreme situation in the United States. Benoite Groult, editor of the pro-feminist *F-Magazine* in the late 1970s, wrote in 1994 (quoted by Louis, 1994: 63), "In the United States, sexual harassment is talked about a lot, but in France it is a national sport which is played in public! And in our official institutions!" While in the United States the term "sexual harassment" was coined to identify the use of sexuality to affirm gender domination and referred to behaviour based on gender, in France this definition has been distorted. The law against sexual harassment in France refers only to the abuse of a position of authority to obtain sexual favours. There is a striking absence of an awareness of gendered power relations both in the French legislation and in the debate which surrounded it (Delphy, 1996: 152).

But how can we explain the fact that French women, including some feminists, defend their "right" to seduce and be seduced against what they perceive as American thought-police? How do we explain the representation of sexuality in France as specifically French? Although recognizing the dangers of falling into the trap of perpetuating national stereotypes, Lisa Appignanesi (1994) asserts that women in public places in France *do* have different experiences to women in public places in Britain. It is also true that, while an extramarital affair is frequently a reason for the resignation of a British public figure, in France it is seen as barely worthy of a mention, and the idea that someone should resign for this reason is perceived as ludicrous. Furthermore, women who reach positions of power in France go to great lengths to stress that they nevertheless still value their femininity and sexual attractiveness.

This preoccupation with seduction represents a striking difference between Anglophone and French feminism. It means that feminists are concerned not only with changing gender relations on a societal level, but also within the couple, which occupies a far more important place in French than in Anglo-American feminist thought.

To summarize, then: anti-feminism is frequently found in the media. It is often constructed in conjunction with anti-Americanism and with a portrayal of French gender relations as particularly consensual and sexy. This has implications for feminists, whose debates around sexual harassment, political correctness and, as we shall see in Chapter 4, gender have also been constructed, in part, around a reductionist view of the American debate. It also has implications for popular interpretations of changes in masculinity. The effects of feminism on French society, and in particular on masculine identity and on relations within the couple, are taken as a starting-point for the analysis of the French male psyche in the popular interpretations of masculinity examined in Chapter 2.

French feminism or "French feminism"

French feminism as it is understood by feminists in France is very different to "French feminism" as it is perceived in Britain and the United States. This difference has important implications for the choice of materials covered in this book and needs careful explanation. This section aims to clarify what is labelled "French feminist" in France and outside; to explain the absence from this book of two of the three theorists who represent French feminism in many Anglo-American publications – Luce Irigaray, Hélène Cixous and Julia Kristeva – and to examine the relation between these theorists and feminism in France.

American feminists and women's studies departments have been particularly keen to import "French feminism", but the texts they have chosen for translation, critique and popularization have often been severely limited to a narrow band of French women theorists, which is sometimes reduced to only three: Luce Irigaray, Hélène Cixous and Julia Kristeva. The inverted commas which almost always accompany the Anglo-American "French feminism" demonstrate the authors' detachment, hesitation or recognition that the term does not really mean what it says. A multitude of footnotes attest to this knowledge. For example, Nancy Fraser writes: *"New French feminisms* . . . was the book that first constructed 'French feminism' as a distinctive cultural object for English-speaking readers" (Fraser & Bartky, 1992: 1). She adds in a footnote:

> We could doubtless learn much about the workings of our culture and its institutions if we could reconstruct the precise process of this synecdochic reduction. It is all the more striking in that it occurred despite the strenuous protests of Monique Wittig, Simone de Beauvoir, and the editors of the journal *Questions féministes*. (ibid.)

And yet the rest of the book consists almost entirely of articles by and about Irigaray, Kristeva and Sarah Kofman, as well as by American academics writing in the "French" tradition.

A binary opposition has been constructed between "French feminism", which is highly theoretical and influenced by psychoanalysis, deconstruction and post-structuralism, and "Anglo-American feminism", which is empiricist, pragmatic and concerned with producing change at a social and political, rather than a discursive level. This opposition is dependent on maintaining a clear distinction between the two types of feminism. So the aspects of French feminism which provide the starkest contrast with the equally reductionist representation of "Anglo-American feminism" are emphasized, while more familiar forms of feminist theory and practice are ignored. In order to maintain the distinction between French and Anglo-American theory, some curious adjustments have been made to the meaning of the terms "French" and "Anglo-American". The literary critic Toril Moi (1987: 6) points out, for example, that the texts which are considered particularly "French" are those which have more of an "exotic flavour", rather than the materialist-feminist texts, which in fact have much in common with British socialist feminism. While materialist feminists are excluded from the category "French feminism", American feminists can be included in it, by virtue of their style and use of theory. Toril Moi (1985: xiv) writes:

A final point: the terms "Anglo-American" and "French" must not be taken to represent purely national demarcations: they do not signal the critics' birthplace but the intellectual tradition within which they work. Thus I do not consider the many British and American women deeply influenced by French thought to be "Anglo-American" critics.

This has produced the paradoxical situation in which the poststructuralist feminist theory referred to by Anglo-American feminist critics as "French feminism" is described in France as particularly American (Collin, 1992).

The nature of feminism in France is, then, very different to that suggested by many studies of "French feminism". Significantly, two of the three theorists most frequently referred to as "the French feminists" are not seen as important actors in French feminism by French feminists themselves. Julia Kristeva, a linguist and psychoanalyst, receives little attention from French feminists: "She is neither a feminist, nor, I suppose, an anti-feminist. . . . For us, what she writes is outside feminism" (Delphy, interview, 1993). Hélène Cixous, a novelist, playwright and professor of literature at Paris VIII, was involved in the feminist movement in the 1970s, but has not written on the subject for many years. Not only do French feminists pay little attention to the work of these theorists; some even express amazement or incredulity at the thought that this work is considered "feminist" by otherwise critical British and American feminists. Christine Delphy (1985: 151) writes:

In the United States, Cixous, Kristeva and Irigaray, among others, are studied, and what is more, they are studied as feminists. This is, to say the least, shocking with regard to the first two, who proclaim their distance from feminism high and low.

In contrast to Hélène Cixous and Julia Kristeva, who are labelled "feminist" only outside France, the philosopher and psychoanalyst Luce Irigaray has a following in the movement. She has many critics, some of them overtly hostile (Guerlais, 1991: 64; Planté, 1993: 114), but her theories of difference are highly influential and are examined in Chapter 3.

The construction of "French feminism" has exaggerated the place occupied by Cixous, Irigaray and Kristeva and ignored the developments in feminist practice and theory in France. It presents a picture distorted in several respects. Firstly, it groups together theorists whose work has little in common. Secondly, of the three theorists most often referred to as "French feminists" two do not refer to themselves as feminists and have expressed differing degrees of hostility towards feminism. Elizabeth Grosz (1989: 234) argues that we cannot, however, use this factor to claim either that they are not feminist or that, as feminists, they are politically inactive and ineffective. She claims that the implications of their theories are highly political, challenging, as they do, the very basis of male-dominated knowledges. The production of meanings, discourses and knowledges which challenge existing ones is an essential part of the feminist struggle, even though it could not achieve feminism's aims alone. Grosz argues that "Without a critical feminist awareness of the ways patriarchal knowledges inform everyday language and life and without alternative frameworks of knowledge and representation, women will remain tied to a series of concepts and values which oppress them."

However, the recognition that the dismantling of patriarchal discourses is an important aspect of feminism's project does not justify its construction as the only, or most important, part of the French feminist struggle. As Marie-Victoire Louis comments (interview, 1993), "Feminism is not three women. Feminism is a social movement, it is currents and contradictions, and if there were an important aspect of French feminism, it would be found in the work of historians and sociologists."

Thirdly, there are now French feminists who have been advised not to refer to themselves as such outside France in case it should mislead English-speaking readers. But if they cannot call themselves French feminists, then what can they call themselves? Eleni Varikas (1993: 63) writes:

The "national" modifier thus effaces or trivializes any other feminist positions; it implies that any reference which falls outside those selected and defined as French theory or French feminism, *is not theoretical* (or *is not feminist*) and that it therefore does not need to be discussed. However, reducing "French" feminism to certain theoretical positions not only obscures the fact that the majority of feminist struggles have been led outside and sometimes against these positions; not only does it obscure the most influential theoretical positions in feminist thought in France (Colette Guillaumin, Christine Delphy, Michèle Le Doeuff, Nicole-Claude Mathieu, to cite just a few); it prevents the analysis of the conditions in

which these numerous positions emerged, of their relation to the political practice of women, of what makes them socially and academically
acceptable or unacceptable, and of their subversive dynamic.

The theories of masculinity examined in this book emerged from a feminism
which is diverse, dynamic and contradictory. It is important to situate them in
this context. They also need to be situated within the context of a broader debate
on masculinity which is taking place in France. This is the subject of Chapter 2.

2   French theories of masculinity

Writing on men and masculinity is on the increase in France. However, the literature is much thinner than it is in Britain. Individual researchers are working on specific aspects such as fatherhood, but it is difficult to identify areas of interest or dominant themes other than this. By tracing the development of specific discourses on masculinity, we can situate the feminist discourse in relation to the others. We can also assess the varying weight carried by these discourses. A salient feature of the discourses on masculinity which are examined here is that they are almost all constructed around a certain representation of feminism. Examining the masculinity debate therefore also enables us to consider the various ways in which feminism is represented and the implications of these representations for feminist politics.

Three categories of texts have been selected: early texts produced by men involved in men's groups; articles from the popular press; and a number of recently published books.

Early critiques of men and masculinity

It was critiques of masculinity which emerged from the early men's groups which established a debate around men and masculinity. Men's groups began to form in the 1970s as a response to feminism and with the aim of discussing some aspect of gender relations. They varied considerably in terms of their attitudes towards women and feminism and in terms of their ideals for future relations between the sexes. For example, some aimed to protect the rights of fathers in the face of women's increasing control over reproduction, while others met to discuss ways of freeing themselves and their partners from what they saw as the harmful constraints of masculinity.

The early texts on men and masculinity are far from homogeneous. They include writing by heterosexuals and homosexuals, by pro-feminist and anti-feminist men, and by men who remain ambivalent to feminism. An examination of these texts can reveal the relation between them and early feminist writings on masculinity. Much of the early questioning of masculinity was carried out by men as a response to feminism. The form this response took varied considerably. One indication that men were responding to feminism was the creation of a number of men's groups, beginning in 1972. The number increased, gradually at first, but then more rapidly from 1977. Men's groups differed greatly both in theory and in practice. Some were sympathetic to feminism, some were indifferent to it, and some were ardently anti-feminist. It was men's groups' interest in masculinity which provoked a feminist response and led to the creation of a dialogue on the subject between feminists and men's groups in reviews and journals. Feminists did not join in this debate until later, although it must not be forgotten that there were other ways in which their theories were very much concerned with masculinity, as will be explained below.

A characteristic shared by much of the early writing on masculinity by men in France and in Britain is that it concentrated almost entirely on the authors themselves and on other men, without examining the connections between masculinity and femininity. Masculinity was portrayed as an unfortunate burden, causing men pain and anguish. This writing tended towards the confessional and was often autobiographical. Although credited with exposing much more of their subjectivity as authors than was traditionally acceptable in male academic work, they were criticized by feminists and pro-feminist men for not progressing beyond this step, and for failing to provide any further analysis of masculinity, ignoring, for example, the social structures which reproduce not only this painful suffering, but also the social effects of masculinity and the power relations surrounding it. This approach, which sought individual solutions to the problems of masculinity, and failed to advance beyond coming to terms with this "affliction" on a personal level, was prevalent in the 1980s and can be found in discussions of fatherhood in particular.

Two publications on masculinity have been particularly influential in France. The first is *La fabrication des mâles*, in which Georges Falconnet and Nadine Lefaucheur (1975) argue that both masculinity and femininity need to be challenged and that new ways of relating to each other need to be established. The book draws on the personal experiences of the 32 men that they interviewed, discussing the unease felt by many men in the face of feminist demands, how they acquire their masculine identities, what masculinity means to them and how they perceive women. It explores the contradictory and heterogeneous nature of constructs of masculinity, as well as discussing future alternatives to the models of masculinity the interviewees feel are available to them. It also examines representations of men and masculinity in advertisements, schoolbooks, songs, etc., discussing the relationship between representations of masculinity and consumption, colonialism and imperialism.

The second influential publication on masculinity is an article entitled "La sainte virilité" by Gisèle Fournier and Emmanuel Reynaud (1978).[22] It is a harsh critique of masculinity and of the ways in which it oppresses men as well as women. It begins (p. 31):

> It has rarely occurred to men to criticize masculinity. It is their territory, they identify themselves by it. In its name they undergo all kinds

of suffering and commit all kinds of atrocities, but they do not question it. They see masculinity as a law of nature. It makes them feel at ease; it is the proof of their power. They do not imagine that it could be their prison.

Fournier and Reynaud discuss men's relationships to their bodies; the importance of the penis; competition between men; male violence towards women; and homophobia as a means of maintaining dominant models of masculinity. Arguing that the pressures men are under to conform to a certain model of behaviour are oppressive, they conclude (Fournier & Reynaud, 1978: 61) that men need to free themselves of masculinity in order to discover a new identity: "There is no reason why masculinity and femininity should exist. They are the foundations on which a whole world is built. Questioning them shakes these foundations; destroying them could be the prelude to liberation."

The significance of these two publications lies in their identification of masculinity as a construct which causes problems and which should be challenged and either redefined or destroyed. Several other articles and special issues of reviews which appeared in 1978 were devoted to the question of men and masculinity. Most of them were written by men involved in one way or another with the various men's groups, some of which also produced their own publications, for example, *Pas rôles d'hommes*. This ran for four numbers, then, following a split in the group, it was replaced by *Contraception masculine – paternité*, which published two issues in 1980 and *Types – paroles d'hommes* which appeared between 1981 and 1984 (Welzer-Lang, 1992a: 16). Whereas the former was concerned with male contraception and men's experiences of paternity, the latter was a broader attempt to explore and challenge the construct of masculinity.

In 1982, Guido de Ridder published *Du côté des hommes: à la recherche de nouveaux rapports avec les femmes*. In an attempt to give a voice to a minority of men who are challenging existing models of masculinity and looking for ways to change relations between men and women, Ridder draws on a series of interviews with men involved in the same men's group as himself. He examines the emergence of men's groups, the reaction of those involved to feminism, their reasons for wanting an alternative to "traditional" masculinity, and the difficulties that confront them in their attempts to change. In an optimistic conclusion, he writes (Ridder, 1982: 184) that, "everything seems to indicate that the current changes in relations between men and women are just the beginnings of a far bigger change to come".

Other men's groups were motivated less by the prospect of change in gender relations than by resistance to it. One of the most anti-feminist men's groups was the Mouvement pour la condition masculine et le soutien de l'enfance (MCM), an organization consisting mostly of divorced fathers. Its general secretary, André Perrot (quoted in Ridder, 1982: 50), wrote in the editorial of its journal *Condition masculine*, "The most important thing, to start with, is to realize to what extent the masculine condition as a whole has deteriorated, whether we look at divorce, fatherhood, marriage or social roles, bringing with it disastrous consequences for society."

The Mouvement de la condition masculine et paternelle (MCMP) was created in 1975 in the belief that men are worse off than women, particularly in the family. They abhorred the excesses of feminism and the way in which politicians have given in to feminists' "intellectual terrorism" (*Le monde*, 14 May 1975). Like similar groups in Britain and the United States, reactionary men's groups such as the MCM and the MCMP organized around the issues of fatherhood and "men's rights" and therefore produced less in the way of deconstructions of masculinity than did the more pro-feminist groups.

Critiques of masculinity also emerged from the gay movement. For example, Guy Hocquenghem (1978) argued that the decline of the revolutionary ideas so bound up with representations of working-class masculinity has produced a fragility in masculine identity. Many men are now searching vainly for a new gender identity at a time when they also feel threatened by feminism. The model of the virile working-class man has, he claims, been replaced by American-inspired models. The fact that so many men have been affected by this change, he adds in parenthesis, can only demonstrate just how fragile their identities are. He argues that May 1968 marked the end of a certain type of heroic masculinity, a masculinity which enabled men to position themselves at the forefront of the revolution, while "their" women made the coffee, and gay men were kept at a distance. The gay movement and the feminist movement emerged out of this, bringing their oppression from the private into the public domain. Hocquenghem asserts that there has been a shift in power. The disappearance of "hard" masculinity has left a space for new ways of behaving. Feminist and gay challenges, along with the crisis of masculinity, have made possible the creation of new power relations. But, he adds, not until gay men cease to be seen as a threat to heterosexual men who are desperately trying to repress their homosexuality will the tension be broken.

In October 1984 a conference entitled Men against Sexism was held at St Cloud. It was organized by the review *Types – parole d'hommes* and the organization Association pour la disparition des archétypes masculins. Opinions differ on whether the conference was pro-feminist or not. At the time, feminists were wary, as will be seen below. Daniel Welzer-Lang, from RIME (Recherches et interventions masculines) in Lyons, on the other hand, emphasizes the importance of this conference, since, he claims, it was the first time feminists and "pro-feminist" men had met and discussed the subject in public. A selection of papers from the conference was published in *Les temps modernes* (462, 1985). The interpretations offered in these papers vary, but one aspect receives particular criticism from feminists. This is the view that men are as oppressed by sexism as women, a view which is expressed in the introduction (*Les temps modernes*, 462, 1985, 1303–4) and echoed in some of the papers, for example, Jean-Louis Viovy's (1985) critique of the media's invention of the "new man", in which he discusses how much more difficult it is for men than for women to acquire their gender identity.

Similar analyses were being produced by British and American men's groups and in men's studies departments, which had recently appeared in American universities. They were also the subject of feminist criticism, which has been echoed more recently in writing by pro-feminist men. Joseph Bristow (1990: 191) writes, "It is hard not to notice the reactionary dimensions to this emergent politics of masculinity. Apparently transformed by feminism, some of these men seem caught up in a desire to have their own version of it."

Collections of articles representing a variety of positions in relation to feminism appeared as special issues of some journals. For example, a 1984 special issue of *Le genre humain* included an article by Colette Guillaumin (1984), a member of the editorial collective of *QF* and currently on the editorial board of *NQF*, as well as an article by philosopher Alain Finkielkraut (1984), which reads as a nostalgic lament for the passing of the rites of passage which, he argues, used to play an important part in the construction of masculine identity.[23]

Finally, some authors on the subject have tried to place themselves "outside" feminism. For example, a special number of *Dialogue* (1980) on "male unease" was unequivocal in its position on feminism. Taking as its starting-point the assertion that there was a certain "male unease", visible in contemporary films, in articles and papers, and in the emergence of men's groups, it argued that men were suffering from the effects of feminism, and that their suffering needed to be examined within the context of the heterosexual couple and the family. Marie-Rose Roussier (1980, 7) stated in the very first pages, "Have we, in choosing such a subject, given in to feminist ideology? This was not the intention of our association and we do not intend to employ feminist ideology any more than any other kind of ideology." Inherent in this was the claim that knowledge about masculinity must be objective. Subjective ideas about masculinity, such as those of feminist and other "ideologies", were belittled in such a way that they did not even need to be seen as contenders in a debate.

Early critiques of masculinity, then, represented a variety of positions in relation to feminism, ranging from the extreme anti-feminism of the MCM to the pro-feminism of *Types – paroles d'hommes*, and not forgetting the attempt in *Dialogue* to adopt a position "outside" feminism. The analyses of masculinity they produced varied widely. While some were attempts to reclaim for men the power which women were said to have removed from them, others sought to explain the harmful effects of masculinity for men as well as women. As the number of conferences, special issues and men's group publications increased, feminists began to respond.

Feminist responses to men's groups' critiques

It must be stressed that feminists in France as elsewhere have always been indirectly concerned with masculinity. For example, early theories of patriarchy or sex class systems attempted to explain how men as a group held power over women as a group; and, as will be discussed in Chapter 5, feminist attempts in the early 1970s to explain rape raised questions about the nature or the construction of masculinity. However, the explicit treatment of masculinity by feminists began with their reactions to men's groups' analyses.

While the first analyses of masculinity were emerging from men's groups, feminist priorities lay elsewhere. Feminists joined the debate as a response to these early men's groups' explorations of the subject, although many feminists considered that it was a problem which should be dealt with by men. Even while launching frequent and severe attacks against much that emerged from men's groups, many feminists continued to call for men to examine the problems of masculinity themselves and to consider ways to change it. This contradiction is visible throughout the debate between feminists and men's groups, although there is now some evidence of a greater willingness on the part of feminists to work together with men. For example, a collection of articles published in 1992 as *Des hommes et du masculin* was produced jointly by CEFUP and the Centre de recherches et d'études anthropologiques. The involvement of CEFUP is an indication not only of feminist recognition of this area of research, but of their willingness to publish a collection of articles by men and to invite a man, Daniel Welzer-Lang, to edit it. As Daniel Welzer-Lang and Marie-France Pichevin (1992: 8) write in the introduction:

> It [CEFUP] is demonstrating the theoretical support that feminists are giving to the work carried out by men whose aim is to understand the social construction of masculinity. This collection would probably not have been possible a few years ago, for want of authors. What is new here is the joint willingness, in the scientific field, of men and feminist women . . . to consider together the effects on men of the domination of the masculine gender over the feminine gender.

While this co-operation between feminists and men involved in the study of masculinity is portrayed here as a significant step forward, the last phrase of the above quotation reveals that the motivation for this project is still focused on men's experiences of masculinity and its effects on them.

Before about 1978, feminists did not write explicitly about masculinity, and there was more interest in the more immediate question of whether or not men had a role in feminism. At the time, one of the most important feminist issues was whether the movement should be for women only, and what role, if any, men could play in feminism. For example, Christine Delphy's article, "Nos amis et nous" (1977), which appeared in *QF*, was a criticism of what she saw as men's attempts to co-opt the movement and to dictate the priorities of the feminist struggle. In 1981 a number of articles published in a special issue of *La revue d'en face* on men addressed similar questions.[24] For example, Catherine Lapierre (1981) argued that men's groups were just an expression of men's desire to have an equivalent oppression to women. Most of them ignore feminist work, she continued, leading a "struggle" against masculinity which has nothing to do with what feminists want. Moreover, men involved in these groups often see themselves as no longer "afflicted" by masculinity, thus placing themselves outside the problem. In the same issue, Irène Théry (1981) discussed the legitimacy of men's groups and Françoise Gilles (1981) expressed doubts about the motives of men involved in experimental trials of male contraceptives.

An examination of these early feminist reactions reveals a number of contradictions. On the one hand, many feminists had been insisting for years that men should reflect on masculinity and try to solve some of the problems it caused. On the other hand, they were critical of some men's attempts to do just this. Some feminists accused men of ignoring their masculine identity, while others criticized their self-indulgence in "crises of masculinity". For example, Annelise Maugue (1987) wrote *L'identité masculine en crise au tournant du siècle* as an attempt to break the silence surrounding masculinity which, she claims (Maugue, 1987: 7), has always hidden behind the mask of the universal and the norm: "Men, for their part, hardly seem to feel the need to situate themselves as far as masculinity is concerned. . . . Firmly placed in the role of subject, they watch, study and judge the other."

Maugue argues that, even after 20 years of feminist pressure, men are only slowly beginning to respond and to search for alternative models of masculinity. Maugue's call for men to examine their own masculinity is echoed by Simone Iff (1988: 242), but Iff is critical of men's groups, which prioritize the defence of men's own interests. She writes, "What women want of men is something else entirely. They want men to look at themselves critically; to find out who they really are . . . to understand their *own* cultural conditioning and work on its critique."

Many feminists were critical of men's groups. For example, a report in *Paris féministe* (D., D., B. and B., 1984: 26) on the 1984 St-Cloud conference began: "'Men against Sexism.' The intention was honourable, but it became in fact: 'Men and Sexism' . . ." The authors of this report argued that, although most of the contributors were trying to demonstrate the ubiquity of sexism, the organizers, and some of the male contributors, insisted that the main problem was sexism in the private sphere, and that men should therefore fight sexism at home, but not extend their critique to the public domain or to models of masculinity. *Paris féministe* states (ibid., 27):

> Quite obviously, the aims of the men present were primarily to give [themselves] a more positive self-image than that conveyed by most men, and therefore to create for themselves more comfortable positions in the sexist system. But they were evidently not concerned with destroying this system!

This view is not uncommon in Anglo-American criticisms of certain types of men's groups' critiques. The British historian Michael Roper (1990: 185), for example, discusses the competitive element in men's attempts to "demonstrate moral rectitude", and Lois Banner suggests, in a review article which appeared in *Signs* (1989), that men involved in men's studies have constructed the notion of "hegemonic masculinity" in order to demonstrate how it is a minority of men (to which the authors do not belong) whose masculinity is of the dominant type.

Masculinity in the press

As was mentioned in Chapter 1, the media began to proclaim the death of feminism and the advent of a postfeminist era as early as 1978, and their representation of a postfeminist climate has played an important part in the growing interest in men and masculinity. Feminism, which is represented as belonging to a historical period, usually the 1970s, is said to have had an enormous impact, which now needs to be rebalanced. Women have gained so much power that we now need to turn our attention to men and masculinity and consider how they have been affected by these changes. Françoise Picq (1993: 349) writes:

> So feminist discourse, unprecedented in 1970, became inaudible in the 1980s. A new consensus was established, which proclaimed the end of the battle. Feminism was said to be dead because its aims were achieved. Patriarchy was said to have disappeared. The problem henceforth was that of men, thrown by their loss of power and searching for a new identity.

An increasing number of articles about the "new man" and "new fathers" began to appear in the press around 1980. For example, Mariella Righini in *Le nouvel observateur* (1979) asked what had become of "our" men after ten years of feminism. In September 1980 seven pages of *Le monde-dimanche* (Mamou, 1980) were devoted to a survey on "Unease among new men". It was revealed that men were experiencing an identity crisis. This was caused by the increase in the numbers of women who work, meaning that work no longer functions as a basis of masculine identity. Moreover, women have been liberated by access to contraception and abortion. Women now control all decisions concerning reproduction. "In a couple of decades, men have lost everything" (Mamou, 1980: 1). Media interest has not waned: collections of articles on men and masculinity appeared in *Le nouvel observateur* in 1991 (no.1338, 13–19 June) and in *L'événement du jeudi* in 1992 (13–19 August). In addition to these, the 1980s saw the appearance of magazines created specifically for the "new man" market (*Vogue hommes, Il, Cosmo hommes, Nouvel homme*, etc.).

If we examine a selection of interpretations of masculinity which have appeared in the press, we can discern certain attitudes towards feminism, as well as towards masculinities, which most suggest are changing or in crisis. The changing representations in the weekly press of sexual identity, men, masculinity, feminism, etc. are of interest, despite the predictable recurrence every summer of articles in one way or another concerned with sexuality. The attention that is currently being paid to masculinity in articles such as these is related to the publication of new books on the subject[25], and their popularity makes them worthy of consideration.

One example chosen from a large number of magazine articles, special numbers, surveys and studies, all in one way or another concerned with changing masculinities, is a collection of articles in an issue of the centre-left intellectual weekly, *Le nouvel observateur*, which appeared in 1991, called "Ça va les hommes?". Like many others, this can be seen as an attempt to identify the "new man" and the reasons for his emergence. The articles are written by regular *Nouvel observateur* journalists, and include a commentary by Josette Alia on what she claims to be the first-ever survey about men, carried out among men; interviews; and articles on advertising's portrayal of contemporary masculinity, and changing attitudes to male homosexuality.

Alia states that the appearance of the new man in the 1990s came at the end of a process which began 20 years ago. In the 1970s, she claims, men responded to feminist demands by becoming ideal househusbands and fathers. However, in the 1980s, bored of housework and deprived of their positions of power in the home, these men changed from "feminized man" into "infantilized man", and women, apparently, could not resist mothering them. In the 1980s, then, men had the best of everything: they no longer had to make all the decisions, they could enjoy being the object of women's desires. . . . And it was out of this that the new man is supposed to have appeared. However, Josette Alia (1991: 8) does express doubts about how "new" the new man is, and whether he is not exaggerating the changes: not only are "our nice anti-macho husbands . . . less liberated than they claim", but a good third of the men interviewed have not changed at all.

Despite Josette Alia's interpretation of the survey as revealing a hazy picture of today's man, full of contradictions and uncertainties, her conclusion is firmly situated in the postfeminist discourse which structures this collection of articles. Here, feminism is portrayed as a passing phase, which is no longer relevant to the way we live. Alia identifies what she perceives as a comforting return to traditional gender roles after the upheavals brought about by feminism, and an emphasis among young people on the importance of maintaining differences between the sexes. So Alia begins by looking for the "real" new man, setting up different models of masculinity as reference points ("feminized man", "infantilized man" and "new man"). Then she claims that, in fact, they have not changed as much as we think and they would like to pretend. Finally, in the conclusion, she denies the need for change in men, since, she claims, young people no longer want change; they just want to return to traditional expectations of gendered behaviour.

While claiming to illustrate the plurality of masculinities in contemporary French society, these articles mock variants which threaten to blur the division of the sexes. By situating the discussion within a context of postfeminism, where there are no significant differences between men and women, the question of power relations is ignored, and men can be represented as the victims of feminism.

The feminism that is supposed to have led to men's loss of power and to crises in masculine identity is presented by these authors as a coherent, unified movement, whose ideals have reached every section of society, and whose effects have been tremendous. Feminism, claim the authors, has produced a fragile male identity. Men, uncertain of their own masculinity, are struggling to define themselves in the face of feminist demands. It is feminism which has produced reactions in men, ranging from taking refuge in a defensive, macho masculinity to various efforts to reform. The articles imply that men are to be pitied for their suffering and admired for their attempts to change. The authors concentrate, on the one hand, on the ways in which men feel feminism has caused them to lose power that was theirs by right, and on the other hand, on the power that women are said to exert in the home.

These articles undermine any calls for change in gender relations in their espousal of discourses of postfeminism and equality. Feminism is perceived as complete and no longer relevant now that total equality has supposedly been achieved. Feminism's only relevance, in the view of these authors, is one of its consequences, namely that men have had to adjust themselves to it. Despite claiming to be concerned with how men and masculinities are changing, these articles in fact do little to encourage change. Instead, they favour an end to what they portray as the petty fighting between the sexes and a return to what they imply is the comforting stability of traditional gendered behaviour.

As a cultural phenomenon, these texts can tell us something about the ways in which feminism and feminist thought is presented in France, and the ways in which the debate on masculinity is being popularized. It seems that feminism is derided, caricatured and marginalized by authors who claim to be writing within the context of a widely accepted postfeminism. In this respect, it is interesting to note that, while the tone of these texts does not seem to differ much from many British and American postfeminist representations of feminism, they see themselves as being involved in a debate which is noticeably different to the equivalent Anglo-American debate. The former French Prime Minister, Edith Cresson (Attallah, 1991), for example, can argue that, whereas in the United States public men cannot have affairs without it causing a scandal, in France it is not important. Or indeed, it is seen as being to the credit of the man concerned. "I think we order things better here," she says.

Books on men and masculinity

A more difficult category of publications includes Christine Castelain-Meunier's (1988), *Les hommes aujourd'hui*; Elisabeth Badinter's (1992) *XY: de l'identité masculine*; and Evelyne Sullerot's (1992) *Quels pères? Quels fils?* These are worthy of particular attention here because of the position that they occupy in the masculinity debate. They have all reached a wide audience. Sullerot's and Badinter's books reached the top of the bestseller list within weeks of publication. All three of these authors are, or have been, represented as feminists, but these books can all be read as firmly situated within postfeminism, presenting a defence of men's interests rather than a critique of masculinity. Their representation as feminists is widespread, and this has implications for feminism. The popularity and visibility of Sullerot and Badinter mean that they are perceived as representative of feminism and their views as current feminist dogma.

Les hommes aujourd'hui: virilité et identité

Christine Castelain-Meunier's book, *Les hommes aujourd'hui: virilité et identité* (1988) is concerned with the changes that men have had to make in order to adjust to the demands of feminism. It is, according to the introduction, an attempt to "understand [men]: their efforts; their failures; their wounds; their satisfactions; their new aspirations" (p. 11). The book is divided into three parts, the first of which is an uncritical, narrative account of a universal history of civilization, which does not seem to differ much from the myths that feminists have been trying to deconstruct for the past two decades. The major argument is that, now that physical strength is no longer necessary for men's work (having been replaced by intellectual ability in a society based on communication, services and images), men's dominance over women, which the difference in physical strength legitimated, can no longer be taken for granted. It remains to be seen, she says, who (men or women) will come out on top in the new society; it all depends who is the most competent at acquiring the skills required for modern jobs.

The first part of the book also examines the impact of feminism and men's reactions to it. "Feminism" is portrayed as a single, coherent movement, with no mention of the many conflicts and divisions that have dominated much of its history. Along with an atmosphere of crisis (economic and cultural), feminism is supposed to have produced a fragile male identity. Men, she claims, uncertain of their own masculinity, are struggling to define themselves in the face of feminist demands. Their reactions, which are examined in detail later in the book, are here outlined as being either a defensive, macho masculinity or various attempts to change. And it is clear that some men have made an effort to change, in a direct response to feminism, even where this has meant confronting certain difficulties.

The visible gains of feminism, especially increased access to contraception and abortion, as well as the gradual influence of certain feminist values on at least some sections of society, have indeed challenged traditional masculinity, and Castelain-Meunier tries to unravel the contradictions and complexities both of women's gains and men's responses. However, having devoted only half a paragraph of the introduction to an explanation of how her study was carried out, including the vital information that it was among an unrepresentative male population from the new middle classes, Castelain-Meunier makes no further mention of considerations of class. Her selectivity is justified on the grounds that it is in this section of society that the values of the future can be identified: "their questioning of the situation was clearly an indication of a profound cultural evolution" (ibid., p. 12). However, the specificity of the groups of men that she interviewed is soon lost in generalizing statements about "men" and "women", and it becomes noticeable that considerations both of variations in models of masculinity according to class and of the extent to which positive effects of feminism have been felt among women from different classes are, therefore, almost completely absent from the book. Moreover, although it is undeniable that the effects of feminism have led to change in some men, the assertion that men have been victimized by it ignores the many occasions on which they still dominate women, and refuses to examine the contradiction inherent in the notion that the dominant party in an oppressive relationship can be a victim.

The second part of the book concentrates on new models of masculinity which have appeared in the past two decades. The types of masculinity that Castelain-Meunier identifies in this section are the following: defensive masculinity, which is a regression to traditional values, often accompanied by violence; homosexual masculinity, which is a paradoxical combination of marginalization and the feeling of community; the "new hedonists", whose identity is constructed around fashion, conspicuous consumption and expensive leisure activities; yuppies, whose focus on professional success is seen as a retrograde move towards emphasis on the public sphere in the face of feminist demands that the private gain greater importance; feminized men, who, as a product of 1968, are already on the decline; and "l'homme en changement", who is making every effort to reform, and is presented here as being the ideal "new man".

The third section looks at the changes apparent in the 1970s and the 1980s. The 1970s are presented as the decade in which women profited from sexual liberation, and rejected male power and traditional models of the family and marriage. They also learnt to make sexual advances and to challenge their status as objects. Castelain-Meunier claims that during the 1970s "We moved from a generation in which men were dominant and prevented women from achieving sexual and social fulfilment, to one in which women prevent men from achieving sexual and social fulfilment." (ibid., p. 152)

In contrast, the 1980s are portrayed as the decade in which men reacted to the new behaviour of women, who were searching for ways out of crises in relationships, refusing to be seen as objects and rejecting power relations in the couple. For men and women, it was a time of choice and plurality, the variety of living arrangements available to them including single-parent families, living alone, homosexual relationships, etc. Men were fighting to solve their identity crisis, their feelings of disorientation, which had been provoked by feminism.

The question of fatherhood is at the centre of the fourth part of the book, with considerations of male contraception and the changing significance of fatherhood for men, since:

Fatherhood is one of the main axes on which today's masculine identity is situated and if a man's children no longer prove that he is virile, the way in which he behaves as a father situates him in relation to models of masculinity. (ibid., p. 196)

In conclusion, Castelain-Meunier emphasizes the plurality of "new men" in contemporary French society, who do not conform to a single model, yet all fulfil at least three conditions. Firstly, they are characterized by a refusal of the limitations of traditional models of masculinity, a refusal to fit into a single category which can be opposed to women, while at the same time coping with the insecurities caused by the loss of traditional masculinity. This implies not falling into the traps of androgyny, feminization or inverted sexism. Secondly, the "new man" believes in egalitarianism in all domains. And thirdly, Castelain-Meunier's "new man" is not stupid: he believes in equality only as an ideal. She writes.

Those who take the principles of equality all the way discover its dangers and the impasses to which it can sometimes lead. . . . By creating a situation in which relationships are too transparent and negotiations are always necessary, equality can kill the mystery of difference or become castrating. (ibid., p. 242)

Quels pères? Quels fils?

Evelyne Sullerot's aim (1992) is to break the silence surrounding the question of fathers and the changes that have affected them in the last 20 years. The first part of the book is concerned with the discovery of paternity; the construction of patriarchy; the representation of fathers in mythology and religion; and a history of the power exerted in the family by the father in France since the Revolution. This is followed by an examination of the changes that have affected fathers since 1965: the increase in the number of single-parent families, divorces and unmarried couples with children; legislative changes; and the availability of contraception and abortion, allowing women more control over their fertility. Claiming that fathers are disadvantaged by all these changes, Sullerot investigates the demands of associations for divorced fathers, and the hostility towards them. The last chapter is based on a survey carried out among an unrepresentative population of 15–18-year-olds "all from well-off backgrounds and cultured families" which is supposed to illustrate the attitudes of the fathers of the future.

Sullerot describes men forced to pay maintenance to the mothers of children they never wanted, nor even knew about; men whose wives initiate a divorce and receive custody of the children; and men deceived by women who now have all the power to decide when, whether and how to have children. She claims that men are now powerless in relationships, and it is for this reason that she advocates certain changes in men's favour. For example, she suggests that men should have the right to prevent women having an abortion if they are the biological father; and she supports the availability to individuals of genetic paternity tests, which would, she claims, bring an end to women's "deceit", "scientific evidence exposing feminine mystifications". (ibid., p. 24)

Sullerot argues that only children and their biological parents can be called "families", and expresses scorn for any alternative arrangement for bringing up children. She denies the possibility of anyone who is not the biological father being able to replace him (ibid.), and states that children conceived by artificial insemination should be given the details of the sperm donor, who is, she claims, their only "real" father:

> Any adult can love a child who is not his . . . but, when the parental links are certain, there is something more than love, something stronger and less sentimental which cannot be described. It is a link, a bond, an inexplicable tie. There is something shared, at a deep and primitive physical level, even if the parent and child do not get on at all.

For Sullerot it seems that "ownership" of a child is more important than any love or understanding. Men are the victims of feminism: "Some of them have done nothing wrong at all and have made no mistakes as fathers. But they are beaten, because they are men, in a war which they never wanted" (ibid., p. 111).

In common with many feminists, Sullerot criticizes the unfairness of the system that awards custody almost invariably to the mother after divorce, despite the fact that the magistrate has to take nothing other than the child's best interests into account. However, she interprets this and other differences in society's attitudes to mothers and fathers as being wholly in women's interests, a contention that feminists would not accept. Sullerot's assumption that the present situation, in which women are more likely than men to have custody of the children after the break-up of a relationship, is uncomplicatedly advantageous for women is contradicted by Irène Théry's argument in *La revue d'en face* (1980). Firstly, states Théry, there is the problem of the non-payment of maintenance which is almost always awarded in favour of the mother. But even when the payments are made, Théry argues (ibid., p. 66) that awarding custody and maintenance payments to the mother means that she remains in the same role after divorce as she was before: financially dependent on a man and responsible for childcare:

> Even if it provides a "comfortable" standard of living, financial dependence is never more than a necessary evil, and is certainly not a means of solving the problems of women's free labour. It would be better to concentrate on the search for ways of giving them priority in finding training and a paid job (without implying that this would solve everything). It would be better to concentrate on the emotional and social implications of a financial relation than to ignore them on the pretext of making it seem less dramatic.

Neither would feminists accept Sullerot's differing expectations of parenting depending on the gender of the parent:

> It is not the time spent with the child which can indicate the benefits of the father's role, but rather the attention he pays to the child's demands for love. The paternal role can be played by a father who is very busy and rarely there if, when he is there, he agrees to be a father in the eyes of his child; if he agrees to introduce the child to sport, reading, nature, making things, and if he is firm and fair. (ibid., p. 226)

XY: de l'identité masculine

Whereas Sullerot limits herself to pleading the cause of fathers, Badinter's contention (1992) is that men are disadvantaged from the moment of conception. Not only do men have to struggle from the embryonic stage to differentiate themselves from the original female state, but they then have the misfortune to be born to someone of the opposite sex. The construction of a masculine identity is therefore one long, hard struggle against a "désavantage naturel", and because it is a natural disadvantage, there is absolutely nothing they can do about it. (Women, on the other hand, can at least struggle against social disadvantages.)

Badinter describes what can go wrong during the difficult construction of masculine identity, thus producing two types of "mutilated men" (*homme mutilé*): "the hard man" (*homme dur*) and "the soft man" (*homme mou*). "The hard man", she argues (ibid., p. 230), was replaced during the 1970s by "the soft man", "mutilated" because he is not "masculine enough", and detested by other men, "tired of having to do the washing-up and housework in order to have the right to sleep with their wife". A third section of the chapter entitled "the mutilated man" considers whether or not gay men fall into this category. The last chapter of the book describes Badinter's future ideal, "reconciled man" (*l'homme réconcilié*), and the revolution in fatherhood that will be necessary in order to create him.

Although this revolution in fatherhood entails structural and organizational changes facilitating equal parenting (giving women recognition and power in other domains and reorganizing men's work in order to enable them to participate fully), Badinter does not expect fathers to be anything less than "real men". Although a new father may, for the first year, behave as a "père/mère", he must then assert his virility and become "père/mentor". If he fails to do this, he will be unable to transmit a model of masculinity to his sons, who will consequently suffer from identity crises (although even in Badinter's own lengthy account of numerous studies on this subject, it is difficult to find much evidence that this is the case).

Badinter's models of masculinity do not expose any conflict and contradictions between them nor examine their coexistence. There is no consideration of how masculinities vary according to class, age and ethnicity, beyond one passing comment, and, throughout the book, there is a constant refusal to examine the problems associated with masculinity in France. All negative aspects of masculinity are presented as being a problem only in Britain and the United States. It has been harshly criticized by French feminists for its methodology, analysis and lack of logical argument (Trat, 1992/3; Le Doeuff, 1993).

Feminism and changing masculinities

Badinter, Sullerot and Castelain-Meunier very rarely quote, refer to, or even name feminists. Sullerot talks of "some feminists" or "feminists in the 1970s" and "quotations" are unattributed. She sometimes writes "we" when referring to feminists, and sometimes "they", associating and dissociating herself from certain feminist positions by adopting or rejecting "feminism" according to her arguments. Badinter, on the other hand, always refers to feminists as "they", and it is "they" who are responsible for the problems which men are currently experiencing:

> The feminist critique of patriarchal men has led to an unbearable identity crisis. The traditional pressure on men to hide their femininity has been joined by pressure to hide their masculinity. The new equation "*mâle = mal*" [male = bad] has led to a loss of identity for a whole generation of men. (Badinter, 1992: 190)

In common with Castelain-Meunier and Badinter, Sullerot (1992) sees feminism as having had a significant impact. For example, she claims that: "Of course, we would need to go further. But we can only do this if public opinion abandons its blind conformism to feminism" (ibid., p. 289). Badinter (1992) writes: "By bringing an end to the distinction between the roles, and by entering all the areas previously reserved for men, women have made the universal male characteristic disappear: the superiority of men over women" (ibid., p. 17).

The authors discussed here repeatedly mock types of masculinity which they perceive as being in some way deviant or marginal. The "feminized man", for example, is treated with contempt. This has the effect of reinforcing dominant types of masculinity at the expense of any variants. This is despite the claim to illustrate the plurality of masculinities in contemporary French society. It seems that a variety of masculinities is acceptable, as long as none of them actually leads to a decrease in the patriarchal power which depends for its existence on the difference between the sexes. The second way in which these studies serve to reinforce dominant models of masculinity is by stressing the importance of the differences between the sexes. Castelain-Meunier, for example, sees it as vital that sexual difference be maintained, that the sexes should not be allowed to merge.

It is not impossible to find examples of very similar arguments in Britain and the United States. For instance, in *The rites of man: love, sex and death in the making of the male,* Rosalind Miles (1991) also adopts a postfeminist stance, and portrays men as feminism's victims. *The rites of man* has many similarities with *XY*. Both contain detailed descriptions of particularly horrific male violence. The explanation for this violence is claimed to lie in the social construct of masculinity, which is instilled through certain rites of passage. Both books examine the ways in which men acquire masculinity, and the effects that it has on them and on other men. Finally Miles, like Badinter, holds women responsible for men's behaviour, and blames mothers for much that goes wrong with masculinity; feminism is presented as a further pressure on men to assert their masculinity in response to more independent women. However, as was mentioned above, what is interesting about the French articles and books discussed here is that the authors portray the French situation as completely different from the Anglo-American.

By examining the broader debate on masculinity which is taking place in France, this chapter establishes the second context in which feminist theories of masculinity need to be situated. The masculinity debate which emerged from men's groups in the 1970s and which is now taking place in a popularized form is constructed around a particular representation of feminism and its impact on gender relations and, more specifically, on men. While some men's groups' critiques of masculinity are pro-feminist, the majority of the examples considered here portray men as the victims of feminism. They concentrate largely on the way in which constructions of masculinity since the advent of feminism have affected men's lives, paying little attention to gender relations. This is in contrast to feminist theories of masculinity, in which gender relations are central. These are discussed in Chapter 4. First, however, it is necessary to describe one further context in which these theories have developed: the difference debate within French feminism.

3   Difference

This chapter presents a third context in which feminist theories of masculinity are situated. This is the "difference debate", which has occupied centre stage in the history of French feminism and which has determined the conditions of the theories of masculinity which have emerged from it. The importance of the difference debate for the feminist theorization of masculinity is that it has raised questions about the nature and origins of the differences between men and women; the meaning of masculinity and femininity; and the implications of sexual difference for individual identity and for gendered power relations. Theories of masculinity which emerge directly from feminist debates around these questions will be examined in the latter part of this chapter and in Chapter 4. First, however, it is important to map out the contours of a debate which has had a determining influence on feminist practice and theory, beginning with Anglo-American perspectives on difference, then focusing on the specificities of the French case. This will expose some of the differences between approaches to masculinity in French and Anglo-American feminisms, as well as explaining why some French feminists have shown more interest in developing theories of masculinity than others. Chapter 4 will then discuss in detail, firstly, the development on one side of the difference debate of a framework within which theories of masculinity could emerge and, secondly, the theories of masculinity themselves.

If feminism is the assertion that there is a power relation between women and men and that this power relation should be removed, then, put schematically, there are two main ways that feminists might attempt to bring this about. The first is through the argument that men and women are different, but that this difference should not form the basis of a hierarchy. This position attempts to define femininity, while resisting the definitions imposed upon women by the patriarchy. It is often referred to as "difference" feminism. Difference feminists have focused mainly on femininity; their theoretical explorations of masculinity have rarely extended beyond a critique of the falsely universal or gender-neutral.

The second way in which feminism might achieve its aim of removing the power relation between men and women is through the argument that there are no significant differences between them and that they should therefore be equal. The aim of this position is to abolish the categories of femininity and masculinity, in the belief that there is no natural basis for the definition of men and women. This position is often referred to as "equality" feminism, although a more appropriate term is "sameness" feminism. This is because difference and equality are neither opposites nor mutually exclusive. The opposite of equality is inequality, and the opposite of difference is sameness or identity. Creating an opposition between difference and equality obscures the common objective of feminists. Whatever their position on difference, feminists aim for the elimination of the gendered power relation, or "equality". The belief that masculinity, like femininity, is socially constructed has proved fertile ground for explorations of this construct on an individual level and within structures and organizations, as will be discussed in Chapter 4.

Obviously these two positions, sameness and difference, do not tell the whole story. Feminists occupy every possible point between these two poles and may move around between them in what can appear to be contradictory ways according to the issue in question. Some feminists argue that the difference debate has been imposed on feminism and does not suit its complex and heterogeneous range of views and experiences. While feminist debates are still often represented in terms of a clear-cut distinction between sameness and difference, in Anglo-American feminism this opposition has been severely challenged from two angles: identity politics and poststructuralism.

Identity politics became an issue in the British and American women's movements during the 1980s, as a result of criticisms by women who felt excluded. These included black and lesbian women and women from the third world. Their criticisms brought into question the existence of a category "women", for they did not feel included in the one that had been constructed by white Western heterosexual feminists. They changed the terms of the difference debate from seeking to explain the difference between women and men to exploring the differences within the category "women". This led feminists to ask whether these differences are so great as to defy the notion of the category completely. The idea of sisterhood, which had enabled feminism to form a strong identity in the early 1970s, was fragmented by the growing awareness of the divisions between women. The assertion of women's identities other than gender (black, gay, working-class, etc.) can make a feminist politics very difficult (Lovenduski & Randall, 1993: 57–92). The issues which have risen out of these challenges to feminism have forced the rethinking of many categories and concepts including the opposition between sameness and difference. In the context of theories of masculinity, they have led to the recognition of multiple identities within the category "men" and to an examination of the power relations within this category, as well as between men and women.

In France, feminism has been cut through by divisions between women on the basis of class and sexuality, but the question of multiple identities and differences between women in ethnicity, disability, etc. has not been prominent in the way it has in Britain and the United States. Similarly, French feminist theories of masculinity have paid less attention to the relations between masculinities than to its relation with femininity. Some of the reasons why this should be the case will be discussed later in this chapter.

Another challenge to the binary oppositions of equality and difference was made by the influence within feminism of poststructuralist theories. Poststructuralism is a loosely defined collection of theories whose main themes are language, difference, subjectivity and power. Poststructuralism derives from Saussurean linguistic theory. This sees language as a system of relations between its constituent units, which are themselves constituted by the differences between them and other units. No one word would have a meaning if it were not for the existence of other words with different meanings, since that one word could apply to anything and everything; it is difference which gives meaning. Saussure argues that linguistic signs are arbitrary and conventional and that each sign is defined not by some essential property but by the differences which distinguish it from other signs. The sign is a purely relational unit and "in language there are only differences, without positive terms" (quoted in Sturrock, 1979: 166).

In poststructuralist theory, language is not a transparent conveyor of meaning, but a continuous process of difference. There is nothing which is meaningful *in itself* and is outside the endless play of linguistic deferral and difference (Moi, 1985: 9). There is no reality external to discourse that can be described and represented and there is no absolute truth waiting to be discovered. Meaning is created by discourses, which are constantly vying for power. If there are no fixed meanings and no stable identities, the binary oppositions of Western metaphysical thought are meaningless. This has important implications for feminist thought, since it opens up the possibility of difference being thought in other ways. For example, it offers a way of thinking the feminine which does not make it the negative pole of the masculine/feminine binary opposition (Duchen, 1986: 75–6).

The main premise of poststructuralist theory (and one of the few common themes among its theoreticians) is that, in contrast to the claims of humanist theories, subjectivity is not innate, but produced socially through language. As we acquire language, we give meaning to our experience and learn to understand it according to particular ways of thinking which existed prior to our entry into language. These ways of thinking constitute our consciousness, and the positions with which we identify and structure our sense of ourselves constitute our subjectivity (Weedon, 1987: 33). Subjectivity is neither unified nor fixed, but a site of disunity and conflict (Weedon, 1989: 21). It is "precarious, contradictory and in process, constantly being reconstituted in discourse each time we think or speak" (Weedon, 1989: 33). The political significance of this, and one of the main attractions of poststructuralism for feminists, is that subjectivity, instead of being a fixed, immutable entity, can be changed.

The implications for feminism and for feminist theories of masculinity are many. Anglo-American feminists in particular have drawn on poststructuralism to question the categories of men and women, unified rational subjects and the stability of identities. Poststructuralist feminist theory seemed to represent a way of moving beyond the sterility of the difference debate which was deeply rooted in notions of the unified subject. Poststructuralism has offered ways of breaking down the masculine/feminine, nature/nurture oppositions and contributed to the emphasis laid on multiplicity and plurality. It has provided an alternative to the choice between "different from" and "equal to" which had blocked feminism in a theoretical impasse. Joan Scott (1988: 46) argues that feminists need to reject this opposition and insist on differences "as the condition of individual and collective identities, differences as the constant challenge to the fixing of those identities, history as the repeated illustration of the play of differences, differences as the very meaning of equality itself". Scott concludes:

> The resolution of the "difference dilemma" comes neither from ignoring nor embracing difference as it is normatively constituted. Instead, it seems to me that the crucial feminist position must always involve two moves. The first is the systematic criticism of the operations of categorical difference, the exposure of the kinds of exclusions and inclusions – the hierarchies – it constructs, and a refusal of their ultimate "truth". A refusal, however, not in the name of an equality that implies sameness or identity, but rather (and this is the second move) in the name of an equality that rests on differences – differences that confound, disrupt, and render ambiguous the meaning of any fixed binary opposition. To do anything else is to buy into the political argument that sameness is a requirement for equality, an untenable position for feminists (and historians) who know that power is constructed on and so must be challenged from the ground of difference. (p. 48)

Ironically, the effects of poststructuralism, which is often referred to as "French theory" and even, in some contexts, "French feminist theory", have had a weaker impact within French feminism than within American and British feminism. The work of Irigaray and Cixous is clearly influenced by these theorists, but, as has already been shown, it occupies a marginalized position within French feminist theory. In France, the use of poststructuralism by feminists is seen as a particularly American phenomenon and criticisms of this practice are directed at American feminist theorists (Varikas, 1993).

As a result of the now widely recognized problems associated with identity politics (including the emphasis on the accumulation of oppressed identities, which leads to a hierarchy of oppression and divisiveness), some feminists are now suggesting that we need to hold on simultaneously to sameness and difference: recognizing that women have common interests at certain specific moments, yet recognizing the diversity of their existences, experiences and needs. Nira Yuval-Davis (1993) argues for a "coalition politics" which would achieve specific political aims. She quotes Caryn McTighe Musil who wrote in 1990:

> If the seventies were dominated by the exhilaration of discovering and naming ourselves as women, bound together in sisterhood, the eighties

have been dominated by the discovery and definition of our differences as women. . . . The challenge of the nineties is to hold on simultaneously to these two contradictory truths: as women, we are the same and we are different. The bridges, power, alliances and social change possible will be determined by how well we define ourselves through a matrix that encompasses our gendered particularities while not losing sight of our unity. (Yuval-Davies, 1993: 4)

Difference is central to feminism because it defines its raison d'être. Feminism as a political project rests on the notion of a category of women which is oppressed by a category of men. The issue of what constitutes these categories and what is the relation between them is central to feminist politics. If these categories do not exist in relation to each other, then feminism cannot exist. It is for this reason that the challenge to these categories by identity politics and poststructuralism has raised such important questions for the future of feminism.

Difference is central to relations between women, to feminist theory and feminist practice. It is also central to the theorization of masculinity and practice aimed at its transformation. For example, the feminist project of bringing an end to male violence raises questions such as why violence is perpetrated overwhelmingly by men and how masculinity and violence are related. Difference affects the strategies feminism employs to reach its main goal, which is the removal of the power exercised by men over women. It raises the question of separatism, claims for equality or the rejection of institutions and power structures perceived as masculine. For example, feminists might demand the equal representation of men and women in political institutions because men and women are the same and should therefore be equally represented or because men and women are different and should therefore be equally present in sites of decision-making, in order that both points of view or approaches to politics are represented. But they might also reject politics on the grounds that it is a masculine domain, which women have no interest in entering. Let us now examine these debates in the context of French feminist theory and practice.

The difference debate in France

French feminism began with largely egalitarian and androgynous theories. Early second-wave feminists, including Simone de Beauvoir, wanted to minimize the differences between men and women, or rather, the effects of these differences, which they saw as products of patriarchy, constructed in order to justify the oppression of women. Difference, for these feminists, meant inferiorization. "Equality" feminism has since been dominant in France despite the distorted image of French feminism which predominates outside France and which suggests the opposite (Collin, 1995: 671).

In contrast, "difference" feminists claimed that this can leave masculine values and norms unchallenged, by simply claiming them for women as well as men. They rejected male definitions and male politics, arguing that it was important to stress women's specificities, rather than to try to join men in a world they created by, and for, themselves. This risks attaching fixed definitions to men and women. It is often criticised for being essentialist and for failing to recognize the historical specificities of masculinity and femininity and of gender relations.

The difference debate in France has been deeply influenced by the opposition between universalism and particularism. Accounts of the difference debate in French feminism are often expressed within the framework of this opposition. The notion of universalism dates from the Enlightenment and is at the heart of the principles of the Revolution. It attempts to guarantee the equality of all citizens by seeing them as undifferentiated. Within the universalist tradition, differentiation is seen to bring with it the danger of marginalization or exclusion. Since difference could be used to justify inequality, the subject of the Republic must be *l'homme en général* (the undifferentiated man/person). The aim of feminism within the universalist tradition is to ensure that women are included in the universal, which has, until now, excluded women, while claiming to be gender-neutral. The "difference" current runs counter to the universalist republican tradition and Françoise Collin (1995: 672) claims that this is why it has not been as popular in France as sameness feminism.

The influence of the concept of the universal could also account for the resistance in France to identity politics, which are seen as fragmentary (Duchen, 1995). In the French republican tradition, differences between individuals are minimized or ignored, and groups are not formed around a common identity. The social project is to produce a homogeneous society. Immigrants are integrated into French cultural life as effectively as possible through the education system and the media. This is in contrast to the American celebration of cultural differences, which form part of the national identity. The French approach can be difficult to accept from the outside, and the accusation of racism has been directed at French feminists by British and American feminists, who are not accustomed to such insistent denial of difference (Duchen, 1995). As far as masculinity is concerned, it has limited the consideration of differences between men in their relation to each other and to women.

In contrast to the British and American feminist difference debates, the French version has not been cut through by either deconstruction or identity politics. It is still frequently expressed in dichotomous terms. However, it is at the level of strategy, rather than more abstract theory, that ways of moving beyond the difference debate are becoming apparent. Feminist strategy in relation to the law raises questions such as whether the undifferentiated universal subject of republican ideology should be the subject of the law or whether this simply hides inequalities, denying their relevance. Can true equality be achieved only through the recognition of existing inequalities and the resolution to use the law to remove these inequalities? The campaign for the equal representation of men and women in politics has brought these questions to the forefront of feminist debate. It is forcing a more complex and nuanced negotiation of the concepts of sameness, difference, equality and identity, which is difficult to present in terms of binary oppositions to which certain groups of feminists adhere. This debate could represent a way of moving beyond the difference/equality stalemate and open up a way of perceiving differences in terms of multiplicity.

The difference debate in French feminism today: the campaign for parity

A feminist-led campaign for the greater representation of women in political institutions in France has been gathering momentum since 1992.[26] The aim of the campaign is to add an article to the Constitution stating that elected bodies must be composed of an equal number of women and men. It has attracted the support of a broad range of feminists, cutting through previous sites of division and conflict; it has provoked responses from mainstream politicians across the political spectrum, particularly around election time; and numerous surveys have demonstrated that it has broad popular support. The media debate which has accompanied the campaign is evidence of its impact. The debate which this campaign has fuelled has centred on questions of difference/equality; universalism/ particularism; citizenship/democracy; as well as exclusion/inclusion/marginalization. In this debate, sexual difference is cut through by other differences, and there is a growing awareness of the need to rethink all of these concepts. While the variety of claims for sameness and difference may well have been present for much of the second wave, the questions raised by the campaign for parity have forced further reflection because difference plays such a large role in the justification of its claim.

One of the main questions posed by the claim for parity is why the inclusion in the Constitution of a law imposing the equal representation of men and women should further the feminist project. Responses to this are linked to the question of difference. One response is that women are the same as men and therefore equally competent. They have been excluded from the political arena which is falsely represented as open to all. There is no reason to exclude them, and they should be given the same rights and opportunities to do politics as men. A second response is that women are different from men. They do politics differently, have a different agenda and different interests. The argument for their inclusion is that they can contribute something specific to the political arena, or even transform it. Unless their difference is made explicit and given a space in which to express itself and to exert an influence, women will continue to be obscured by the universal, which is, in fact, masculine. Support for the campaign for parity can come from feminists who advocate difference as well as those who advocate equality through sameness, or the inclusion of women in the universal.

At the centre of the claim for parity is the criticism of universalism from which women are excluded. It is argued that the concept of the universal citizen has served only men's interests for two centuries and has obscured the gendered nature of citizenship. Universalism pretends that there is no difference between men and women, but in doing this it denies the possibility of discrimination. Many commentators have pointed out the false universalism of the term "homme" in the Déclaration des droits de l'homme. But should women be included in universal citizenship on the same basis as men, or should a new feminine citizenship be defined? Advocates of women's inclusion in universal citizenship argue that there is nothing wrong with universalism itself, as long as it is truly universal. The problem is that access to the universal is denied to 50 per cent of humanity. Eliane Viennot and others from the parity campaign argue that the demand for the recognition in the law of gender difference is a fight for the elimination of this difference as a major factor in the identity of individuals. Even if it necessitates a preliminary stage in which difference is recognized, it is a difference which has been constructed historically and politically, and not biological difference. At the end of the process, women will come to be seen as being equally as capable of running the country as men, and there will be no political, social or symbolic difference between men and women. In order for women to become equal to men, we must first admit that they are not. When these differences have disappeared, the law will no longer be needed. But it is an important phase in the transformation towards that situation. The aim of the parity campaign is not, asserts Françoise Gaspard (1994), to have women in parliament representing women, but to have equality in parliament, and therefore true universality.

While Gaspard and Viennot stress that the recognition of difference is just one stage in the elimination of its significance, the feminist lawyer Gisèle Halimi (1994) claims access to the universal on the grounds of sexual difference, in this case experiential. Very real differences and inequalities are denied in the claim that everyone is the same and equal. Access to the universal will be open to women only once it is admitted that there are gendered specificities. These specificities may be biological, social or psychological in origin, but they are very real: women are not present in elected bodies. So the recognition of difference is essential to change. It is only by highlighting the fact that humanity is made up of two sexes that each will be considered equal to the other. This differentiation must not be confused with the sexist, racist and xenophobic use of difference to justify exclusion. But we need to recognize that sexual difference has mattered in the past and continues to do so (Halimi, 1994: 17).

Women's difference, claims Gisèle Halimi (1994: 18), needs to be used to found their equality, not to justify their inferiorization. The future of democracy will be "enriched by the contribution of both identities". In this, Halimi does not question the existence of these "two identities": their existence seems to flow effortlessly from the assertion of the existence of material differences in the lives of women and men in French society. So while Gaspard is aiming for true universality, represented by equality in parliament, Halimi is aiming for the representation of both masculine and feminine identities which will contribute to democracy.

Luce Irigaray (1994) argues that feminism runs the risk of achieving only the inclusion of women in what will remain a masculine "universal". This "universal" needs to be exposed as masculine through the assertion of the feminine. Irigaray wants gender difference written into all aspects of the law. She believes that women are different and should remain so. Dismissing the nature/nurture debate as a false dilemma, Irigaray (1994: 107) claims that feminism's objective should be to construct a feminine identity, "a different way of being and loving, without perpetual conflict, but remaining oneself in relations with the other gender". Parity must be demanded on the grounds that women are different. And women must achieve full citizenship – not "gender-neutral"/"universal" citizenship, which is in fact masculine, but feminine citizenship:

> Before trying to enter institutions whose democratic nature needs to be rethought, we first need to make the necessary and fully justifiable demand for full civil rights and for the right to represent ourselves, instead of claiming the right to represent others before we have gained legal recognition of our own identities. (Irigaray, 1994: 107)

However, others fear that the inscription of sexual difference in the law will represent a regression in feminist politics. Large sections of the feminist movement have been trying for decades to insist that sexual difference is socially and historically constructed. If it were inscribed in the law, would this not simply serve the interests of those who use sexual difference to justify discrimination?

There is no doubt that the sameness/difference opposition continues to dominate many discussions within French feminism. But what is interesting about the parity debate is that there is evidence that it offers a way beyond this theoretical stalemate. Eleni Varikas (1995) criticizes the parity campaign in *NQF*, on the grounds that assimilating women into male structures is not enough. What is needed is a redefinition of democracy in which women would enjoy full citizenship and in which key concepts such as justice, power and the relation between the public and the private domain would be redefined. One of the main problems with the current political system is the opposition between equality and difference, which forces impossible choices. Women seem to have the "choice" between assimilation into a universal law which was created by and for men, or marginalization by a specific law imposed on some members of society. New alternatives need to be worked out in a series of coalitions around specific projects.

This critique of democracy, coming mainly from feminists on the far left, has been prominent in the contributions to the parity debate by *Cahiers du féminisme*. The critique offered by *Cahiers du féminisme* of the terms of the debate raises many more questions about the representation of a diverse electorate, democratic citizenship and the republican ideal of universalism. Their involvement in the debate began with a criticism of its class blindness. The campaign, which focuses closely on a change in legislation forcing the equal representation in elected bodies of men and women, does not address the question of which women would benefit from this. Nor does it consider the varying levels of access to public politics of women. *Cahiers du féminisme* pointed out that many women do not have the resources to participate in politics and that the priority was not to enable a female elite to join the existing male one, but to redistribute the resources necessary for everyone to become active citizens. Admittedly the emphasis is on class, and it is arguable that in this respect there is no change; the difference debate continues to be constructed largely in terms of sameness versus difference, with *Cahiers du féminisme* drawing attention to the class divisions among feminists and women, as they always have. However, there does seem to be evidence in their arguments of a concern with multiple differences including those between women. For example, how other differences or specificities, including race, class and disability, can be represented. Can a multiple or diverse electorate be properly represented by an elected body? And if so, should their differences be glossed over in claims of universality or should they be highlighted? Is there a case for prioritizing the recognition of the discrimination against and exclusion of women from traditional parliamentary politics above that of other excluded groups, for example, immigrants?

These issues were avoided by the supporters of parity in the early days of the campaign. Initially, parity supporters argued that women do not constitute a social category in the same way as the working class, immigrants, blacks, etc., but instead form 50 per cent of all social categories. They argued that the demand for parity is not a demand for the representation of social groups, but for the representation of the human race which is composed of two sexes. This avoids discussion of all other excluded groups and claims that women's difference is special. However, the debate is now progressing at such speed that consideration of these issues is becoming unavoidable and it is here that we might find French feminists moving beyond the sameness/difference debate and trying to work out a way that women can be equivalent to men, while retaining specificities when appropriate. Through it, feminism might be able to negotiate a way in which equal rights for everyone can be combined with a consideration of specific and collective oppressions.

The feminist philosopher and editor of *Cahiers du* GRIF Françoise Collin (1995) suggests that the difference debate is irreconcilable. Nature and culture are inextricably intertwined. We should no longer see sameness and difference as either/or positions but rather as "both one and the other", since each individual is at the same time a member of humanity and a sexed/gendered being. Universalism has always thought equality in terms of sameness. It appeared neutral only because it excluded that which was different. But it needs to find a way of taking into account cultural, linguistic, sexual and religious differences within the same country. It needs to recognize the right to equality and the right to difference. It needs to create a universal which is plural. Collin (1995: 674) advocates the use, in feminist practice and theory, of both universality and specificity. Feminists should adopt one position or the other strategically and as necessary. Nevertheless, many feminists remain sceptical and it is clear that conflict around the way to proceed will continue.

Difference feminism and theories of masculinity

French feminist theories of masculinity have developed within the framework of a difference debate which has until very recently been conducted on either/or terms, the emphasis on the differences between men and women playing a more important part than the differences within these categories. In Chapter 4 it will be argued that feminists who have adopted a social constructionist stance within the nature/nurture debate have elaborated theories of gender which could provide the means to consider conflicting identities in individual men and women. First, however, theories emanating from the "difference" end of the spectrum will be examined, and it will be argued that, while they provide useful critiques of the masculinity of structures and discourses previously perceived as gender-neutral, their main interest has been the exploration of feminine, rather than masculine, identity.

In the 1970s, the theoretical explorations of the group Psych et po formed an important part of "difference" analyses of women's oppression. Psych et po undertook a radical critique of masculine institutions and structures, especially at the level of language. They sought the discovery of the feminine, which was, they argued, repressed by the masculine. Women, as well as men, were dominated by the masculine even at the level of the unconscious, and the aim of the group was to "chase the phallus from our heads", leaving room for the feminine to express itself (Duchen, 1986: 20).

Psych et po's project is continued today by Luce Irigaray, the best-known defender of the difference position in France. Irigaray's project is two-fold. Firstly, she aims to expose the masculinity of discourses which have been represented as universal or neutral. These include philosophy, psychoanalysis, science and religion, which have excluded women by constructing them as other. Secondly, Irigaray aims to create a feminine discourse which would allow the feminine to exist in its own terms, not as it has been defined by phallocentrism, the process of cultural and representational assimilation which defines subjectivity in relation to the male model (Grosz, 1989: 103). For example, Irigaray criticizes Freud's and Lacan's emphasis on the masculine and their construction of femininity as masculinity's other. She criticizes Freud for universalizing a model of human subjectivity which is based on the white Western male, femininity constituting a lack or absence of the qualities defining masculinity. Irigaray interprets this as instituting a phallic economy, an economy based on sameness, oneness or identity with the masculine subject, and this is phallocentrism (Grosz, 1989: 103).

In order for the feminine to be brought into existence, phallocentrism must be challenged and other forms of discourse must be created, which allow women to speak *as* women. Irigaray (1984: 105) insists on the autonomy and specificity of the feminine which must no longer be absorbed into the masculine-posing-as-neutral. Irigaray (1994: 106) claims that "feminism's most obvious impasse is its desire to decondition itself of its feminine identity in order to join a neutral universal".

Irigaray theorizes sexual difference through a combination of influences, including Lacanian psychoanalysis, structuralist and poststructuralist linguistics and language (Grosz, 1989). A major influence is Derrida and particularly his reading of difference through the concept of *différance*, which Irigaray uses to clear a space in which women's self-description becomes possible in terms other than those which define men's self-sameness. Her method is to construct a critique of phallocentric discourse in terms which both expose its phallocentrism and subvert it. She aims to represent women and femininity in terms other than those used by phallocentrism. Elizabeth Grosz (1989: 102) writes:

> Irigaray's texts are . . . simultaneously "serious" philosophical critiques of phallocentric discourses; and experiments in new conceptual and rep-resentational practices, carried out within *and* beyond phallocentric constraints. . . . Irigaray presents "constructive", poetic, exploratory texts capable of multiple readings and different associations. . . . Her writings perform what they announce.

Irigaray recognizes that women's autonomy cannot be achieved at a discursive level alone; change is also necessary at a social and individual level. But this will not suffice if language and cultural representations are left unchallenged (Grosz, 1989: 110).

For Irigaray, male sexuality and patriarchal language are isomorphic. This means that they correspond in form and shape. This does not mean that patriarchal language is produced by or reflects anatomy or a male essence. The body, for Irigaray, is constituted and given meaning only socially and historically through power relations and systems of representation. The body, then, is given meaning in and by culture. The male is constituted as virile and phallic; the female as passive and castrated. The male body is socially produced, constructed by the discourses dominant in patriarchal social relations. Male sexuality is produced through the internalization of images and representations. Elisabeth Grosz (1989: 112) writes, "In other words, men do not form discourse in their own image(s); rather, phallocentric discourses form male sexuality in their image(s)." Irigaray argues that knowledges and discourses which are valued in our culture are isomorphic with male sexuality. What she aims to do is to create the conditions in which discourses isomorphic with female sexuality and corporeality can be produced (Grosz, 1989: 128).

Critiques

Irigaray's work is important in that it represents a fundamental challenge to Western thought. It offers possibilities for explorations of alternative ways of thinking and writing which undermine dominant ideas of knowledge and truth. While raising new questions for feminism and opening up opportunities for the development of feminist theory, Irigaray's work has also provoked serious criticism from feminists in France. The most common criticisms are that her work is ahistorical, essentialist and denies the differences between women. Outside France, where Irigaray's work is nevertheless regarded more kindly, a debate rages over whether the accusation of essentialism can be justified, and to what extent her work can be seen as political.[27]

Irigaray's aim is to realize the feminine, which has so long been obscured by the masculinity of discourses such as science, religion and medicine. Irigaray's concern with masculinity, then, is exposing its prevalence, then seeking to subvert and undermine its influence, creating a space in which the feminine can come into existence. Masculinity is examined because it is important to understand its workings in order for them to be undone. Irigaray examines the construction of masculine identity, showing how it differs from feminine identity. She does not, however, attempt to account for the way in which individual men live their masculinity and the way in which this interacts with male power and its material manifestations, including violence towards women. According to Irigaray the world and human experiences are constituted as meaningful through discourse. Male sexuality is constructed and given meaning only through discourse. This analysis offers advantages to feminist theory, primarily that it can enable the production of theories which are clearly anti-essentialist. Problems arise, however, when feminists attempt to account for the material realities of physical violence exercised by men. This does *not* occur only at the level of discourse, and it is difficult to explain in Irigaray's terms. While it is important not to essentialize sexuality, feminism cannot ignore the physical reality of bodies which are not produced only by discourses. It is for this reason that attention here will be turned to theories of masculinity which are more concerned with these questions and which relate more directly to the issue of male violence, examined in detail in Chapter 5.

4   Gender

On the sameness or social construction side of the difference debate, it is possible to trace a development from questions of biological difference versus social construction; to seeing gender as a relation; to stressing the importance of both sides of the relation; and finally to emphasizing the importance of the relation itself. If gender is seen as a relation, then it becomes important to understand both sides of this relation. This, therefore, necessitates an investigation of masculinity as well as femininity. This chapter examines theorists who have attempted to account for sexual difference by viewing it as a social construction. The social construction of sexual difference is almost invariably referred to as gender in English. However, there has been considerable debate in France over the use of the terms "gender" and "social relations of sex", and this debate is examined later in this chapter.

The following account of the development of theories of gender and social relations of sex aims to demonstrate how this has led to an explicit interest in masculinity.[28] It concentrates on three things. Firstly, it analyzes the major stages in the development of these theories, in order to demonstrate how the importance of both terms of the social relations of sex and of the relation itself has increased. It will be argued that this has both facilitated and necessitated the construction of men and masculinity as objects of research. Secondly, it considers how masculinity was interpreted, more or less implicitly, by the various theorists involved in the production of these theories. Thirdly, it examines some examples of attempts to produce specific theories of masculinity within a framework of gender or social relations of sex. It should not be inferred from the following that masculinity has been the major concern of these theorists, but interest has clearly existed, and it is therefore worth examining the ideas which have emerged.

1970s: from sexual difference to gender

The idea that gender or sexual difference is socially constructed has its roots in sex role theory, which became very popular with sociologists during the 1950s and 1960s and was the dominant paradigm in American psychology until the 1970s. Sex role theory was used by early feminists, who in their search for an explanation for the differences between men and women developed various ideas about how gender was constructed and why masculinity and femininity were so different. They tried to explain how individuals learned to behave in gender-appropriate ways, mainly through the agency of the family and school (Edley & Wetherell, 1995: 70–95).

It is easy to see why role theory proved so attractive. It has the advantage over psychoanalytic theories of describing a process which continues throughout an individual's life, rather than being completed at an early age. It can explain the relation between society and the individual and it offers hope for change: if roles can be learned, this suggests that they can be unlearned (ibid.). Role theory has, however, been subject to many criticisms in recent years. Some of the main criticisms have been summarized by Nigel Edley and Margaret Wetherell (1995). They include the failure of role theory to explain where sex roles come from and why there should be different roles for men and women. Sex role theory seems to accept a social division based on biological sex. Sexual difference comes first, and sex roles are built on this difference. Many versions of role theory assume that there is a "real" natural self beneath the roles which individuals are socially required to fulfil. Secondly, the role itself is difficult to define. Is the male sex role the way in which most men behave or is it an ideal to which they aspire? The confusion of these two possibilities has led to the labelling of individuals who do not conform to the norm as deviant, even if so-called "deviant" behaviour actually corresponds to the behaviour of most men. Moreover, the concentration on the normative case has led to an almost complete silence on black, working-class and gay masculinities. Role theory can also ignore the power difference between men and women and the ways in which the definitions of masculinity and femininity have come to reinforce this difference. However, some feminists were able to incorporate this aspect into work which was situated within a sex role framework (Delphy, 1993).

These shortcomings accounted for the gradual replacement of role theory by the concept of gender. Gender, like sex roles, could demonstrate that not all the differences between the sexes were natural. There were disagreements about which differences were natural or social and to what extent, but many feminists agreed that some differences at least were socially constructed. So gender started out as referring to those characteristics, values, etc. which were not biological, but which were different for women and men. The way in which boys and girls acquired their gender identity was explained first in terms of sex roles and later with the help of psychoanalysis. The asymmetry and hierarchy between the two terms was not always emphasized in these analyses (Delphy, 1993). Later, it was the relation between the genders, the division of humanity into two sexes and two genders, that became the object of feminist interest. And it was this understanding of gender as a power relation that led to feminist interest in men and masculinity. For some, this was seen as a need to theorize both sides of the relation between masculinity and femininity (e.g. Anne-Marie Devreux); for others, it was the relation itself which needed to be theorized (e.g. APRE); or the relation between gender and sex (e.g. Christine Delphy).

The development of theories of gender and social relations of sex began with feminist attacks on naturalism and their arguments in support of social constructionism. This was already present in sex role theory, but was reinforced and developed by feminists in the 1970s and 1980s. The term "naturalism" refers to ideologies which attempt to justify women's social situation with arguments resting on so-called natural features. An example of naturalist ideology is the argument that the sexual division of labour is natural, since it follows on from the different roles that men and women play in reproduction (Combes et al., 1988: 172). Naturalist ideologies assume that what is natural precedes what is social, and therefore that society is organized according to the dictates of nature. The importance for feminism of challenging naturalism is that it attacks one of the ideological bases which justify the relations of oppression between the sexes. Social constructionist feminists denounce the social use which is made of ana-tomical differences between the sexes, reject a hierarchy which is based on an immutable nature and look more carefully at what exactly constitutes the differ-ences between women and men. Feminist critiques of naturalism have included the claim made by feminist biologists that there is nothing simple or natural about sex categorization, that sexes are situated on a continuum, and that only socially can we divide humanity into two groups (Ferrand & Langevin, 1986: 4–9).

One of the most consistent and ardent opponents of naturalism in feminist and anti-feminist thought is Christine Delphy, co-founder and editor of *QF* and *NQF*. Naturalism, argues Delphy, is the ideology which is now used to justify the oppression of women, but scarcely a century ago it was used to justify the oppression of the proletariat. Delphy insists that she is not denying that women and men are anatomically different and play different parts in reproduction. But, she argues, why should that be used to explain the oppression of one by the other? Delphy (1984: 23) contests that, since biological explanations of the oppression of the working class or non-whites have lost all scientific credibility, this should have brought into question the use of such an explanation for the oppression of women: "Why should we, in trying to explain the division of society into hierarchical groups, attach ourselves to the bodily type of the indi-viduals who compose, or are thought to compose, these groups?"

Many of the early feminist critiques of naturalist arguments took place in *QF*, which played a vital role in the elaboration of social constructionist theories. Before examining some aspects of their work, however, it is necessary to define materialism in the context of French radical feminism. Stevi Jackson (1996: 36–9) offers a detailed and informative explanation, whose main points are summarized here.

Materialist feminism

Firstly, it is important to distinguish between philosophical and Marxist uses of the term "materialism". Philosophical materialism emphasizes the primacy of matter over mind. Historical materialism perceives historical, social conditions as more important than nature. It argues that human activity transforms nature and that we are social, not natural, beings. "Historical materialism" was the term used by Marx to describe his method of social analysis, and it is the method which is of interest to radical feminists. French radical feminists, while rejecting the type of Marxism which subordinates women's oppression to the oppression of the working class, have used historical materialism to try to explain gender inequality.

Marx's materialism stood in opposition to idealism, according to which ideas are the motor of historical change and determine social and cultural life. Materialism posits that ideas cannot cause social division or oppression; inequalities are rooted in social practices, the way in which we live our lives. Ideology can conceal or justify inequalities and becomes embedded in the social practices it legitimizes, but gender inequality is not primarily ideology or the product of discourse. Jackson (1996: 39) writes, "It is not ideas about women and men that create inequality between them, but material inequality which gives rise to certain ideas about women and men."

Materialist feminism looks for social causes of male dominance, rather than ideological, psychological or biological causes. Materialism is anti-psychologist. What goes on in our heads is seen to be determined by our material conditions. The materialist theory of gender means that femininity and masculinity cannot be understood as psychological differences between men and women, but are related to their material situations (Jackson, 1996: 41).

Questions féministes

QF's "anti-difference" position was established in the editorial of the first issue, in which the editors criticized arguments, particularly from Psych et po, according to which women's "natural" difference made them superior to men. This current, which they called "*néo-féminité*", was criticized for being ahistorical and for ignoring social factors in its search for the essential Woman. Concentrating on the body and on the physical difference between women and men is, they argued, exactly what patriarchy does in order to justify women's oppression. If women, too, begin to assert their difference, then this can only serve patriarchal interests: "It is the patriarchal system which posits us as 'different' in order to justify our exploitation, to mask it. It is the patriarchal system which forces the idea of a feminine 'nature' or 'essence' on us" (*QF*, 1977: 5). They stressed that: "The social existence of men and women is not at all dependent on their being male or female, on their anatomical sex." (ibid.)

The editors of *QF*, then, asserted their opposition to any defence of feminine difference, whether this was biologically or socially justified (see Guillaumin, 1979). They argued that it is not women's biological sex which places them in a single social class, but their position in the power relations which exist between the sexes, namely as the oppressed. The priority must therefore be to "analyze and destroy the mechanisms of oppression", masculine behaviour, discourse and violence (*QF*, 1977: 13–14). The theorization of femininity and the glorification of women's corporeal or psychological differences was portrayed by *QF* as politically regressive. According to *QF*, this facilitated the continuing domination of women by men on the grounds that this was natural, since they were different. *QF*'s major concern was bringing an end to the oppression of women by men. They searched for an explanation of this oppression and the ways in which male power was maintained. Part of this theoretical project was an attempt to understand masculinity: how it is constructed and reproduced and how it functions as a support for male power. A fundamental point in *QF*'s reasoning was that masculinity was a social construct and not a biological given, and was therefore not immutable. The aim was the destruction of the political class of men, not of men themselves. As Monique Wittig (1980: 80) wrote:

> It is therefore up to us, historically, to define in materialist terms what we mean by oppression, and to analyze women as a class. This amounts to saying that the category "woman", as well as the category "man" are political categories and are therefore not eternal. Our struggle aims to wipe out men as a class, as part of a political class struggle – its aim is not genocide.

In this context, three of the most important questions addressed in *QF* can be represented at their simplest as "What is difference (and masculinity)?"; "Why are men dominant?"; and "Can men change?". The answers to these questions, as will be demonstrated below, can be summarized as follows: firstly, that difference (and therefore masculinity and femininity) are social constructs; secondly, that the social construct of difference/masculinity/femininity is responsible for women's oppression and male power; and thirdly, that it is historically variable and therefore can be changed.

The publications of three members of the original *QF* editorial collective, Christine Delphy, Nicole-Claude Mathieu and Colette Guillaumin, illustrate this position. The early work of these theorists set the terms of the debate on gender which has developed among French academic feminists. Their stress on the social construction of difference has continued to play a central role in discussions of gender and is now one of the basic premises on which these discussions depend. Academic feminists who explicitly used the early work of Guillaumin, Mathieu and Delphy as a basis for their continuing development of theories of gender and social relations of sex acknowledge their theoretical debt to them, while at the same time producing critiques of certain aspects of their work. This "second generation" of gender theorists, and in particular the group APRE, are discussed later.

Christine Delphy

Since 1970, Christine Delphy has argued against naturalist explanations of women's oppression. Her article "L'ennemi principal" (1970) was an early attempt to theorize the sex system. It stressed the systemic nature of men's dominance of women. It aimed to find the structural reasons why the abolition of capitalist relations of production would not by itself liberate women and to develop a materialist analysis of women's oppression. Using Marxist analyses, but refusing to subordinate the oppression of women to the oppression of the working class, Delphy developed the concept of the domestic mode of production. A mode of production is a set of strategies for dealing with basic economic questions. In the capitalist mode of production, goods and services are produced when the proletariat sells its labour to the bourgeoisie, who own the means of production. Because the bourgeoisie does not pay the full cost of the labour and extracts "surplus value" from the proletarians, the social relations between these two classes are relations of exploitation. Delphy viewed the family as an economic system in its own right and saw women's subordination within the family as independent of capitalism. In the domestic mode of production, women's unpaid labour is appropriated by male heads of household (Jackson, 1996: 95). According to Delphy, the domestic mode of production was the site of the economic exploitation of women by individual men, to whom they gave their labour free of charge. In this system, men and women are divided into antagonistic classes. Women constitute a class, she argued, since most women marry, but patriarchy hides the fact that women constitute a separate class by pretending that they belong in the same one as their husbands.

Delphy argued that patriarchy is a class system, like capitalism, and that the exploitation of women by the patriarchy is common to all women, specific to women and their main oppression. Whereas men belong to different classes according to the position they occupy in the capitalist mode of production, women share a common class because they occupy the same position within the domestic mode of production. Whether they are the wives of capitalists or proletarians, their labour is appropriated by their husbands. Patriarchal oppression is common to all women, she argued, because 80 per cent of women are married at any one time; it is specific to women because only women have to provide domestic labour free of charge; and it is their main oppression because even when women work outside the home, they are exploited as women. Therefore, since all women are oppressed by patriarchy, they all need to join together to overthrow this system (Delphy, 1970: 170).

Delphy has always placed an emphasis on the relation between women and men, which she argues is a power relation. For example, in 1981 she wrote (Delphy, 1981: 66):

This starting-point has led us to stress the *relation* which positions women and men in two groups, which are not only different, but first and foremost hierarchical. In other words, we have to analyze it within a framework of class. In this analytical framework, what is important is not the contents of each role, but the relation between them, between the two groups. The defining characteristic of this relation is hierarchy, and it is this which explains the contents of each role, and not the other way round. In this framework, it is clear that the key concept is *oppression*, which is, or should be, the key concept of any class analysis.

Delphy's use of the term "sex class" stresses the relation between them. It is the relationship between the classes that defines their existence:

> The concept of class . . . implies that each group cannot be considered separately from the other, because they are bound together by a relationship of domination; nor can they even be considered together but independently of this relationship. . . . The concept of class starts from the idea of social construction and specifies the implications of it. Groups are no longer *sui generis* constructed before coming into relation with one another. On the contrary, it is their relationship which constitutes them as such. (Delphy, 1984: 25–6)

By seeing male dominance as systemic and institutional, Delphy excludes the possibility of individual men acting outside the system. The system of male dominance exists outside and before the individual. No man can escape his dominant position, because, no matter how egalitarian his relation with his partner, he owes his material situation to the discrimination faced by women as a class (a class to which his own partner belongs) on the labour market. Delphy (1977: 32) insists that none of this is due to the man's *desire* or *intent* to dominate a particular woman or women in general, but:

> An individual man does not have to lift a finger to be at an advantage in relation to women on the labour market. But on the other hand, he cannot prevent himself from being at an advantage, nor can he refuse this advantage. Similarly, he does not need actively to take advantage of his institutional privileges in marriage.

According to Delphy, there are structural reasons why individual men cannot bring about change. The general oppression of women by men pre-dates any interpersonal relations between individual women and men and determines their nature. Therefore, nothing can be done to change this situation on an individual level. It is this aspect of Delphy's early work which seems to express too much intransigence for current gender theorists, such as APRE, who are keen to explore the ways in which individual men *can* escape from the inevitability of male dominance.

The advantage of Delphy's analysis is that it addresses the issue of the systemic oppression of women by men. However, it has difficulty accounting for the huge variations experienced by individuals engaged in very different social relations. While analyzing the way in which the material conditions of men's and women's lives impact on the relations between them, it does not consider, for example, how these relations are affected by other social relations, including those of race or disability.

One of the main criticisms of Delphy is that she does not attempt to theorize subjectivity. In other words, neither she nor other materialist feminists provides a theory of the way in which the gender identity of the individual interacts with the social structure of gender hierarchy. How do men and women acquire masculine and feminine identities? Delphy has paid this little attention, although Stevi Jackson (1996: 139–40) has isolated some references to subjectivity in Delphy's work. According to Jackson's reading, Delphy "implies that a materialist perspective should treat subjectivity as embedded in social practice as shaped by material social relations". But this has not been developed, and to date only psychoanalysis offers theories of the way in which gender is acquired on an individual level.

Nicole-Claude Mathieu

Nicole-Claude Mathieu, who was a member of the editorial collective of *QF*, was arguably the first feminist in France to begin an analysis of masculinity. This was in an article published in 1973 in the anthropological journal *L'homme*, entitled "Homme-culture et femme-nature?". Mathieu also made a vital contribution to the development in France of the concepts of biological sex and social gender, and to theories of gender as a relation. An examination of Mathieu's publications during the 1970s illustrates the development of the thesis that difference/masculinity/femininity are social constructs; that it is these constructs which are responsible for maintaining women's oppression; and that, as social constructs, they are *not* fixed immutable states.

Gender is just one social relation within which individuals may hold more or less power. In this social relation, men dominate women, but they also dominate young boys. The basis of the relation is therefore not biological sex, as is often claimed, but the social relation between the two sex categories. Mathieu argues that through the masculine discourse which structures our society, society is both interpreted and constructed as divided into two categories of sex, and the difference between them is used to justify and maintain the power exerted by one category over the other. Mathieu introduces the idea of multiple axes of power on which individuals are situated differently according to the social relations involved, but does not develop the discussion of social relations this could apply to, for example race and physical ability.

In 1977, Mathieu was theorizing gender, which she called "social sex". In questioning the connection between the biological reality of men and women and what is defined as masculine and feminine, Mathieu was establishing the same distinction between biological and social sex as British and American feminists at the same time. Mathieu's early work was resolutely opposed to biological explanations of the social hierarchy between men and women. Mathieu (1977: 52) argued that the social construction of masculinity and femininity needs to be exposed, so that these constructions can be destroyed. Masculinity and femininity, she stressed (Mathieu, 1977: 59), *can* be changed, "for femininity and masculinity have no sex. Or rather, they only have a statistical relation to biological sex and, moreover, this relation is arbitrary, as has been shown above, and therefore temporary in a historical society."

Colette Guillaumin

Colette Guillaumin argues that women's time, labour and energy are appropriated by men. This appropriation is justified by the definition of the difference between the sexes as natural. Guillaumin compares the way in which naturalist arguments are applied to sexual and racial differences in order to justify domination. The argument that women are different by nature, she states (Guillaumin, 1978), is used to justify all sorts of material disadvantages, including physical violence. Natural differences are presented as the cause of women's oppression, and, since they are natural and exist outside history and all social relations, they are immutable.

Guillaumin uses the term *sexage* to describe the domination of women by men, by analogy with *esclavage* – slavery and *servage* – serfdom. The appropriation of women's bodies includes not only their labour, but also for sexual and reproductive purposes. *Sexage* takes place on two levels, the collective and the individual. The first is the appropriation of all women by all men; the second is the particular form of appropriation which takes place in marriage. Marriage is the individual expression of the appropriation of one sex by the other (Daune-Richard & Devreux, 1986: 27).

The "ideology of difference" is used to maintain women's oppression and defines the differences between the sexes. These differences include physical characteristics and emotional, psychological and experiential characteristics, but also a multitude of other differences between women and men, for example, how much space they occupy, how much they earn, the clothes they wear, their rights, etc. Guillaumin (1979) points out that it is only women who are defined as different, while men constitute the norm or the referent to which they are compared. The ideology of difference presents sexual difference as natural. However, if it were natural, surely it would not need to be so energetically protected. If masculinity were really natural and inherent to males, then why would so many measures have to be introduced to protect it (Guillaumin, 1984)? And why do men feel so threatened by anything which brings into question the clear distinction between the sexes, for example, "effeminate" or homosexual men? Guillaumin (1984: 68) asks,

> If the instinctual nature of sexual characteristics is what its advocates claim it to be, then why do they exhibit such a great fear, why do they enforce such rigorous controls in order to prevent the disappearance of something which by definition cannot disappear?

So masculinity and femininity are not natural but socially constructed and they exist only in relation to each other. Since masculinity and femininity have no essential existence outside of their relation to each other, then they are historical constructs and can therefore be changed.

The contribution of the QF theorists

The theories produced in *QF* have not been accepted uncritically. The systemic nature of the oppression of women as a sex class by men as a sex class, as portrayed by Delphy in "L'ennemi principal" and "Nos amis et nous", leaves no room for change in the relations between them without overthrowing the whole system. While in the 1970s the importance of such arguments was that they joined women together in the notion of sisterhood, there was an increasing sense during the 1980s that this did not reflect the reality of many women's experiences. It could not account for heterosexual relationships which *were* experienced as egalitarian; it could not account for differences between individual men or between individual women. Certainly in the United States, and to a lesser extent in Britain, the notion of sisterhood was challenged by black and lesbian women, as was noted in Chapter 3. They pointed out that sisterhood excluded them and stressed the differences between women. Third world women also criticized western feminism for its cultural imperialism and ethnocentrism. They demonstrated how western feminists ignored the many different needs, experiences and priorities of third world feminists. For example, if free and legal contraception and abortion was a major demand for Western feminists, it did not have the same meaning for women who were sterilized by force, or who had their pregnancies terminated against their will. This was to have a significant effect on the theoretical developments around the question of difference, and during the 1980s differences between women became more central to Anglo-American feminist debate than differences between women and men.

In France, this kind of discussion has not taken place to anywhere near the same extent as in Britain and the United States. It is very difficult to find any references to the specific oppression of North African women in France, for instance, and the difference debate continues to centre on the question of whether or not women and men are essentially the same or different.

While it is important to recognize the limitations of the early theories of gender which appeared in *QF*, they did make a considerable contribution to the development of subsequent ideas about sex, gender and masculinity. The roots of theories of gender and social relations of sex can be easily identified in their analyses. Delphy, Mathieu and Guillaumin stressed that gender or social relations of sex are a construct which maintain women's oppression. They are historically and culturally specific and can be changed. Nicole-Claude Mathieu (1977), for example, argued that it is the social hierarchy between the genders which is more important than sexual difference; Colette Guillaumin (1979) that difference only exists in the relation between masculinity and femininity, and that neither of these terms has any meaning outside of this relation; Christine Delphy (1981) that gender constructs sexual difference, in that the physical differences between the sexes acquire meaning in excess of their actual importance because of the social hierarchy of gender. Similarly, Colette Guillaumin (1984) argued that the belief that social inequalities are the result and not the cause of sexual difference is untenable. That the male anatomy is invested with such symbolic meaning is not due to its inherent qualities, but to the social power enjoyed by men. *QF* was critical of feminists who appeared to assert an essential difference between the sexes. This was seen as providing evidence for the argument that sexual difference was natural and could therefore not be changed. For example, Monique Wittig (1980: 77) wrote in 1980:

> . . . if we accept that there is a "natural" division between women and men, we naturalize history. We pretend that men and women have always existed and always will do. And not only do we naturalize history, but we also as a consequence naturalize the social phenomena which are the manifestation of our oppression. This amounts to making any change impossible.

Gender in the 1980s and 1990s

As the stress laid by feminists on the unequal and hierarchical relation between women and men grew, feminists broke free of the sociological and anthropological tradition of considering the sexes as natural and therefore separable. Instead, they argued that they could only be considered in relation to each other, and that it was also important to study men as gendered individuals (Daune-Richard & Devreux, 1986: 22). During the 1980s, theories of gender were developed by feminists who drew on the work of Mathieu, Guillaumin and Delphy and continued the debate in the terms in which they had constructed it. Thus, many of them took as a basic premise the belief that difference, masculinity and femininity are socially constructed. Major themes which structured the continuing debate were the social construction of what is often portrayed as immutable biological fact; and variations in the relations between individuals and the structure of male dominance, which early "structuralist" theories of patriarchy and sex class (such as Delphy's) were unable to account for. In this respect, the gender debate in France in the 1980s was similar to its British and American counterparts.

"Gender" in each country took on a similar range of meanings. However, French feminists engaged in a prolonged debate over the terms "gender" and "social relations of sex", a debate which is often misleading in its representation of the use of each term by others. As will be argued below, this debate seems to rely on a limited representation of the wealth of meanings of one term, in order to portray another as more useful. It also often depends on an opposition between French and Anglophone gender theories, which is based on a simplistic representation of the use of the term "gender" in Britain and the United States. Before discussing this debate, however, let us first consider the ways in which the concept of the social construction of sex was being developed during the early 1980s.

"Biological" sex as a social construct

An important development of the 1980s was the argument that even biological sex could not be seen as two neatly divided categories. Feminists in the 1970s had accepted the existence of two sexes, and had argued that it was the socially constructed gender laid on top of these sexes which needed to be challenged and removed. Now, feminists were arguing that there are not even two natural biological categories of sex. Sex is often ascribed according to the different positions occupied by men and women in reproduction, but even then, it is not clear that they can be neatly divided into two categories. As psychologists Marie-Claude Hurtig and Marie-France Pichevin (cited by Dhavernas & Kandel, 1983: 1) assert, sex is a complex and heterogeneous reality and there is no single indicator which can be used to define it.

Evidence presented to the conference at Toulouse in 1982 by biologists Evelyne Peyre and Joelle Wiels (1984) aimed to demonstrate the complexity of the biological determination of the sexes and to show how the criteria used are not always appropriate. They concluded (ibid., p. 823) that biological differences between individuals certainly exist, but that it is reductionist to divide them into just two sexes: "Just as human diversity cannot be reduced to a few 'races', we feel that it is important to show that neither can it be reduced to two sexes."

It is clear to feminists even in the 1990s that the constant battle against naturalist ideology must continue. This is undertaken by feminist psychologists, such as Marie-Claude Hurtig and Marie-France Pichevin, and biologists such as Evelyne Peyre, Joelle Wiels and Michèle Fonton, among others. In a paper published in 1991, for example, Peyre, Wiels and Fonton (1991) aimed to demonstrate that there is no biological basis for the division of humans into two categories of sex. They argued that the sex of individuals is distributed along a continuum from male to female and that there are huge variations from population to population and within any one population over time. They challenged the belief that sex can be determined without complications on the basis of the role of the individual in reproduction, arguing that given the number of heterosexual couples who are, for one reason or another, incapable of producing children this definition is imprecise. The target of their criticisms was the belief that sex is naturally and clearly divided into two categories; individuals who deviate from the norm being defined as pathological. They (Peyre et al., 1991: 33–4) asked, "But would it not be better to admit, given the number of people concerned who are in fact not ill, that it is not these individuals who are abnormal, but the conceptual framework of bicategorization, into which they are being forced?"

Peyre et al. (1991: 48) concluded that "The link between social sex and biological sex which exists in contemporary western societies seems to be based principally on a social division of roles which seeks to justify the oppression of women by anchoring it in the Natural Order."

Finally, changing attitudes to biology have affected theories of gender and social relations of sex, and have necessitated a reconsideration not only of the relations between the sexes, but also between sex and gender. In particular, the work of Christine Delphy (1993) and Nicole-Claude Mathieu (1991: 227–66) rejects the belief that sex and gender can be easily separated, and asserts that the boundaries between them need to be examined. For sex is not simply an unchanging natural base upon which gender can be constructed; rather it is constructed through the hierarchical relations of gender itself. Mathieu (1991) uses examples from non-western societies as well as phenomena marginalized in our own society to argue that neither the definitions of sex nor the boundaries between sex and gender are that clear.

In common with feminists in Britain and the United States, some French feminists are also beginning to reintroduce the question of biology and the body into their considerations of gender. This does not mean that they are claiming that gender derives from biological sex, but rather that the body cannot be ignored out of fear of accusations of essentialism. As Danièle Combes, Anne-Marie Devreux and Michèle Ferrand (1988: 173–4) have stated:

> The sociological construction of relations between men and women, of relations between the sexes, has taken place through a fundamental break with a "naturalist" or "biologistic" definition of the sexes. A consequence of this is that it is more difficult to integrate a consideration of the body into the analysis of social relations of sex. On closer inspection, the problem is probably the endless confusion between the body and sex. . . . One way in which the body and biology could be re-integrated into relations between the sexes is possibly, as is being suggested by some researchers, by re-introducing the biological, after having de-naturalised relations of sex. . . .

"Genre" or "rapports sociaux de sexe"?

Since Toulouse, an increasing amount of attention has been paid to the development of theories of gender and social relations of sex, and, especially in the last few years, a number of attempts have been made to clarify the various meanings that these terms have acquired in France. Delphy was an early advocate of the use of the term "gender" ("*genre*") and has continued to use it, despite the opposition to the term by other French feminist theorists, such as Colette Guillaumin, Nicole-Claude Mathieu and Monique Wittig (Delphy, 1993: 5).[29] Such opposition was based on the view that the distinction between sex and gender was itself essentialist. It recognized that sex is natural, rather than rejecting sexual categories as a whole (Jackson, 1996: 120). In "Le patriarcat, le féminisme et leurs intellectuelles" Delphy (1981) claimed that for most people, including many feminists, sexual difference is perceived as leading to at least a minimal division of labour, which is called gender. This division of labour, she states, is used as an explanation of the domination of one group over the other. Delphy (1981: 65), however, suggests that the opposite is true: that gender is created by oppression; that the hierarchical division of labour comes before the technical division of labour, which it creates, along with sex roles or gender; and that gender, in turn, creates anatomical sex in the sense that the hierarchical division of humanity into two transforms an anatomical difference, which in itself is devoid of any meaning, into an important distinction.

For Delphy, gender is an important term, in that it stresses the social aspect of the division between women and men. Nevertheless, in the introduction to *Close to home* she elaborates on some of the problems with the term, the most important being that it is too often used in conjunction with "sex", and that it therefore loses some of its potential meaning. Delphy (1984: 24–5) argues that too many feminists readily accept the social division of women and men, questioning the variations in the form it takes, but not necessarily the division itself. She criticizes the way in which gender is seen as a social dichotomy which is determined by a natural dichotomy: sex. Delphy claims that gender is seen to vary, but sex is supposed to be fixed. No-one asks *why* sex should give rise to any form of social categorization, just *which* form it gives rise to. For Delphy (1991b), it is not sexual *difference* which matters, but the social division and the hierarchy between the genders.

For APRE, which can be seen in many ways as the successor to *QF* in terms of producing gender theory, the most important quality of "social relations of sex" is the emphasis it places on the relation between the two terms.[30]

With the increasing use of theories of social relations of sex, especially within feminist sociology in France, came a growing critique of the perceived limitations of the Anglo-American concept of gender. The use of "gender" by some French feminists by the late 1980s was seen by others as a stylistic device, rather than an analytical tool, which, if anything, detracted from the meaning. It was claimed (Doaré, 1991: 8) that social relations of sex has the advantage over gender, firstly, of drawing attention to the dialectical relation between the sexes, rather than their fixed biological nature, and secondly, of introducing the notion of multiple social relations, rather than two sexes.

Danièle Kergoat (1992: 16–17) argues that, like gender, the concept of social relations of sex emphasizes the social construction of sexual difference. It also indicates the material as well as the ideological base of this construction, which must therefore be understood historically. Finally, it stresses that the social relations of sex are hierarchical. Kergoat's analysis is unusual in that it takes into account the way in which different social relations interact and affect the individual's identity and social practices. Kergoat argues that, instead of concentrating solely on the social relations of sex, we should theorize all social relations simultaneously. Each individual is involved not only in social relations of sex, but in a whole network of social relations. For example, individuals may think of themselves as workers, unemployed, young, black, etc. Within each social relation they may be either dominant or dominated. And the combination of these axes of power and their position on them constitutes their identity, accounts for their social practices and determines which, if any, groups they are going to feel part of. Kergoat argues, therefore, that although all social relations are gendered (*sexué*), social relations of sex are cut through by other social relations (for example, class). This approach allows for the co-existence of conflicting identities. It also enables a consideration of the interaction between individuals and social relations. Individuals are affected by social relations in the way in which they construct their life through their social practices.

Kergoat then introduces a debate around the terms "genre", "rapports de genre" (which, she explains, is the equivalent of the term "gender" in English) and "rapports sociaux de sexe". It is interesting that she does not mention "rapports de genre" again, and does not discuss its advantages or disadvantages in relation to "rapports sociaux de sexe". Instead, she polarizes the debate around a simple choice between "genre" and "rapports sociaux de sexe". Despite explaining that these terms cannot be opposed, since they are both used in a wide variety of ways, and since the meanings attributed to them often overlap, she then presents a list of reasons why "rapports sociaux de sexe" is the more useful term. These reasons include the fact that it stresses the *relation* between the two sexes and therefore less easily becomes a synonym for "women". However, the "debate" which Kergoat presents does not have the appearance of a balanced and informed comparison of the relative advantages of the three analytical terms. In order to highlight the advantages of "rapports sociaux de sexe", she interprets very narrowly the uses made by other French theorists of the term "genre" and conveniently ignores the sophistication of the Anglo-American debate around the term "gender". Perhaps, as Kergoat mentions briefly in this article, it is more a question of personal preference for one term rather than the other than of a significant difference in meaning. Interestingly, in an article published a year later in *Politis*, Kergoat (Hirata & Kergoat, 1993: 55) decides to use the term "genre" "par commodité d'écriture" (out of convenience).

Theories of gender and social relations of sex

Since the aim here is to demonstrate how the development of theories of gender and social relations of sex enabled feminists to begin studying men and masculinity within this framework, it is unnecessary to review all the aspects of the more recent developments of these theories. However, a brief overview of the major themes that recur in this work will help to contextualize the specific examples which follow of the ways in which these theories have been used to think about masculinity. A major insistence in much of this work is on the asymmetry and hierarchy which these theorists argue are inherent to social relations of sex. From this basis, Christine Delphy (1981), for example, argues that gender exists only because of these power relations. It is the relation which determines gender, which creates the differences between women and men. If this power relation were removed, the differences between the sexes would be reduced to anatomical differences devoid of any social significance.

Other major themes include the reproduction of gender relations, which highlights both their fixed and changing nature; the relations between individuals and structures; the way in which gender relations cut through society and interact with other social relations in the construction of an individual's identity; the contradictions in the social relations of sex; the historical specificity and hence changeability of social relations of sex; the relation between material realities and representation of gender; and why and how the binary division of the sexes has been maintained.

APRE has paid particular attention to the reproduction of the relations between women and men and of dominant masculine identities. It is argued that not only are the differences between the sexes socially constructed, but on a systemic, if not on an individual level, they act in the interests of the dominant group – men – and that the members of this group therefore attempt to maintain them. This is why the reproduction of social relations of sex is of interest to feminists. When talking of the reproduction of gender relations, these theorists do not mean the replication of an unchanged and unchanging relation, but rather a constant process of change. They recognize the importance for feminism of having exposed the structural functioning of gender relations, but argue that it is important now to look at how they change. They state that social relations of sex occur everywhere, in every sphere, but that they change according to historical situation.

Gender/social relations of sex and masculinity

The development of theories of gender and social relations of sex in France has led some feminist theorists to argue that it is necessary to theorize men and masculinity, in order to understand how these relations work. Men have consequently been constructed as objects of study who are not only gendered, but whose gendered identity exists only within the power relation between the sexes. One of the few feminists to have published work in this area is Anne-Marie Devreux (1992), the only woman to contribute an article to a recent book attempting to illustrate the variety of theories of masculinity in France, *Des hommes et du masculin*. Commenting on the scarcity of feminist theories of masculinity within the context of gender relations, Devreux (1992: 149) claims that feminists, although they have developed the necessary theoretical frameworks, have on the whole left this particular line of analysis to men. She argues that it is now time for feminists to develop their own theories in this direction. Men should be taken as objects of analysis and as gendered social actors. They should be theorized within the context of the social relations of sex in which they dominate women. By doing this, feminist sociologists would reinforce their critique of universal claims and neuter referents and would at the same time move beyond a gynocentrism which hides the power relations between men and women.

French gender theories have contributed to the theorization of masculinity in three main areas. They have addressed, firstly, the problem of the relation between the individual and the structure of social relations of sex; secondly, the reproduction of the power relations between the sexes and of dominant masculine identities; and thirdly, the tension and conflicts between the reality and the representation of gender and masculinity.

The individual and the structure of gender relations

In an important development from structuralist explanations of male power which could not account for individual variations and could not explain the interaction of the individual with the structure, more recent theories have begun to do just this. By examining the different positions of individual men on this axis, it can also explain cases where individual women exert power and/or violence over individual men. Anne-Marie Devreux (1992: 150–51) argues that, although men as a group are dominant in the power relations between the sexes and as a group maintain the conditions necessary to reproduce these relations, individual men occupy different positions in these relations at different times in their personal history. This is because of the interaction between social relations of sex and other social relations and also because of the environment in which these relations exist. So some men will be more marginal or more central to their sex category than others and occupy a more or less powerful position in relation to women and other men. If a man's career slows down because he shares parenting with his partner, he could be seen to experience social disadvantages normally reserved for women. In this respect, he is marginalized in his sex category in relation to men who do nothing at home and succeed at work.

However, despite APRE's repeated recognition of the importance of examining the intersection of gender and other social relations, there is little evidence in their work of serious attempts to develop this.[31] In contrast, British and American feminist and pro-feminist theorists have placed great emphasis on the interaction of many different social relations in the construction of an individual's identity. The way in which the Anglo-American difference debate has been cut through by issues of ethnicity, sexuality and physical ability has influenced the approach taken in the study of masculinity, since Anglo-American writers quickly began to examine the differences between men and the power relations which exist within, and not just between, the sex categories (Segal, 1990; Connell, 1987; Chapman & Rutherford, 1988). In an article which is much cited in the masculinity literature, Tim Carrigan, Bob Connell and John Lee (1987) argue that although men in general are advantaged through the subordination of women, this is complicated by the fact that, at a local level, there are many instances where individual women hold power over individual men. The global picture is thus modified by the intersections of the various axes of power on which social relations are situated at any one time, for example age, race, class, etc. These contradictions between local situations and the global relationships are a vital site of conflict and hope for future change. Lynne Segal (1990: x) states that "it is an understanding of the differences between men which is central to the struggle for change". If men are presented as a homogeneous entity, all equally responsible for male domination of women, then all it can produce is a paralyzing sense of guilt, they argue. Instead, it is necessary to examine the relations between heterosexual and homosexual masculinities, to establish which types of masculinity are hegemonic, or, in other words, which types of masculinity define other types of masculinity. According to Carrigan, Connell and Lee (1987: 179), "Hegemonic masculinity . . . is a question of how particular groups of men inhabit positions of power and wealth and how they legitimate and reproduce the social relationships that generate their dominance." They argue that hegemonic masculinity actually corresponds to the reality of the lives of very few real men. However, many men are responsible for sustaining the hegemonic model. Most men benefit from the subordination of women, and hegemonic masculinity plays an important role in the institutionalisation of men's dominance over women.

While the concept of hegemonic masculinity has gone a long way towards offering an explanation of the variety of masculinities and the relation between them, it has not been accepted by all feminists. Some argue that there is a danger attached to the acceptance of multiple masculinities, and in particular the notion of hegemonic masculinity. Men could use this to absolve themselves of any responsibility for male dominance, arguing that their masculinity is not hegemonic, for example. Stressing the multiplicity of masculinities can obscure the systemic nature of male dominance (Banner, 1989). The problem is that we need to be able to explain why, on a global level, men are advantaged over women. But at the same time, we need to be able to explain how, on a local level, individual men are situated in very different positions in relation to other individual men and individual women. And this is why it is important to examine different systems of social relations and the interaction between them. While this is recognized by some French feminists, the literature is still thin.

The reproduction of power relations between the sexes

How is power maintained and how and where is it reproduced? According to Devreux (1988: 151) and the previous work of the APRE research teams, social relations of sex are reproduced as a structure by individuals. Their reproduction can mean both the maintenance of the structure as it is or its change. The social actors involved in these relations (and at the same time in other relations) re-create indefinitely the conditions necessary to the existence of these relations:

> If the relation between the two terms has changed in one way or the other, it is indeed because the relative status of each social category in relation to the other has changed. But it is also because the individuals (this time biological men and women) have moved within the relation, either within their own category or even from one category to the other. (Devreux, 1988: 152)

The reproduction of the gender system currently requires the reproduction of men as dominant and the reproduction of women as subordinated. So how is masculinity reproduced so that men retain power over women? Devreux (1992) looks at the reproduction of masculinity in the army and at the interaction between the family and the army in the socialization of these men. She examines in particular the way in which domestic chores are represented in this all-male environment. They are seen as boring, repetitive and representing servitude and femininity. They are therefore seen as a punishment and are used in order to emphasize power and hierarchy in the context of what is perceived as "women's work". At a time when young men are preparing to leave home, the army teaches them to associate washing and housework with inferiority. At the same time, it shows them how to escape from these tasks and the inferior status associated with them. So when they leave the army and begin living in a couple, these young men are intent on regaining the masculinity which was temporarily removed from them in the army when they had to do domestic chores, and this they do by refusing to do anything associated in their minds with femininity and inferiority, in particular washing and housework. So masculinity in this context is defined in opposition to femininity. In order to "be a man" these men learn that they must avoid doing anything associated with femininity and inferiority.

Therefore, although the army may appear to be a masculine institution, it is none the less a site of gender relations and of gendered socialization. The army teaches men the hierarchy between what is feminine and what is masculine, and also teaches strategies for maintaining a dominant position in the sexual division of labour. In this non-mixed social space, explanations of the sexual division of labour cannot be based on arguments of natural biological difference. The hierarchy is defined only in terms of social relations of power. This makes an interesting case study which can offer some convincing conclusions. But what appears to be uncomplicated role-learning takes place in a social site which is relatively free of contradictions. There are few conflicting pressures on the men. They are taught or coerced into behaving in a certain way, and refusal to do this is harshly sanctioned. The options available to them are limited. Further case studies which could shed light on the reproduction and maintenance of male power through particular constructions of masculinity will contribute to knowledge in this area of research.

The reproduction of male dominance and a dominant masculine identity is of particular interest to feminists. It is clear that men have an interest in maintaining the situation as it is, although to do this it can be necessary to incorporate a certain amount of flexibility. But while feminists have highlighted the variable and contradictory nature of gender relations and masculinity, they have also stressed the invariable occurrence of male power. The boundaries between sex categories change, for example, as the result of new reproductive technologies or new ways of doing masculinity, but what is striking is that the power relations never seem to be affected (Daune-Richard & Hurtig, 1995: 428). Why should this be so? The psychologist Marie-France Pichevin (1995) in the same volume suggests that stereotypes learned at a very early age emerge automatically in response to an indication of sex categories (including physical markers and inferences drawn from these markers). She points to research demonstrating that these stereotypes emerge automatically whatever the conscious attitudes of the research subject. The psychologist Annick Durand-Delvigne (1995) suggests that power is a more important determinant of gender than sex. This perhaps explains the paradox of a gender system which is stable and intransigent while consisting of categories whose boundaries are fluid and ever-changing.

French and Anglo-American theories of gender

The similarities between the ways in which masculinity has been examined in Anglo-American and French feminist theory are more striking than the differences. The development from sex role to gender theory, for example, took a similar course in France, Britain and the United States. Early structuralist theories of patriarchy and sex class were replaced by more adaptable theories of gender allowing for individual variations on models. Patriarchy, sisterhood and the systemic nature of men's domination of women have been modified to take into account variations in the nature of this domination. In order to do this, some theorists have rejected the term "patriarchy", which they feel is too inflexible, while others have adapted its meaning to incorporate elements of flexibility.[32]

There has also been a common trend from the optimistic belief that masculinity, since it was socially constructed, could be changed, to a re-examination of the mechanisms of social change or reproduction of existing relations. Thus, Lynne Segal (1990) examines men's resistance to changes in the sex system, which she describes as understandable, given the threat they could represent for men's dominance, while Rowena Chapman (1988) claims that one of the elements of the successful reproduction of male dominance is men's shrewd adaptations to current demands. She argues, for example, that:

> . . . the new man represents not so much a rebellion but an adaptation in masculinity. Men change, but only in order to hold on to power, not to

relinquish it. The combination of feminism and social change may have produced a fragmentation in male identity by questioning its assumptions, but the effect of the emergence of the new man has been to reinforce the existing power structure, by producing a hybrid masculinity which is better able and more suited to retain control. (ibid., p. 235)

This highlights an important question for feminists. Evidence that the gender system can adapt itself while maintaining the balance of power brings into question the usefulness for feminists of seeking change only at a local level. The existence of a few "new men" may be represented by the media as a revolution in gender relations, but for feminists this does not seem to be the case. Feminist strategy needs to take into account men's resistance to change.

Tension and conflicts between reality and representation

French feminists have also shown an interest in the conflict between the reality and representation of masculinity, revealing, for example, the way in which scientific research is portrayed as being a particularly masculine affair, even when it is performed by women (Le Doeuff, 1992). In politics, there is a similar insistence on projecting a masculine image, although in this case men are vastly over-represented in relation to women. The effect of this insistence that politics is a masculine activity is to perpetuate the exclusion of women (Sineau, 1992).

The representation of institutions or sites of power as masculine has implications for the reproduction of power relations between women and men, and contributes to the continued exclusion of women from scientific knowledge and from political power. Revealing the ways in which this image is maintained, whether or not it matches reality, Michelle Le Doeuff and Mariette Sineau reject the gender-neutral status of masculinity, and instead examine it as gendered. Once politics is seen as masculine rather than gender-neutral, it is easier to identify the mechanisms by which it continues to exclude women. This type of research forms part of the much broader project of exposing the gendered nature of much that is presumed neutral, whether institutions, discourses or activities. While it is concerned with the structure of masculinity and appears to have little to do with the masculinity of the individual men involved, it does have effects on individuals. For example, the creation of a masculine culture in political institutions means that individual men can enter politics far more easily than individual women. It is one way in which men's power can be maintained.

Difference revisited

Papers presented to the pre-Beijing conference in Paris in March 1995 (Ephesia, 1995) demonstrate that research activity explicitly concerned with gender relations continues. Interest was focused on the boundaries between the sex categories and the role played by definitions of masculinity and femininity in defining these boundaries; on the implicit representations in the law and politics of each sex and the relations between them; and on the relation between the division of the sexes into two categories and the gendered power relation (Daune-Richard & Hurtig, 1995). A central question was whether sex categorization necessarily involves power differentials. Can there be difference without hierarchy? The answer to this question determines feminist strategy. If difference without hierarchy is possible, then feminism can be based on women's specificity without this playing into the hands of patriarchal ideology, which continues to use naturalist justifications for the inequality of men and women. However, if sex categorization necessarily implies hierarchy, then feminists must struggle for access to a true universal in which the differences between men and women disappear. The debate which took place at the pre-Beijing conference provides further evidence that the either/or nature of difference may be breaking down. The debate concluded with the suggestion that it might be necessary to recognize difference in the first instance in order to achieve equality (Daune-Richard & Hurtig, 1995). It is increasingly being argued, as we have already seen in relation to the parity campaign, that equality and difference are not as irreconcilable as they may seem.

5   Feminism and male violence

This chapter examines the attention paid by the French women's movement to the question of male violence towards women. Its aim is to identify certain trends in the way in which the problem has been approached and the implications of changing practice for the search for explanations of this violence. The main argument is that feminists in France concerned with male violence towards women have shown a growing interest in the perpetrators, opening up a space where ideas about violent men and the construction of masculine identity can emerge. This chapter discusses how this interest developed through the practice of French feminist activists.[33] Chapter 6 will then focus on the development of French feminist theories of violence which focus on the perpetrator and explore the links between violence, power and masculine identity. Given the nature of the relation between theory and practice in this area, the questions addressed in these two chapters are intertwined. The main distinction, however, is that this chapter aims to explain how changes in feminist practice led to a growing belief that the theorization of masculinity was necessary to the understanding and prevention of male violence, while Chapter 6 examines more closely theories which focus on the perpetrator of this violence in a search for explanations for it and possible ways of preventing it.

The first trend which will be identified is in feminist action around the problem. It will be argued that from an exclusive interest in the survivor of male violence, some feminists have now begun to pay more attention to the perpetrator. So, whereas in the 1970s and early 1980s the immediate priority was to open refuges for the women survivors, by the late 1980s some feminists were advocating the creation of centres for violent men.

The second trend concerns the changing ideas about male violence, where questions such as why particular women are subjected to certain kinds of violence are increasingly giving way to questions such as why some men become violent.

A third and closely related trend can also be identified. This is the shift in practical feminist priorities from dealing with the effects of male violence (for example, helping the survivors to speak out or campaigning for the proper trial and punishment of the perpetrators), to searching for ways to prevent it, through therapy for violent men or campaigns for better sex education in schools.

The increasing interest in prevention has necessitated a better understanding of *why* some men are violent towards women. The analyses of the reasons behind male violence, which were produced in an attempt to find ways to reduce the problem, and the way in which these analyses began to look at the problem of male violence as an expression of the power relations between the sexes will be examined in Chapter 6.

A problem with the organization of the narrative is, however, that the development of feminist action and ideas did not always occur at the same rate. Although they sometimes developed in parallel, the theory emerging directly out of the practice and changing with it, there were also times when they were not so closely linked. This chapter, then, will attempt to demonstrate the development firstly in feminist practice, then in feminist ideas resulting from this practice, and to explain both the connections and the discontinuities between the two.

A final point which needs to be clarified before this account can begin is that of terminology, beginning with the terms "victim" and "survivor". Feminists working in this area prefer to use the term "survivor", which is seen as being more empowering than that of victim. In France, the term "victim" has also been largely avoided by feminists. The availability in the French language of the term *"femme violentée"*, which does not have the same connotations as "victim", simply stating that the woman has experienced violence, offers a non-problematic solution. Given that I am writing in English, I have chosen to use "survivor" in recognition of the importance of this differentiation.

The fact that I have concentrated almost exclusively on male violence towards women does not mean that it is the most prevalent; survivors of male violence are far more often men than women. Neither does it mean that this type of violence is sexual (in the sense of genital), whereas male violence towards men is not; men (and especially boys) are also raped by other men. Finally, it should not obscure the fact that some women are also violent, beating and raping men, children or other women. The specificity of male violence towards women is, as far as feminists are concerned, that it is an expression of a much broader system of domination of women by men, and it is within this context that the following account of French feminist considerations of this violence is situated.

In France, feminist interest in male violence towards women at the beginning of the 1970s concentrated initially on rape, but other forms followed one after another, from domestic violence, incest, female excision, marital rape and pornography to sexual harassment. While this progression will be pointed out during the following account, not all of the debates can be examined in detail. In the early sections of this chapter, which deal with feminist events and theories in the 1970s, I have chosen to concentrate mainly on rape and domestic violence, since these were the major feminist interests in France at the time. However, during the 1980s many more feminists began to connect different types of male violence and to talk of "violences" in the plural, which were then theorized as different expressions of male power. For example, much of the theorization of sexual harassment which has taken place in the last few years, particularly by

Marie-Victoire Louis and other members of AVFT, sees sexual harassment as just one type of male violence towards women, all of which, they argue, are situated on a continuum. So, whereas in the early parts of this chapter rape and violence are examined separately, later (and especially in Chapter 6) the different forms of violence are examined together as aspects of a more coherent whole, thus reflecting the changes that have taken place in the way that these different aspects of male violence towards women are seen by French feminists.

Feminist action around male violence during the 1970s

In France, as in Britain, violence against women has been a major concern for feminists since the early 1970s, when they first began to expose the seriousness of the problem and its massive occurrence. Initially the priorities were raising public consciousness, campaigning for legislative reform and providing aid for the women survivors. This feminist action will be examined here, and then the ideas which emerged from it will be discussed.

The problem of violence against women mobilized feminists in France as early as 1972, when the first demonstration against crimes against women took place in Paris (Casalis, 1988: 262). Until the Loi Veil was passed on 29 November 1974, legalizing abortion under certain circumstances, abortion remained the major issue for feminist campaigns. However, although it was only a partial victory for feminism, given the initial temporary status of the law and its limitations, it seemed to many feminists in 1974 as though the abortion issue was now over. Consequently, during the second half of the 1970s violence replaced abortion as the main focal point of French feminist interest, as can be seen from the contents page of any feminist journal from this period.[34] The initial priorities were to raise public awareness of the extent of the problem and to provide aid for the survivors.

Aid for the survivors of violence

One of the first feminist organizations formed specifically to provide aid for women survivors of violence was SOS femmes-alternative, which was created in 1975 by two of the groups within the Ligue du droit des femmes: the legal group and the group which produced their journal *Les nouvelles féministes*. In October 1975 they set up a telephone helpline. Within the first month they had answered 200 calls from all over France (*Les nouvelles féministes*, 1980).

Helplines enabled women to talk about the violence they had experienced (and for many, this was the first time they had done that); to discover that they were not alone as survivors of violence; and to discuss the possibilities of escaping from it and/or beginning legal proceedings. However, a growing understanding of the tremendous problems confronting survivors of domestic violence when they finally decide to try to leave home provoked an awareness of the need for women's refuges, and the long struggle began which culminated in the opening of the first: the Refuge Flora Tristan at Clichy in 1978.[35] The idea was to provide a place where women – and their children – could stay, where they would be safe from violence and where they would receive the help they needed to begin a new life. This included finding a job and somewhere to live, perhaps moving the children to a new school, beginning divorce proceedings, as well as regaining the self-esteem and independence which had been crushed by years of abuse and humiliation. The provision of the material and psychological support required by women in this situation was the main priority for feminists. Feminist publications from the 1970s suggest that their main interest was in the survivor, and there is little evidence of the explicit consideration of men and masculinity and its relation to male violence towards women.

Public awareness campaigns

In France, as elsewhere, the main aims of the feminist campaigns around rape during the 1970s were to break the silence, to explain to women that they should not be ashamed of having been raped, and to encourage them to press charges. In 1974 several hundred women joined in a night-time demonstration organized by the Féministes révolutionnaires and the Pétroleuses to protest against the fact that women were unable to go out safely at night. In 1976 feminists published a "Manifeste contre le viol" in *Libération* (16 June 1976). On 26 June 1976 the signatories organized a demonstration against rape, in which around 4,000 women took part (Mossuz-Lavau, 1991: 195).

Their aim was to raise public awareness of the extent and seriousness of male violence towards women, and to destroy the myths surrounding it. The importance of the "demystification" of rape was that it aimed to lay the responsibility for this crime fully on men, instead of blaming women for "getting themselves raped", or worse, "asking for it". For instance, feminists insisted that rapists are not a species apart, but ordinary men, often married and from all social classes. They challenged the belief that women enjoy being raped, and that they *unconsciously* "ask for it". By stating that this desire is unconscious, the insistence of the survivor that it was the last thing she wanted is undermined; even if she did not recognize it, the desire was present in her subconscious, and this led her to behave in a provocative manner. This, feminists insisted, is a male fantasy, which they attacked with the slogan "When a woman says no, she means no!" (Granger, 1987: 9). They argued that women are not responsible for male violence; they do not "ask to be raped", nor can they be said to provoke some kind of uncontrollable sexual desire in men. This idea of men's sexuality as uncontrollable was also attacked. Feminist lawyer, Martine Le Péron (1978: 87), for example, wrote the following in *QF*:

... we dispute the notion of men's "uncontrollable sexuality". This "theory" is generally put forward during rape trials when the assistant public prosecutor ... attempts to find something in the victim's behaviour which could have stimulated the rapist's sexual desires and caused him to lose control. Implicit in this approach is the idea that men – because of their nature – can suddenly lose all the characteristics normally attributed to human beings (reason, intelligence, etc.) and can be taken over by their most basic drives.

That the myths surrounding rape played a prominent part in the proceedings of rape trials, and that this also served to perpetuate and reinforce these myths, was becoming a common feminist accusation. Martine Le Péron (1978: 88) cited, for example, the defence of one woman's rapists, "But isn't she lucky to have been raped by good-looking lads like these! Of course, she is an attractive woman, but just take a look at these rapists and you will realize that she cannot have experienced anything other than pleasure. In which case, can we continue to speak of rape?"

The way that rape trials are conducted and the attitudes of the courts towards the survivors are still criticized today, as will be seen at later points in this chapter. However, during the 1970s feminists were involved in another struggle, this time for a new law against rape.

The fight for legal reform

As far as feminists were concerned, there were two major problems with the French legal situation as it stood. These were, firstly, that during rape trials all sorts of myths and prejudices were expressed which operated in the favour of the rapist(s), and, secondly, that the existing laws against rape were inadequate. As will be shown in this section, the main problem was that there was no legal definition of rape, leaving it to the judges and magistrates, operating within the context of the very myths feminists were denouncing, to decide whether or not the act committed constituted "rape". Feminist criticisms of the judges' practical understanding of rape will be discussed, along with other criticisms of the law and the proceedings of rape trials. This will be followed by a consideration of the law passed in 1980, and the effects of this change.

Before 1980 the law against rape was found in article 332 of the Penal Code, which was passed on 28 April 1832. According to this, the crime of rape was punishable with a prison sentence of ten to twenty years. Article 333, instituted by a law passed on 13 May 1863, allowed for the harsher sentence of life imprisonment under particular circumstances, and especially in the case of group rapes. Other indecent acts with violence were considered to be *attentats à la pudeur* (attacks on public decency), and were punishable with a sentence of five to ten years' imprisonment, ten to twenty years' if the survivor was under 15 (Mossuz-Lavau, 1991: 194–5).

Laws existed, therefore, according to which rape was a crime punishable with relatively severe prison sentences. However, the major problem in translating this law into the practical conviction of rapists was that there was no legal definition of rape. In Britain rape is defined by the Sexual Offences Act 1956, although the restrictive nature of this definition, which concentrates only on sexual intercourse without the woman's consent, has also posed problems (Lees, 1993). In France rape was not legally defined and gradually acquired an accepted meaning as a result of the decisions made by judges. A verdict reached by the Cour de cassation (court of appeal) on 25 June 1857 stated that:

> It is up to the judge to ascertain and to record the constitutive elements
> of this crime, according to its own particular characteristics and the
> seriousness of the consequences which it might have for the survivors
> and for the honour of the family involved; whether this crime consists
> in the abuse of a person against their will, or whether it is the result of
> any other method of constraint or surprise which enables the per-
> petrator to achieve their aim against the will of the victim (quoted
> by Mossuz-Lavau, 1991: 190).

Déspite the law against rape, the absence of a legal definition meant that, in practice, rape was very narrowly interpreted. For feminists there were three major problems. Firstly, they argued, the assessment made by judges of the seriousness of the consequences often concentrated more on whether or not the honour of the survivor's family was harmed than on the consequences for the woman herself. In other words, the decision about whether an attack could be defined as rape in practice often depended on whether or not it could lead to the birth of an illegitimate child. Based on this view, it was clear that a rape, in order to be recognized as such, must include penetration, and did not include, for example, sodomy nor penetration with an object, nor could it be committed on a man. Secondly, it could only be committed by a man on a woman who was not his wife; marital rape did not exist because it contradicted the notion of "marital duties", and because a child who was born as the result of such a rape would not be illegitimate. Thirdly, there was the question of consent, which became the linchpin of rape trials. This meant that many defence lawyers based their defence on the argument that the survivor did in fact consent, or that her behaviour had led the accused to believe that she did. The possibility that this could be used as a defence and that the trial could in fact turn out to be the trial of the woman's responsibility in provoking the rape, her behaviour, her habits, etc., discouraged many rape survivors from reporting the crime (Mossuz-Lavau, 1991: 191). The question of consent has held a similar central position in rape trials in Britain, with the same consequences for the survivors. This has led to feminist action aiming to achieve legal reform, although it has not yet been successful (Lees, 1993).

In France, one of the consequences of the absence of a legal definition and the narrow interpretation of the term by the courts was that many rape cases which were brought before the courts were subsequently downgraded, and the rapists were tried instead for assault and grievous bodily harm or indecent acts. In the French judicial system assault and grievous bodily harm and indecent acts constitute criminal offences (*délits*), whereas rape constitutes a crime, which is more serious. This means that, whereas rape is judged by the Cour d'assises, assault and grievous bodily harm and indecent acts are judged by *tribunaux correctionnels*, which award less severe sentences than the ten to twenty years' imprisonment which could be imposed by the Cour d'assises until the introduction of the new law in December 1980. French feminists, therefore, saw the struggle to have cases defined as rape, and therefore as a crime, as important.

As will be shown below, it was not the imprisonment of individual rapists for long periods of time which was at issue for many feminists. In fact, a vicious debate surrounded the question of imprisonment both between feminists and the left, and among feminists themselves. What feminists did want was the recognition that rape was serious, and one way to reinforce this point was through the conviction of rapists (Le Péron, 1978). A feminist strategy which was employed in order to draw attention to the seriousness of rape and the need for its condemnation was to focus public attention on individual trials. Several feminist lawyers were involved in this strategy, including Gisèle Halimi, who had pleaded for the defence in the Bobigny abortion trial in 1972, which had been a watershed in the progression to the legalization of abortion. It was Halimi again who defended Anne Tonglet and Aracelli Castellano in the trial which was to play a central part in the subsequent feminist campaigns for the introduction of a new law against rape.[36]

It concerned the rape in 1974 of these two young Belgian women who were camping close to Marseilles. The three men who raped them had been charged with the lesser offence of assault and grievous bodily harm, because, according to the judge, the women had not struggled hard enough to demonstrate a lack of consent. About 40 feminists were present at the first hearing on 17 September 1975, during which the women's lawyers pleaded incompetence of the court on the grounds that the men were not being charged for rape. The court and the court of appeal both judged that the case should be defined as a crime and that it should therefore go before the Cour d'assises in Aix-en-Provence. The court found the rapists guilty, sentencing one to six years' imprisonment and the other two to four years. This case convinced feminists that rape should move to the top of the agenda. During the 1970s feminist lawyers demanded more and more often that rape cases which had been downgraded to assault and grievous bodily harm or indecent acts should go before the Cour d'assises (Mossuz-Lavau, 1991: 195).

Following this trial, the definition of rape as a crime and the recognition of this by the courts became a feminist priority. A long battle began to achieve this aim, a battle which was not helped by accusations by men on the left that, by insisting on the conviction of rapists for their crime, feminists were supporting the bourgeois legal system.[37] In response to this, feminists argued that if rapists were not brought before the courts, as other criminals were, this did not bring into question the current form of punishment (many feminists were equally opposed to imprisonment); it simply demonstrated that rape was not considered a crime (des féministes révolutionnaires, 1977: 15).

Between 1975 and 1978 most feminists were in favour of using the legal system in the fight against rape; only a small minority advocated other means of punishing rapists, such as publicizing their crime in the vicinity of their home or workplace. However, the debate around imprisonment came to split feminists too, and the divide was aggravated by a series of heavy sentences passed in 1978. The main split was between, on the one hand, Choisir, led by Gisèle Halimi, and La ligue du droit des femmes, who supported the incarceration of rapists in the same way as other criminals, and, on the other hand, Colette Auger, Monique Antoine and Josyane Moutet of the Collectif juridique de défense des femmes, who supported suspended sentences for rapists along with the payment of damages to the survivor (Auger, 1985: 11).

Whether or not they agreed on the type of punishment, all feminists saw the recognition of rape as a crime as a vital step, and the need for a change in the law became more and more evident. In 1978 a series of bills was brought before the Assemblée nationale and the Senate[38], and two years later the new law was passed.[39] Feminist pressure played an important role in the parliamentary debates, and some of their concerns were reflected in the law. For example, the definition of rape was broadened to include "any act of penetration, of any nature, committed on another person with the use of violence, constraint or surprise" (article 332 of the Penal Code) (Rameau, 1985: 30).

In theory, then, rape now included forced sex between spouses, penetration with any object and fellatio. However, throughout the 1980s feminists argued that the changes in the law had failed to be translated into practice. For instance, they argued that the courts still seemed to have difficulty admitting that fellatio or penetration with objects constituted rape (Granger, 1987: 10).

Rape trials continued to hinge on the question of consent, and feminist attacks on the way in which the trials were conducted did not change much as a result of the new legislation. According to des féministes révolutionnaires (1977), the crucial question for the courts was not whether or not a rape had taken place, but whether or not it was "justified". They (des féministes révolutionnaires, 1977: 16) claimed that it was so difficult for women to prove that they were neither consenting nor responsible for their rape that

> only a woman who is married, at home with the door locked and in company, and clothed from head to toe can be recognised as a victim. That is, when the rape was not only physically impossible, but most of all *socially* unjustified from the point of view of the patriarchal system.

Feminists protested that the conduct of the rape trial turns the survivor into the defendant, in that she has to undergo various tests and investigations into her personal life. This, they argued, positions rape as different to all other crimes, in that it is potentially the survivor who is guilty (of provocation). As Gisèle Halimi (1992: 286) argued in her bill proposing the end to investigations into the personal history of rape survivors in 1984:

> The police enquiry which is carried out on the victim in fact forms part of a judicial practice in which the presumption of innocence operates in favour of the accused. The victim, on the other hand, is presumed guilty, or at least suspect. A woman who has been raped is expected to prove her own resistance towards her attacker and her lack of consent. The plaintiff becomes the accused, and is subjected to the sarcastic allegations of police officers, judges and lawyers.

As will be seen later in this chapter, feminists continued to criticize these investigations into the survivor's personal history throughout the 1980s and early 1990s.

Feminist theories concerning male violence during the 1970s

On a theoretical level, feminists during the 1970s were developing critiques of violence as a form of social control. Violence, they argued, is fundamental to the functioning of patriarchy, and rape, or the threat of rape, operates as a means of limiting women's freedom. For example, in an article published in *Alternatives* in 1977, des féministes révolutionnaires (1977) argued that women were unable to do certain things unaccompanied by a man, such as going out after dark, hitch-hiking or camping. The féministes révolutionnaires claimed that, although this behaviour would not necessarily result in their being raped, if they were they would be expected to explain why they had been there without a man, and to provide a good defence against accusations that through this behaviour they had provoked the attack. Women are therefore controlled by a socially constructed risk of rape which keeps women in their place in the patriarchal order, they concluded. The feminist lawyer Martine Le Péron (1978: 89–90) argued that the rapist maintains the patriarchal order in that women, through fear of rape, restrict their own movements. She stated that the judicial system sees no reason why it should suppress rape, since it is part of the patriarchal structure whose interests the rapist serves.

Part of the construction of a theory of violence as a form of social control was the deconstruction of biological explanations. Feminists argued that male violence was not the result of men's "natural aggression" or "uncontrollable sexuality", but rather an expression of the power relations between men and women. To support this argument, Françoise Collin (1976: 3) argued, for example, that in positions of institutional power women have shown themselves to be just as violent as men, as was discovered to be the case in Nazi concentration camps. This was not to deny, however, that the problem of violence was largely one of *male* violence; women are usually the victims, and men are usually the perpetrators. She (Collin, 1976: 5) writes that "there is a form of violence which is committed by men against women as women; a gendered violence which is not reciprocal".

During the 1970s, then, the relationship between violence and power was explored, and the links between the two have been at the centre of much of the theoretical production around the subject since then. All feminists emphasized that rape is a crime, and that this must be recognized. Reflecting the practical concerns of feminists at the time – to provide aid for survivors and to fight for legal reform – interest in the rapist himself was limited. If some theorists took the time to argue against biological explanations of why men rape, they did not go any further in an exploration of the links between masculinity and violence. It was patriarchy as a system which was responsible, and all men, as the beneficiaries of this system, were potential rapists. However, this gradually began to change during the 1980s, as more attention began to be paid to the perpetrators of male violence in a search for an explanation of their actions.

Feminist thought and action against rape in the 1980s

As was explained above, the introduction on 23 December 1980 of a new law on rape did not bring an end to feminist criticisms of the way in which the law was applied. The main objection, made by feminist lawyers in particular, was to the numerous experts' assessments which the survivor has to undergo, even though they are no more compulsory in trials for rape than for any other crime (Auger, 1982: 97). Feminist lawyers object to the fact that, although it is not a legal requirement, the rape survivor usually has to have a psychiatric test in order to establish her "credibility", a notion which, they argue, has no scientific basis and rests on a subjective evaluation by the "expert" involved. The survivor has to have a medical examination to establish whether there is any physical damage and a gynaecological examination to establish the presence of any sexually transmitted diseases. An investigation of her past life and personality is also conducted. Feminist lawyers argue that these expert assessments add little to the evidence of the incident in question. In the case of rape by a stranger or strangers, at least, no knowledge about the survivor's previous life or personality obtained during the police investigation could have any bearing on the rape, since the rapist(s) would not have known any of it. Neither could any knowledge about the survivor's personality or past history help establish whether or not she had consented to sex with that particular person on that particular occasion. The objective of these experts' assessments is, they argue, to establish whether the survivor's behaviour could in any way have "provoked" the rapist, and to establish the likelihood of her having consented. Feminists claim that the notion of "likelihood" or "probability" which is employed in order to assess whether or not there was consent appears particularly spurious when the knowledge that the survivor is a lesbian can be used to demonstrate that her consent was more probable than if she had been heterosexual, as was the case with Marie-Andrée Marion, whose attackers were acquitted in September 1982. The feminist lawyer Colette Auger (1982: 98) argued after this acquittal that the only contribution these experts' assessments could make to a rape trial was to establish whether or not the survivor's personality and past history meant that she *deserved* to be raped, as a punishment for departing from society's norms.

For many feminists, the three rapes which took place in broad daylight in Paris in 1985 without a single witness intervening or coming forward afterwards to testify could only be seen as a sign that nothing had improved since the introduction of the new legislation. Despite the fact that there was still much to be done on the legal front, the most important thing for many feminists was to provide support and help for the survivors. The series of public rapes led to the creation in June 1985 of the Collectif féministe contre le viol, by the Mouvement français pour le planning familial, Mouvement jeunes femmes, Maison des femmes, and Halte aide aux femmes battues (Rojtman, 1991: 217). In 1986 they established a telephone helpline, Viol-femmes-informations (Collectif féministe contre le viol, 1987: 25). Other feminist groups concentrated their efforts on the provision of information, legal aid and support for the survivors of rape. During the 1980s this type of feminist action increased, in contrast to the 1970s which was dominated by efforts to raise public awareness, for example, by focusing attention on certain trials and by publicizing the details of the rape in the area where the rapist lived and worked (Rojtman, 1991: 217).

Although the emphasis was still on women as survivors of violence, the 1980s also saw a growing (if still limited) interest in men and masculinity. Feminists had begun to consider the violent man and not just the survivor. Attention was drawn to the ordinariness of rapists and men who are violent in the home, and the notion that there is something different about them was slowly being worn away, as this quotation (Devèze, 1984: 21) illustrates: "It seems that men who beat their partners, like rapists, are men just like any others. . . . They are not, as is too often said, notorious alcoholics or savage brutes. There are violent men in all classes of society."

The idea that women are raped by strangers in dark and lonely alleys was also challenged. The Collectif féministe contre le viol (1987: 25), for example, basing their statistics on the calls received by Viol-femmes-informations, stated that 40 per cent of rapes occur in places where women thought they were safe (31.2 per cent at home, 7.5 per cent in the workplace, in sports clubs, etc.) and were committed by men they knew.

Rape continued to be theorized as a means of the social control of women, and feminists argued forcefully against any claims that it was caused by provocation, frustration, or sexual or emotional problems. These excuses, argued Marie-France Casalis (1988: 259) of the Mouvement français pour le planning familial, exist only to absolve men of all responsibility and to shift it onto women.

Domestic violence

Rape was not the only type of male violence experienced by women, and French feminists also began to expose the enormity of the problem of domestic violence. They aimed to bring domestic violence out of the private domain, where men were able to do what they wanted without interference, and to make it a subject for public debate. As Geneviève Devèze (1984: 20) comments:

> Indeed, it is clear to us all that, if a man attacks a woman in the street, the police intervene. But if that same man attacks his wife or his girlfriend every day inside the sacrosanct family home, the police do nothing to stop these violent acts, which he can continue to commit undisturbed.

As with rape, domestic violence was surrounded not only by silence, but also by a number of myths which needed to be destroyed. One of these was that domestic violence is a problem concerning a small minority of individuals from certain classes of society. The experience and knowledge acquired from feminist contact with survivors in refuges and on helplines demonstrated that such violence was, in fact, widespread and occurred in all social classes. Another widely held belief was that women are responsible for the violence that they suffer in the home: that they enjoy it, that they "ask for it", and that if they did not like it then they would not stay with a violent partner. Feminists argued that there were many reasons why women did not, or could not, leave a violent partner. These included the most basic economic reason that most women were financially dependent on their partners, and that the violence that they had experienced over the years had diminished their capacity and their will to assert their independence and overcome these material difficulties. In addition, there is the fear of their partner's reaction and increased violence if they tried to leave, as well as the shame experienced by women survivors of domestic violence, the feeling that they have somehow failed (Devèze, 1984: 22).

In 1987 the national federation Solidarité femmes was set up with the aim of destroying these myths, breaking the silence surrounding domestic violence and allowing women to talk about their experiences. The federation is made up of about 40 associations all over France, which are contacted each year by about 100,000 women. The associations provide support for women trying to escape from domestic violence, from the provision of information to refuges. They also try to educate the various public services who come into contact with this problem (Fédération nationale "solidarité femmes").

In 1989 a national public information campaign on domestic violence was organized by the Secrétariat d'état chargé des droits des femmes. The Collectif féministe contre le viol, the Mouvement français pour le planning familial, the Fédération nationale solidarité femmes, and the association sos-hommes et violence en privé all agreed to participate, answering phone-calls 24 hours a day (Forest, 1990: 7). However, despite recognizing the progress represented by the fact that this campaign had at least taken place[40], feminists were critical of the extent to which it could have any effect, especially given that no extra provisions were made for coping with the response that it would provoke, with the result that all the existing resources were completely overstretched within a couple of days. Isabelle Forest (1990: 9), who was one of the feminists who volunteered to answer phone-calls during the campaign, wrote:

> Domestic violence, as soon as it is revealed, highlights the different aspects of women's oppression. They are not only beaten; they are often financially dependent, since they are, on average, worse paid than men. They are more often unemployed, and any qualifications they may have are not as well recognized on the labour market. At the same time, they generally take responsibility for the children and for the work that this involves, in particular the housework.

Isabelle Forest claimed that what these women need is more than an information campaign. Their most urgent requirement is the material aid necessary for them to leave their violent partner, and to find somewhere new to live.

Equally critical of the provisions made for the duration of the campaign, Marie-Victoire Louis (1990a: 142) points out that the helpline was not free and that, despite the fact that the number of calls it received did not decrease, it was intended only for the length of the campaign, and withdrawn in January 1990. As a result of the campaign, the existing refuges for women survivors of male violence received twice as many appeals for help, but no extra resources. Louis writes (1990a: 143) that the commitment of the Secrétariat d'état chargé des droits des femmes in this campaign was minimal, quoting the minister, Michèle André, who stated, "The aim of the campaign was to improve knowledge of the law, not for women to leave their husbands and the marital home with their children and go instead to a refuge."

At the same time, questions about violent men were being raised. For instance, Geneviève Devèze (1985: 20), despite her primary concerns with the survivors, recognized that research needed to be done on why men are violent:

> This research is necessary, and we are doing it, but in another context, because the main priority in the Louise-Labbé refuge is to offer women, whatever their personal history, a safe haven, completely separate from their violent past and free of fear, in order to allow them to rediscover their personality and quietly plan their full re-integration into society.

Incest and marital rape

The more feminists investigated male violence towards women, the greater the number of forms of violence they "discovered". As their awareness and knowledge increased and as more and more women gained the confidence and support necessary to speak out against the violence they had experienced, the massive exposure of women to male violence in every area of society became evident. Also, the links between the different types of male violence became clearer, and feminists began to integrate them into a larger picture of male power. By the mid-1980s, then, feminist discussions of male violence incorporated pornography, incest[41], sexual harassment in the workplace, female genital mutilations and marital rape. Since, during the 1980s, the similarities between the forms of male violence were increasingly stressed and the differences between them simultaneously minimized, it is unnecessary to discuss each manifestation of violence as though they were separate entities. The exposure of incest and marital violence are examined here as examples of the way in which French feminist thought and practice around male violence developed, and in particular the way in which different forms of violence were "discovered".

Incest

Until 1985 incest in France was a problem completely surrounded by silence. The first publication to break this silence was a book by Viviane Clarac and Nicole Bonnin, *De la honte à la colère*, which the authors published at their own expense, such was the lack of interest at the time. In September 1986 the French television channel, Antenne 2, showed a series of "Dossiers de l'écran" about incest (Rojtman, 1991: 219). The next day, the Collectif féministe contre le viol, which had managed to publicize its telephone number during the programme, was inundated with calls from incest survivors, many of whom were talking about their experiences for the first time (Rojtman, 1991: 219). Information from the helpline Viol-femmes-informations demonstrated the previously unimaginable extent of incest. In an article published in 1987 in *Cette violence dont nous ne voulons plus*, the Collectif féministe contre le viol (1987: 26) stated that out of 264 calls received by their helpline 134 concerned rape and 130 concerned incest (90 by fathers on daughters, and 40 by brothers on sisters). The main problem with incest, they claimed, is silence: on the one hand the silence resulting from the hypocrisy surrounding all violence in the family, and on the other hand, the silence of the survivors. Not only does the survivors' silence contribute to the invisibility of incest, but it is also often interpreted as a form of consent. The real reasons for it are, they claimed, that incest survivors are unable to talk: because of the threats made by the abuser, because of their feelings of guilt and responsibility, because of the fear of breaking up the family, sending their father to prison, or losing their mother. In addition to the great difficulty of telling someone, those who do manage to talk are silenced or disbelieved, especially if their abuser is someone who is seen as socially "respectable" (Collectif féministe contre le viol, 1987: 28). In order to encourage incest survivors to talk about their suffering, the Paris group of the collective produced a video in 1988 entitled "L'inceste, la conspiration des oreilles bouchées" (Granger & Trat, 1990: 8).

The main problem with incest lies with its definition. While the facts are rarely disputed, the attack can be defined as rape only if it can be proved that the child did not consent. The absence of consent is difficult enough to prove in any rape trial, but for a child, whose credibility is suspect from the start, it is especially hard.

In 1989 public attention was brought to the problem of incest by the case of Claudine J., who during a television programme entitled "Les abus sexuels sur les enfants: briser le silence" had described the abuse inflicted on her during her childhood by her father. Despite the fact that he could not be recognized from her testimony, since she gave neither his name nor the region where he lived, and since he lived in a place where no one had ever met Claudine, he pressed charges for slander. The trial became an important focus for feminist action, because it was seen as a struggle to prevent the silencing of incest survivors at a time when they had only just begun to speak out.

At the time of the trial, the Code of criminal law procedure stated that crimes could be tried only within ten years of their occurrence. This meant that fathers guilty of incest were protected from the possibility that their children would bring charges against them when they became adults, since the ten-year time limit began at the time of the abuse. Therefore, any adult saying something along the lines of "my father raped me" could be taken to court for slander, even if they could prove their case. Claudine J.'s trial, therefore, could not consider whether or not she had suffered incest as a child. She was found guilty of slander and had to pay the symbolic one franc compensation (Le Doeuff, 1989). The day after the verdict had been given, a law was passed stating that in the case of crimes committed against children by a parent or anyone with authority over them the ten-year limit would now begin when the survivor reached the age of 18.[42]

The television programme and the media attention which accompanied the ensuing court cases helped to raise public awareness of the problem of incest. However, it was still too often ignored. For example, the 1989 public information campaign about violence barely mentioned incest, and when it did it was presented as a "family problem". Feminists objected to the representation of the problem as one of a dysfunctional family which needs to be treated as a unit. They insisted that only one person was responsible for the crime and that was the abuser. When the family as a whole is blamed, all sorts of charges are made against the mother: she has failed to satisfy the abuser sexually, has failed to protect the children, etc. (Rojtman, 1991: 220).

A CNRS research project entitled Viol et violences contre les femmes (Bordeaux et al., 1989: 73) stated that it would be impossible to understand how the abuse could continue for so long if it were not for the silence and a sort of "complicity by abstention" on the part of the other members of the family. Again, this could be interpreted as shifting the blame onto the rest of family, despite the fact that the researchers also draw attention to the care which the abuser takes in order to ensure that the abuse remains a secret. As Marie-France Casalis (1990: 12) from the Mouvement français pour le planning familial writes:

Responsible and guilty as always, we women.

If we are the survivors and we say nothing, our silence is held against us. It was up to us to denounce our attacker; why did we not do so? Why, as mothers, did we not see or hear or understand that it was because they had been raped by their fathers that our daughters were suffering?

Despair, distress, silence, anorexia, running away, drugs, depression, which one of us would have thought to look for the cause in the sexual abuse of the child by her father?

Despite the legal provisions for the sentencing to between five and ten years for indecent acts and between ten and twenty years for rape, when they were committed by a parent on a child under 15, there were still very few convictions for the crime of incest during the 1980s. This was despite the fact that the Collectif féministe contre le viol received 800 calls from women incest survivors between March 1986 and the beginning of 1990. Only 30 per cent of these women had taken any legal steps, and of those which had led to a court case not one had resulted in a sentence of ten or more years, the sentence which was then applicable to rape (Casalis, 1990: 12).[43]

The importance of incest for feminists attempting to analyze it as an expression of male power is that it demonstrates the same problems involved in breaking the silence around any kind of male violence towards women, but in an accentuated fashion. For not only does it occur within the sanctity of the family, where no-one is supposed to interfere, but it also raises the problem of the silencing and the powerlessness of the survivors, who are doubly silenced for being (usually) girls, and for being children; doubly oppressed by a man who also holds extra power over them, as their father (in the majority of cases). Incest, therefore, is about power and powerlessness on an individual level, but also on a societal level in the taboos which surround it, the refusal to recognize its existence, and the refusal to hold the attacker responsible for his actions and condemn them. As the Collectif féministe contre le viol (1991: 19) wrote in their 1991 report:

Every adult who sexually abuses a child abuses their power and the child's trust in them. In the eyes of children, all grown-ups have authority. Constraint neither has to be proven, nor exercised with violence: there is always at least moral constraint, often emotional blackmail, and at worst, the real sexual exploitation of the child. Even an adolescent who rapes a child is abusing the power they derive from their age. The new Penal Code, by choosing to replace the term "indecent acts" with the term "sexual attacks", which is not defined, designates badly sexual attacks on children which are above all an abuse of power and trust. And the term "attack" must be interpreted in the widest sense as meaning an attack on the person of the child.

Marital rape

By the time French feminists turned their attention to marital rape at the end of the 1980s, the discussion was based within a context of violence as an expression of male power and dominance, and the links between different types of male violence towards women were becoming more important than the differences between them. Feminists argued that, contrary to the opinion often expressed by magistrates, judges and the police, the effects for the woman survivor were no less traumatic if the rapist was her partner than if he was a stranger. The legal situation, however, was ambiguous. In theory, the legal definition of rape which has been in force since 1980 should allow women who have been raped by their husband to press charges, since it defines rape as "any act of penetration, of any nature, committed on another person with the use of violence, constraint or surprise" (article 332 of the Penal Code). However, in practice, very few men have been taken to court charged with the rape of their wife. The French Civil Code also contains several ambiguities. Article 242 on divorce states that one partner can ask for a divorce if the actions of the other partner constitute a serious or repeated violation of marital duties and render their life together unbearable.[44] Among the acts which fall into this category are "abstention" and "non-consecration of the marriage after eleven months". The fulfilment of marital duties is not explicitly mentioned as an essential part of marriage by law, but it has an important place in attitudes and traditions, as well as being explicitly required by canon law. It is difficult, therefore, for a woman to press rape charges against her husband if he has been forcing her to have what is seen as "normal" sexual relations every day throughout their marriage. In the case of "abnormal" sexual practices, he might be tried for indecent acts or violence, but it is unlikely that he would be found guilty of rape (Devèze, 1991: 215).

In theory, then, it has been possible in France since 1980 for a man to be charged and found guilty of having raped his wife, but in practice very few cases have been taken to court. On 13 February 1981 a man was found guilty by the Cour d'assises at Grenoble of raping his wife, and was sentenced to eight years' imprisonment. However, the circumstances of this case were exceptional. As the woman walked home, her husband followed her in his car. He stopped next to a public park, took his wife into it, and cut her repeatedly with a razor-blade while his friend held her down. He then forced her to have intercourse. The husband was charged with raping his wife and with premeditated assault and grievous bodily harm. The rapist's lawyer pleaded that the fact that he was married to the survivor meant that the charge of rape was not applicable. However, the Chambre d'accusation (the court of criminal appeal) ruled that "It is true that, according to traditional case law, rape between husband and wife is not punishable. However, such a conception could not refer to despicable actions far removed from any notion of marriage and intimate relations between husband and wife" (Devèze, 1990: 6).

However, as Devèze (1990: 6) points out, in this case the rape was accompanied by violence, and it is impossible to say what the verdict would have been had this not been the case. Moreover, during the same year a man who had raped and tortured his wife by inserting burning objects into her vagina was found guilty of *outrage à la pudeur* (indecent behaviour) and *actes de barbarité* (acts of barbarity). The charge of rape was dropped by the court, which did not consider that it was applicable within marriage (Devèze, 1991: 215).

During the late 1980s French feminists began a difficult struggle to alert public awareness to marital rape and to insist that it be defined in the law as a crime. The campaign continues. One of the difficulties is that even the women who experience marital rape rarely recognize it as such. According to Geneviève Devèze (1988: 271–2), men experience marital rape as the exercise of their right to sexual satisfaction, whereas women experience it as an abuse of power, sometimes as sexual abuse, but very rarely as rape, believing that rape is something that happens between strangers. This means that men know that, if their wives do not recognize it as rape, they can continue without fear of the consequences. Another difficulty is that when women do decide to talk about their experiences of marital rape, they are told that it must be far less traumatic to be forced to have sex by someone with whom they have previously had consenting sex than by a stranger (Devèze, 1991: 216).

State responses to male violence

Feminists continue to criticize state responses to male violence towards women. The main targets of these criticisms are the police and the courts. In an analysis of the letters received by the Secrétariat d'état chargé des droits des femmes during the public campaign in 1989 against domestic violence, Marie-Victoire Louis (1990a: 151–2) refers to cases in which police officers refused to intervene, held the woman responsible, tried to intimidate the woman into withdrawing her complaint, and refused to register complaints for various reasons. Louis holds the legal system even more responsible than the police for the failure to respond appropriately in the face of this violence. She finds cases closed despite medical evidence of serious injury, "enquiries" which never happened, the failure to take into consideration rape and sexual violence, the failure to take into account the emotional effects of death threats, the tendency to ignore premeditation and verdicts which laid the blame on both partners or solely on the woman.

When considering state responses to violence which is perpetrated almost exclusively by men and in the vast majority of cases against women, it is surely significant to remark on the gendered nature of the institutions which legislate and execute legislation. It is clear that they are numerically dominated by men. For example, the new Penal Code, which came into force in 1994 and has significant implications in the area of male violence, was written and passed by men (Louis, 1994: 42–3). The question of whether the equal representation of men and women in the legislature would change the nature of public policy is still open to debate. However, many feminists argue that in certain key areas, including abortion and violence, policy outcomes *would* be different. One of the questions which emerges from these discussions, and which has exercized feminists throughout the period under consideration, is whether feminists should engage with the state, and in this case the law, at all. Carol Smart (1989) identifies the power of the law to define as its most important characteristic and argues that it is this which feminists should focus on and challenge. For example (Smart, 1989: 165): "Feminism can (re)define harmless flirtation into sexual harassment, misplaced paternal affection into child sexual abuse, enthusiastic seduction into rape, foetal rights into enforced reproduction, and so on." According to this view, feminists should not engage with the law in order to achieve reform, but in order to challenge its very basis. This is not to say that the reforms which feminists have gained are not significant. But they are not necessarily stable. (Consider, for example, the legalization of abortion, which is again under threat.) And they are not necessarily in the control of feminists. For example, feminists attempted to influence legislation against sexual harassment, but the fact that men can counter-sue for defamation could easily backfire on women.

The feminist lawyer Odile Dhavernas (1990) criticizes state responses to male violence from a different angle. She sees victim support, which is now available from state institutions, including the police, as an alternative to state action which would target the causes of male violence and attempts to reduce it. It is true that survivors are better treated than they used to be, but there are just as many of them. Dhavernas (1990: 44) argues that the professionalization of the "management of suffering" is accompanied by the failure of the state to invest in any form of prevention. That state institutions take no interest in prevention, rehabilitation, therapy and alternative policies was demonstrated by the parliamentary debate on the new Penal Code, which has been analyzed by Marie-Victoire Louis (1994). The Penal Code, she explains, is a catalogue of prohibited acts, the penalties for which are ranked according to the seriousness of the offence. Its repressive nature has been criticized by both the AVFT and the French Communist Party (PCF), which continue to assert that prison sentences are ineffective and that alternative approaches need to be sought (Louis, 1994: 46).

This chapter has demonstrated that, in France, feminism has played an important part, firstly, in exposing the extent of male violence towards women, secondly, in forcing changes in the laws relating to it, and now in theorizing its causes and its relationship to masculinity. It has also shown the development in the way in which the problem of male violence has been approached by French feminists. In its most schematic form, this progression has led from a concentration on the victims of male violence (listening to their experiences and attempting to deal with the consequences of the violence they have suffered) to a growing interest in the perpetrators.

These trends obviously interconnect: if the main aim of feminists is prevention, one of the ways to suggest preventive measures is the analysis of violent men. However, the trends identified above are not the only ones to have emerged from this study. For example, there has been an increasing tendency for feminists to connect different forms of male violence towards women. They talk of "violences" in the plural, and join all the different forms together on a continuum as expressions of male power, rather than seeing them as discrete phenomena with independent causes and explanations.

French feminist theory has aimed to establish the connections between male gender identity, male domination of women and male violence. Chapter 6 concentrates, firstly, on what feminists in France have said about violent men and the connections between violence and masculinity, and, secondly, on the attempts that some feminists have made to explain male violence in the context of power relations between the sexes. It focuses particularly on French feminist theorists who emphasize the need to shift the responsibility for male violence from women onto violent men and who claim that the solution to male violence lies in changing men and in changing representations and constructions of masculinity.

6   Gender and violence

In France, as elsewhere, growing feminist interest in the prevention of male violence towards women has raised questions about masculinity and gender relations. The silence has been broken, and it would be wrong to deny the effects of 20 years of feminist campaigns against male violence. Feminist pressure has undoubtedly affected public opinion and forced institutional and legal changes, but while the successes must be recognized, the feminist struggle against male violence is not over. Feminist organizations continue campaigning, offering support for women who have experienced violence, running helplines and refuges, providing legal advice and services. There is some evidence, however, that grassroots activists feel that there is a lack of contact between them and feminist academics, which is limiting the impact of their work (for example, Rojtman, 1991: 223). Activists state that, while steps can be taken to attenuate the effects of male violence, if it is going to be reduced – and this is the goal of all feminists working in the area – then the relation between gender and violence needs to be understood. While feminist academics have shown unrelenting concern with the theorization of gender relations, the theorization of violence is underdeveloped.

As was demonstrated in Chapter 5, insights gained from grassroots activism have led to a growing interest in the perpetrators and to an attempt to explain male violence by focusing on them, rather than on the survivors. The growing interest in prevention has similarly necessitated a focus on violent men. These developments have contributed to the establishment of masculinity as a legitimate object of study. At the same time, feminist academics involved in the theorization of gender relations have also established masculinity as a legitimate object of study. It is at the point where these two areas of feminist theory and practice meet that some of the most interesting questions about masculinity – and about French feminism – can be posed. For example, how male identity is constructed around violence, how male violence functions within a system of male dominance, and how individual acts of male violence fit into this broader system. It is therefore necessary to examine the small amount of work which is situated at this point of convergence, that is, attempts to explain male violence within the framework of gender/social relations of sex. This chapter focuses on violent men and examines the ways in which French feminists have approached the problem from this perspective. It considers the conflicts which arise when the focus shifts from the women who experience violence to the men who perpetrate it, including the question of how resources should be allocated and whether feminists are prepared to work with violent men and with pro-feminist men in order to effect change. It then examines theories produced by feminists which attempt to discover the causes of male violence towards women by focusing on the construction of masculine identity and gendered power relations.

Interest in violent men and the causes of male violence

The growing feminist interest in searching for explanations of why men are violent, rather than why women become the survivors of violence, is based on the increased emphasis placed on the sex of the perpetrator. Françoise Collin (1976), for example, suggested that, since this is the only constant factor in male violence, it should perhaps therefore be the focus of feminist interest.[45] Marie-Victoire Louis (1990a: 149–50) wrote more recently:

> Domestic violence, rape, marital rape, child abuse, sexual harassment: with only a very few exceptions, in all these cases, including when the violence is homosexual, the attackers are men. Why has such an enormous and so obvious a reality not yet been taken into account in France? Why has the relation between the sex of the attacker and that of the survivor not been identified by criminologists, legal sociologists, the police, and researchers as the central question?

The importance of the shift in emphasis from survivor to perpetrator, and its implications for future feminist theory and practice, have been addressed by Anne Zelensky and Mireille Gaussot (1986: 171), who describe it as a "third stage of feminism". In a first stage, they state, feminists concentrated on consciousness-raising and the sharing of experiences between women, especially in women's refuges. The second stage was the feminist fight to change various aspects of the law between 1975 and 1985. And now, "A third phase is taking shape: having first considered the survivors, principally women, the process of questioning domestic violence is beginning to concern the perpetrators of violence as well, who are mostly men" (Zelensky, 1988: 276).

Now that it has become evident that legislative changes, although important, have been unable to change attitudes (for example, many convicted rapists still fail to understand the gravity of their crime), Zelensky (1988: 285) claims that feminists need to focus their attention on "the other side of domestic violence, men". Having sought in the 1970s to destroy popular myths which obscured the causes of male violence towards women, many feminists are now working towards an explanation of these causes.

Daniel Welzer-Lang is the director of RIME in Lyons and author of *Les hommes violents* (1991) and numerous articles on the subject of male violence.

Influenced by work that has already been carried out in Quebec, where this approach has acquired a certain amount of popularity, Welzer-Lang's analysis (1992b: 138) stresses, above all, the *function* of male violence. He argues that for the men involved in domestic violence, the attacks have a clear aim, whether this is to produce a certain type of behaviour in their partner, provoke a certain reaction, or just "teach her a lesson". In other words, violence is a means of controlling women's behaviour. This is nothing new to feminist analysis which has explained male violence as a form of control of women since the 1970s. However, Welzer-Lang's findings are interesting in that they demonstrate how *conscious* the desire for control can be.

Welzer-Lang (1992b) has shown that violence towards women is committed with an objective in mind. Violent men define their violence broadly, seeing it as a continuum of physical, psychological, verbal and sexual violence, any of which can be used to achieve their objective. Their partners, however, define the violence they are subjected to much more narrowly. Violence for them is often only being hit, or perhaps kicked. They see violent acts as isolated incidents, even if they occur frequently. Moreover, they identify only one reason for the violence, and that is the desire to inflict pain. Welzer-Lang shows that women who have been subjected to violence remember the pain above all else. The violence for them is experienced physically. Violent men, however, seem to remember what they wanted to achieve and express little appreciation of the impact of the pain. He uses these findings to support his claim that domestic violence has nothing to do with the common excuses of "losing one's temper", being "out of control". Instead, it is a means of exercizing control, of asserting authority over a partner. The first priority, then, is to make violent men take responsibility for their behaviour.

At RIME common explanations of male violence such as alcohol, frustration and traumatic childhood experiences are dismissed. Welzer-Lang (1991: 55–6) argues that the fact that men choose exactly when and whom they hit demonstrates that their behaviour is both intentional and conditioned and that violence is not due to a loss of control. The solution is not, therefore, learning how to control oneself, but rather removing the desire to control one's partner. Welzer-Lang insists that violent men need to admit that they use violence to control their partner. They can then focus on getting rid of this desire to dominate. Despite his commitment to the work with individual men which takes place at RIME, Welzer-Lang (1990: 24) stresses that violence is only a symptom. At the root of violence towards women is the inequality of gender relations.

An analysis based on gender is essential if we are to explain the connections between male violence towards women, male violence towards men and violence by women. Such an analysis rejects the view that men are violent towards women because they are male. The problem with this view is that it cannot account for violent women and non-violent men. Violence cannot, therefore, be explained in terms of biological difference. Welzer-Lang's study (1989) of male rape demonstrates that whether men rape women or other men, gendered power relations are in play. The male rape victims interviewed in his study all felt that they had been "treated like a woman" and found this aspect of their experience the most difficult to deal with. Welzer-Lang (1989: 42) suggests that the "feminization" of the male rape victim reinforces the subordination of women by men at the same time as it denies that there are gendered power relations *between* men. Studies of pornography for gay men, male prostitution, transvestism and trans-sexuality are slowly adding evidence to support this thesis (Welzer-Lang, 1995).

On a practical level, too, there seems to be a gradual growth in interest in working with violent men. This is not to say that feminist work with survivors has ceased. On the contrary, groups continue to struggle for survivors of domestic violence to have the right to stay in their home if they wish, while the violent man is forced to leave; feminist lawyers such as Odile Dhavernas denounce the "experts' assessments" of rape survivors; and women's refuge workers' struggle to provide enough places to meet demand. However, a number of steps have been taken by feminists and pro-feminist men to provide centres for violent men, including RIME in Lyons and SOS-hommes et violences en privé in Paris, in the belief that this will help to reduce the incidence of this violence.

Marie-Victoire Louis (1992) strongly advocates the acceptance of men in feminist struggles to change the power relations between the sexes. She writes (Louis, 1992: 36):

> How can we believe in the possibility of a change in the power relations between the sexes if we do not try to involve men, to make them accept responsibility, to make them face up to the situation? How can we believe in feminism as a kind of humanism if we reject the possibility that men can change, if we enclose them in the identity of the oppressor?

Louis (1990a: 163) claims that men need to be made to take on responsibility for violence and for the power relations between men and women:

> As long as the "interests of the family" come before the respect of the rights of the individual, as long as the sex of the attacker is ignored as a potential, but probable, explanatory factor in this violence – which is often a simple expression of *the law which men want to impose on their wives* – we remain within a problematic which posits violence as a "woman's problem". And from this moment, it is logical that men will not be held responsible.
>
> Why should women have to put up with being beaten or even lose their lives, just so that their husbands should not end up in prison?

However, Louis insists on the difference between men accepting responsibility for violence and men being made to feel guilty for it. She stresses that although it is important to recognize the function for patriarchy of this violence, it is wrong to say that all men are (potentially) violent or benefit from it. Louis states that while on the one hand it is obvious that the patriarchal system functions because rape carried out by some men controls women's movements, on the other hand, it is wrong to say that all men benefit from this situation. She argues that many men suffer when their wife, partner, sister or mother is attacked and that an increasing number of men are expressing solidarity with women around the problem. For Louis, it is important to recognize these contradictions and to work together with supportive men, because this demonstrates that there *are* men who find this type of violence unacceptable and because it shows other men that there are alternative, non-violent, models of masculinity. It also disproves theories which state that men are naturally violent and cannot help it (Louis, interview, 1993).

Anne Zelensky agrees that men must be included in feminism. A feminist activist who has been consistently active and innovative, despite accusations of "reformism" from other feminists, Zelensky was one of the first, if not the first, French feminists to begin working together with men on the question of male violence. This resulted in the creation in 1988 of the only centre for violent men in Paris, sos-hommes et violences en privé.[46] Zelensky says (interview, 1993), "I think that feminism concerns both women and men, and if we carry on including only women, the gap between the two is going to continue to widen." Men's reactions to feminism have, she states, sometimes resulted in a violent anti-feminism. Therefore, it is better to involve them in it and encourage them to accept certain responsibilities than to make them feel guilty and wait for a reaction. However, this willingness to work with men must not be seen as a universally accepted trend among feminists. Zelensky has received very little support from other feminist activists, who are still reluctant to devote any time or energy to what they see as problems which men should be confronting themselves. She reports (interview, 1993) that "not only do they not work on this subject, but the majority of them are against it. Feminist activists, grassroots feminists, and particularly the feminists who look after battered women, are very hostile. . . . Either they are hostile or they don't want to hear anything about it."

Problems can be expected to arise when feminists find themselves fighting for funding for women survivors of male violence with organizations concerned with violent men.

Prevention

Feminist pressure has been largely responsible for raising public awareness of violence; giving women the confidence to speak out about violence they have experienced; and insisting that survivors are better treated in police stations and in the courts (Dhavernas, 1990: 44). It seems that it is feminist action which will also play an important role in projects aimed at preventing further violence. For feminists, the main question about male violence is, ultimately, how to envisage bringing an end to it, and it is this question which structures feminist involvement both theoretically and practically. The search for a solution depends on the continuing theorization of *why* men are violent, accompanied by suggestions of more immediately practicable measures that would reduce the amount of violence in society. Some feminists claim that although refuges for survivors of male violence have been a tremendous help for many women, they can only deal with the consequences of the problem, not its causes. The measures that need to be taken now, they argue, are largely preventive, focusing on the many different causes of male violence. Suggestions for appropriate preventive measures include self-defence training for women; changing cultural representations of women; offering sex education classes in schools which stress the importance of consent and respect for the autonomy of both partners in a relationship; and therapeutic treatment for violent men (Zelensky, 1988: 284). They argue that children should be brought up in such a way that boys learn to respect girls from an early age and that girls and boys get to know each other, thus destroying the fear they currently have for the other sex. They identify this fear as one of the causes of aggression since sexual violence results partly from the attacker's inability to recognize the existence of the other person (Zelensky & Gaussot, 1986: 171).

As one of the Québecois sources (Macleod, 1990: 45) for much of the French thought around violence stresses:

> The final objective, and one which is not insignificant, is to promote a new idea of men, an idea based less on competition and violence than on co-operation and sharing. This would be done by using all possible means and sites: public education, the media, the education of children, the workplace. It is true that the perpetrators must learn to renounce physical violence. But they also need to get rid of the overwhelming need for inflexibility, domination and control which for them constitute the very essence of masculinity.

Marie-Victoire Louis (1990b) argues that until gender relations are put at the centre of the debate, there is no hope of any decrease in the amount of male violence towards women. Although some men are discovering the constraints imposed on them by masculinity as it is culturally constructed and are trying to escape from it, they cannot do this unless it is within the context of a broader debate on the power relations between the sexes.

Before preventive measures can be introduced to remove the causes and functions of male violence, these need to be identified. Organizations such as the Collectif féministe contre le viol (1991: 2–3) have recognized that if an end is to be brought to male violence, studying the perpetrators is an indispensable part of this project. The first stage in the analysis of the causes of male violence towards women was the identification of the sex of the perpetrator as its most significant characteristic. Following on from this, feminists began to focus on the connections between violence and masculine identity.

Feminist attempts to explain male violence can be divided into two main stages. These are, firstly, those which concentrate on the character and behaviour of individual violent men, and, secondly, those which have introduced wider social factors. Feminists active around the question of male violence towards women first tried to identify characteristics which they believed were common to violent men. While this approach is still widely used by non-feminists, feminist analyses have moved beyond the considerations of the individual or pathological.

Why are some men violent?

The first sign of a consideration of the links between violence and masculinity was the attempt by certain feminists to identify the characteristics of violent men. This was partly in order to expose what feminists saw as the myths surrounding male violence, and partly as a result of the growing mass of information acquired by feminists working in refuges and on helplines, which they realized could enable them to begin describing attackers' behaviour, personalities and methods. This identification of common characteristics in violent men can be seen as a first step in understanding the causes of violence and in undermining certain mythologies. (See Collectif féministe contre le viol, 1991: 2–3.)

Three of the most commonly held beliefs which feminists reject are that rape is due to men's sudden and uncontrollable sexual urges; that rape is always committed by strangers; and that rapists are "mad" or in some way marginal to "normal" society. The Collectif féministe contre le viol use analyses of the calls they receive on their telephone helpline to support their arguments against these beliefs. For instance, they argue that the circumstances in which rapes take place show that the majority are premeditated and sometimes involve intricate plans. In the case of child abuse, the lengths to which the rapist goes in order to ensure that nobody discovers it can be tremendous, and are well documented. In the case of rape by someone outside the family – whether known to the victim or not – the rapist's strategy often consists of luring the victim to a predetermined place, whether this is the victim's home, the rapist's home, or a deserted public place. Sometimes the rapes are planned by watching the victim and noting her habits. Other rapes occur at bogus job interviews or house-viewing appointments. The collective claim that this premeditation proves that rape cannot be explained by sudden uncontrollable urges forcing the rapist to act "against his will". It shows that he is responsible for his actions and able to control himself (Collectif féministe contre le viol, 1991: 10).

The collective's figures also negate the belief that rape is committed by a stranger. Around half of all rapes, they show, are committed by someone known to the victim. In 1991 the collective received 926 calls about rape on their telephone helpline: 524 (56.5 per cent) of these were committed by men outside the victim's family, 358 (38.7 per cent) by members of their family, and 44 (4.8 per cent) by their husbands. Of the rapists who were not members of her own family,

45 per cent were known to the victim (Collectif féministe contre le viol, 1991: 9). In another part of the report, the collective write: "About 50 per cent of rapists are known to their victims. In the case of teenagers, it is more than 50 per cent, and for young children, it is 95 per cent" (ibid., p. 15).

From the information they have obtained from the helpline, and in agreement with what many feminists have been saying since the 1970s, the Collectif féministe contre le viol feel able to state that "contrary to popular belief, rapists are not drop-outs, psychopaths or alcoholics" (ibid.).

Information collected and analyzed by feminists who work in refuges for women victims of male violence supports these claims. Publications by the clinical psychologist Geneviève Devèze draw on her work as director of the Foyer Louise-Labbé, a women's refuge in Paris. Devèze (1990: 7) does not claim that there is a certain type of man who is violent, any more than there is a certain type of woman who becomes the victim of that violence. The well-known case of the loving father playing happily with his children in the park, having only a few hours previously viciously beaten his wife, is evidence enough that it is impossible to provide a description of the "typical violent man". Devèze (1988: 272–3) stresses that social factors interact with an individual's masculine identity to produce acts of violence. However, this does not prevent her from trying to identify certain characteristics which they have in common, and certain patterns of behaviour which seem to recur. For example, Devèze (Devèze & Le Breton-Viala, 1988) claims that violent men tend to have a fragile masculine identity. The insecurity that a violent man feels in his own identity, she argues, leads him to fear that his partner cannot possibly be satisfied with him, and this produces an almost paranoid belief that she must be having an affair. Since these women are usually exceptionally faithful, they cannot understand their partner's accusations. The more they try to explain to their partners that they are making a mistake, the more insecure the men become, and so it continues. According to Devèze, violent men are often possessive, jealous and paranoid about losing their partner. At the same time, they are also often very successful outside the couple, particularly at work. Devèze also mentions immaturity, a tendency to alcoholism and difficulties in their relationship with their mother as typical characteristics.

Feminists have identified several problems with concentrating on the characters of individual violent men. One such problem is that concentrating on the individual makes it difficult to account for the massive occurrence of violence towards women and the widespread social acceptance of it. If we argue that violence is a way in which men react to personal frustration, as a result of unemployment, for example, this suggests that the more the individual is frustrated and unable to exercise his power, the more likely he is to be violent towards women. We would then expect to find more violence within the most disadvantaged classes, and this is not the case: violent men are found in all social classes. Since male violence towards women is common and widely tolerated, feminists suggest that broader social explanations must be sought for the high levels of incidence and tolerance. In France, they have examined the historical development of social attitudes to the violence exerted against women by men; the "complicity" between men accused of violence and the male-dominated legal system; and the social construction of male sexuality around violence.

Many French feminists have argued that today's masculinities have been constructed in and by a society that permits or even encourages violence towards women. They have traced the historical origins of a widespread social acceptance of male violence towards women to Roman Law. The *pater familias* enjoyed total authority in the family, and this included the *droit de correction* (the right to administer physical punishment). This tradition was supported by religious teachings in all European countries throughout the Middle Ages, and was present in the French Penal Code of 1810, which considered the murder of a woman by her husband "excusable" in the case of adultery, if she was caught in the act in the marital home (Zelensky, 1988: 278). Legal reform has been extensive. In 1938 women gained civil rights and were no longer legally obliged to obey their husbands. Paternal authority was replaced by parental authority in 1970, and in 1985 equality was instituted between spouses. However, feminists argue that history has left its mark on the practice and attitudes of many people (Zelensky, 1988: 275–6). While beating one's wife is less socially acceptable than it used to be, violent men are still not held fully responsible for their actions. Excuses such as alcohol are used to justify violent acts. Much violence towards women remains invisible, and it is often up to the woman to prove that it was not her fault, in the face of widely held beliefs that it usually is. Even when the evidence of male violence is irrefutable, it is still possible to label the perpetrators ill, perverted, or in some way marginal to society, and by turning them into scapegoats, the societal origins of male violence are ignored; by referring to them as exceptions, the norm can be perpetuated. Anne Zelensky (1988: 280–81) claims that society encourages violence as part of normal masculine behaviour, whether this is through sport, "standing up for oneself" in the school playground, or war. Male violence is socially permissible, and individual men have some control over the extent to which they use this permission. Even if they choose not to behave in violent ways themselves, they often seem to tolerate violent behaviour in other men. The high tolerance of male violence in society is extremely powerful: "Men beat their wives because they can" (Devèze, 1990: 7). And they can because society has been constructed around men's interests: they have enjoyed the economic power, physical strength and access to information necessary to maintain their dominant position. At the same time, violent men are represented as "unhappy beings, deprived of love throughout their childhood, alcoholic and/or unemployed, misunderstood or, in a word, immature" (ibid.). The consequence of this representation is that women pity their attackers and return to "look after them". Devèze comments that "It is not a stupid decision, but the one which society presents to the victim, and of course, to the attacker" (ibid.).

Arguments that society is organized in such a way that male violence is an acceptable and integral part of its functioning are contested, however. It is a widely held belief that inequalities between women and men have disappeared from French society, for example, in terms of power in the home, or the control of reproduction and parenting. For example, Elisabeth Badinter's *L'un est l'autre* (1986) argues that differences between men and women no longer exist and that, in contrast to the United States, French society has no problems with male violence; Evelyne Sullerot's *Quels pères? Quels fils?* (1992) argues that mothers now have far more power than fathers; and Christine Castelain-Meunier's *Les hommes aujourd'hui: virilité et identité* (1988) argues that, since physical strength is no longer a factor in postindustrial society, there are no remaining salient differences between men and women. Feminists, however, reject these dismissals of inequalities which, in their view, contribute greatly to a very real and very high level of violence in French society.

Feminists have discovered not only a high level of tolerance of violence towards women, but also evidence of complicity between men. In particular, they have presented evidence of ways in which the police and judiciary have protected men accused of violence, especially when they are from the same social class. Marie-Victoire Louis (1990a: 154) argues that men protect each other by means of a widely accepted refusal to act. For example, she refers to a letter written to the Secrétariat d'état chargé des droits des femmes by the wife of a headmaster, whose file had been "lost":

Care was taken not to tarnish the reputation of someone who holds a position of responsibility with children. But does this not represent, in this particular case, a failing or even the complicity of the judiciary because of a feeling of solidarity with people who share common interests, and who are more concerned with protecting each other than with doing their job? . . . Moreover, how can the discretionary power of judges, which actually prevents justice from being done, be justified? What is the point of talking, taking action or complaining, when the judiciary itself refuses to listen to us?

Louis (1990a: 163) claims that this solidarity which exists between men and which operates in their interests increases the impunity enjoyed by violent men. It also raises questions about the responsibilities of the state and the way in which it has, over the centuries, sanctioned male power in the family by positioning them as "heads of household" who must be obeyed by their wives. While evidence suggests that middle-class men are no less often perpetrators of violence towards women than working-class men, it can be much harder for the wives or partners of middle-class men to have their accusations listened to. In other words, the police, the judiciary and public opinion seem much readier to believe that a working-class man has abused his partner than if the accused is seen as someone "respectable".

The third area of feminist interest in the links between masculinity and violence is the social construction of male sexuality around violence. Analyses of calls received by the Collectif féministe contre le viol (1991: 26) from teenagers of both sexes reveal striking differences between attitudes held by boys and by girls. Many of the teenage boys, for example, think that it is normal to have to "force" a girl, or that if he buys her a drink or pays for her cinema entrance then she has already consented to sex. On the other hand, many teenage girls experience their "first time" as rape. The calls they receive from teenage boys lead the collective to state that the difference for teenage boys between "fuck" and "rape" is far from clear and that the notion of consent is never discussed in sex education classes. The frequency with which women in refuges describe being forced by their partners to act out scenes from pornographic films and magazines has been identified by Anne Zelensky (1988: 280–81) as an indication of the influence of pornographic materials, in which sexuality and violence are closely linked. Interestingly, the debate on pornography has been far less prominent in French feminism than in its Anglophone counterparts.

So how do we explain the connections between male violence and sexuality? Françoise Collin (1990: 10) has begun to address the question of the origins of this connection. She argues that masculine identity is constructed on the oppression of women and their negation as subjects with autonomous desires:

> . . . our entire culture gives men a different relationship to their sexuality than women. For men, in fact, their sexuality is from the outset presented and perceived as a unilateral right, a right which is often based on the equation of desire and need, as with hunger and thirst. On the way, however, one slight "detail" is forgotten, namely that this desire does not engage with an object, but with another desire, another human being. In this view, the desire of the other is either completely obscured, the other being reduced to an object, or assumed to be consenting. And this view is reinforced by a long history of the subjection or the submission of women.

For many feminists, male violence is seen as a support for the system of oppression of women. An important point in this argument is that male violence is committed by men against women *as women*, and is a political act, not an incident between individuals. Emmanuèle de Lesseps (1980) argued, for example, that the fact that violence was committed by men against women was inextricably linked to the social construction of women as "other". In order to demonstrate the political status of violence against women, de Lesseps pointed out the similarities between sexist and racist acts of violence. She argues that there is a certain type of violence which is committed by men against women, just as there is a certain type of violence committed by the dominant ethnic group against subordinate groups. However, whereas in the latter case the political implications of this violence are recognized, in the case of violence against women it is seen to stem only from the "desire-hate" of the male attacker – his desire to consume his victim by objectifying her through the destruction of her body. De Lesseps argues that this "desire-hate" is also present in racist attacks, but that racist attacks are never reduced only to this aspect; the fact that by attacking a Black/Jew/Arab the attacker is attacking all Blacks/Jews/Arabs is clearly recognized. But it is not recognized that women are attacked *as women*, as members of an undifferentiated group. Violence against women depends on their existence as "other", on their difference and thus their objectification. These attacks are a fundamental part of the system of oppression, a way of maintaining the representation of subordinate groups as "other", and therefore to be oppressed.

Male violence has continued to be theorized as a means of the social control of women, and the attacker as an agent of the patriarchal system. Feminists have considered the ways in which violence reinforces the system of male dominance and the ways in which this system uses the notion of women's consent and "natural" subordination to justify acts of violence. Frédérique Vinteuil (1985: 10) for example, argues that rape serves to maintain the status quo and to control women's activities:

> The rapist who prevents women from going out late, from going to cafés, from going for a walk on their own, who makes them live in constant fear, does more for the moral order than the Pope and more for the domination of women than all the socio-biology texts on women's natural inferiority put together. Perpetrators of violence are pathetic individuals; they are also the front-line troops in the battle of the sexes that the patriarchal society occasionally sacrifices, but usually supports.

Women's consent to violence

The notion of women's consent, whether it is to sex, violence, or subordination, runs as a theme throughout the debates around male violence towards women. The early feminist campaigns against rape stressed that when a woman says no, she means no; feminist lawyers have criticized both the way in which rape trials hinge on the question of consent and the judges' interpretations of the "proof" of consent; feminists active around domestic violence have emphasized that if women victims of domestic violence stay with a violent partner, this is more likely to be due to their financial dependence than to an acceptance of the violence; and feminist theorists have questioned much of the thought surrounding the notion of consent.[47]

The influential work of the feminist anthropologist Nicole-Claude Mathieu (1985: 169–245) focuses on the claim that women consent to their subordination. She argues that consent presumes consciousness and access to the information necessary to make a free and informed choice. Without the necessary consciousness of their oppression, women do not have the means to consent to it. Mathieu draws on Gramsci's comparison between "culture" which is the dominant class's conception of the world and "folklore" which is the dominated class's conception of it. Gramsci opposes the systematic, unitary, centralized aspects of the former to the unsystematic, fragmentary and multiple aspects of the latter. Mathieu argues that women's experiences of their oppression are full of contradictions, for example the experience shared by many young women of "giving in" to a man's "advances", only later to be called a "slut".

Women's consciousness is constrained by the organization of gender relations and the knowledge about society to which the oppressed have access. Their responsibility for childcare and domestic labour acts as both a physical and mental constraint on their consciousness. They often lack the time and mental energy required to resist their oppression. Men, claims Mathieu, are perfectly aware that women are constrained both physically and mentally by childcare responsibilities, but they invert cause and effect, thereby implying that women's limitations are the reason for their lack of power, and not its consequence.

> Violence against the oppressed does not only occur when their "consent weakens", it exists *before*, and all around, and all the time, as soon as, *in the mind of the oppressor*, the oppressed, even without knowing it, even without "wanting" it, is no longer in her place. But the oppressed is never in her place. She has to be reminded of it constantly: and this is social control. (Mathieu, 1985: 225)

Physical violence, the material and mental constraints which constantly control women's behaviour, are etched in women's consciousness, states Mathieu. If beatings and rapes are no longer necessary all the time, this is not because women consent. Mathieu argues that the oppression of women by men is not maintained by women's recognition of the legitimacy of men's power, nor by their gratitude for the services men offer them. Rather it is the limited and controlled consciousness of the oppressed and the position of ignorance in which they are maintained which constitute, along with the material constraints, *violence*, the controlling force of domination.

Mathieu's attempts to explain why so many women seem to accept their subordination and physical abuse have been enormously influential in French feminist theory. They contribute to an understanding of the way in which inequalities between men and women are represented as normal. They help to refute theories of women's masochism and offer alternative explanations for women's apparent reluctance to leave violent partners. What feminists need to know is how men get women to accept their subordination. How exactly is male dominance of women maintained? Is it through violence or the potential for violence? Is it through a shared sense of masculinity and power? Explaining the nature of male power has always been one of feminism's burning issues and continues to be at the centre of feminist debate.

Violence, gender and power

The question of the relation between the structural elements of male dominance of women and individual expressions of this dominance remains problematic. The contradictions and inconsistencies evident in the expression of gender relations at an individual level disrupt the overall pattern. For example, how do we explain the sexual harassment of men by women or the violence of women towards their partners or children? How do we explain the power relations involved in sexual attacks by men on other men in which the "feminization" of the victim is clearly documented? And do non-violent men and violent women challenge the structures of male power over women? These questions can be addressed only within a feminist analysis of the power relations between men and women, and involve the analysis of the interaction between gender, violence and power.

While feminists have emphasized that the characteristic feature of most violence towards women is that it is committed by men, they have recently admitted that the question of violence by women must also be addressed.[48] Marie-Victoire Louis (1992: 36) insists that we must not confuse the defence of women as a sex and the political struggle to transform power relations between the sexes. Feminists should not hide women's violence out of a sense of solidarity. Instead, they should try to establish why this violence is occurring. Louis' own work represents a significant contribution to this project. However, as is evident from this chapter, the theories being developed by French feminists around the connections between male violence, masculinity and gender relations are still in their early stages. Louis herself claims (interview, 1993) that the only specificity of French work on male violence is that it is so far behind that which has been produced in Britain, the United States and Canada, and this is true in terms of the amount of literature. Nonetheless, it seems that the questions which are being posed by feminists in all of these countries are not dissimilar, with one exception. Anglophone feminist theory and practice around male violence has increasingly considered the multiple ways in which differences between women have affected their experiences of violence and their means of coping with it (Hester et al., 1996: 1). Criticisms of the violence literature are still made on the grounds that not enough attention is paid to the experiences of black women and lesbians and the effects of racism and heterosexism (Maynard, 1993: 119). In France, however, it is even more difficult to find evidence of the interaction of gender, race, sexuality and violence.

The relation between French feminism and its European and international counterparts will be a deciding factor in the way that French feminist theory and practice develops in the near future. Since the mid-1980s women from many European countries have begun to demand that human rights include women's rights (Hanmer, 1996). Violence against women is one of the many ways in which women are denied full citizenship rights. Women are increasingly campaigning on a European and international level to bring an end to male violence.

An examination of the subjects covered in *Projets féministes* demonstrates that violence towards women is seen as a global phenomenon, and its editor, Marie-Victoire Louis, analyzes common features as well as differences throughout history and across cultures. She argues that the concept of human rights needs re-examining in a way which will bring an end to women's subordination in the private sphere, while continuing to guarantee the protection of the individual against the abuse of power by the state.

Conclusion

French feminist theories of masculinity have their origins in the women's movement. In the 1970s feminist practice, including consciousness-raising and campaigns for the right to control one's own body, was closely connected to feminist theory. The theoretical nature of the discussions which dominated the early feminist meetings in Paris is well documented. Numerous publications appeared in which theoretical issues featured. The campaign against rape drew on feminist theories of male domination and the maintenance of the patriarchy to denounce the myths which surround rape. These included the belief that rapists are usually strangers; that rape is a rare phenomenon committed by social deviants; and that when a woman says no, she means yes. This process of exposing the widely held, yet, according to feminists, erroneous beliefs about rape was one which involved the production of evidence supporting feminist arguments, the continuing project of attempting to explain how rape contributed to the maintenance of the patriarchy and, at the same time, the urgent task of providing support for the growing number of women who were becoming able to speak out about their experiences of rape. In turn, the knowledge gained from listening to women talking of their experiences contributed important empirical and experiential evidence to feminist theory, facilitating its development.

Divisions between feminist activists and theorists developed as some feminists moved into universities and research institutes, sometimes breaking their links with the movement and sometimes minimizing the visibility of the feminist aspects of their work. The period around 1980 was one of change in the movement. Feminist activism was in decline. Feminists faced problems renewing the movement with a new generation of women and reconciling feminist demands with the growing institutionalization of some aspects of feminism in the parties and the Ministry for Women's Rights. Despite the insistence on the part of those involved in selecting the projects which would be included in the research programme established in the wake of the landmark conference at Toulouse in 1982, feminists from within the institutions and, to an even greater extent, feminist activists criticized what they perceived as a widening gap between activism and research.

Since the decline of the MLF, which began in the period 1978–81, feminism in France has had difficulty establishing a new identity. The arrival of the Socialists in power in 1981, the creation of the Ministry for Women's Rights and the relative growth at that time of feminist research, which received official recognition in the early 1980s, all contributed to the institutionalization of feminism. But although feminists are still active in the parties, the trades unions and academic institutions, their impact is not strong enough to sustain a new definition of feminism, other than a gradual spread of ideas. This is referred to by Janine Mossuz-Lavau as "everyday feminism" (*le féminisme ordinaire*), and her study (1995) of attitudes towards women's status reveals that there is a widely held acceptance of the legitimacy of women's gains at the same time as a rejection of the label "feminist". While some observers have suggested that the campaign for parity could produce a remobilization of feminism, for this to happen several important conflicts would need to be resolved. These are, firstly, the differences around revolution and reform. While this issue is far less hotly disputed now than it was during the 1970s and early 1980s, it is of particular salience in relation to the question of whether feminists can achieve their goals by bringing women into (male) political institutions. Secondly, the conflict around "ownership" or representation of the movement which surrounded relations between Psych et po and the rest of the MLF is still present and features in the organization and accounts of most major feminist actions, including the campaign for parity. The changes and contradictions in the stance of Antoinette Fouque (once revolutionary, anti-feminist, self-proclaimed founder of the MLF, now MEP, advocate of parity and involved in pro-feminist actions) only add to the complexity of relations within the movement.

During the 1980s and early 1990s the gap between activists and researchers was identified by both as a factor which had a negative effect on the difference feminism could make. This problem is not unique to France. The British radical feminist Liz Kelly (1994/5) calls for a new feminist praxis as a solution to the problem of the widening gap between theory and practice in British feminism. "Praxis" Kelly defines as "an old fashioned, and now unpopular, term meaning the ongoing linkage between theory and practice" (1994/5: 48). She claims that feminist networks and coalitions around specific issues are demonstrating the ability to move beyond some of the impasses faced by feminist theory:

> Through working together to create feminist social change, women are finding ways of working with similarity and difference at the same time. The more isolated and unaware feminist theoreticians become from feminist activism the more they are disconnected from the source which would encourage them and enable them to resolve some of the theoretical knots. (ibid.)

The rejection of theory by activists means that their practice is informed by established ideas which may not be relevant to new developments. The campaign for parity seems to share some of the characteristics Kelly identifies as necessary for the construction of feminist praxis. It is clear that, for some, parity offers the possibility of establishing links between activists and theorists. However, it is less certain that, even if this were to happen, these links would extend to other areas of feminist activity such as violence, where the limited contact between activists and researchers has been identified as an obstacle to change.

The climate in which theories of masculinity are produced and received

Many factors contribute to the social, political and cultural climate in which theories of masculinity are produced and received. Feminism and a multitude of responses to it play an important role in the construction and representation of this climate. While there is little evidence that the "new man" portrayed by the media as sharing domestic chores and childcare actually exists, the changes in masculine identity which inspired his cultural construction do have some basis, and it is these changes which are investigated by many studies of masculinity. The relationship between the rise of the women's movement and the "crisis in masculinity" proclaimed by some journalists and intellectuals is not straightforward. In many journalistic accounts, feminism is held directly responsible for men's loss of power and their resulting identity crisis. The problem with establishing this causal link is that it suggests as a solution the acceptance of blame by feminists and the renunciation of their feminism in the interest of restoring the balance of gender relations in France. The positioning of a particular way of structuring gender relations as a national characteristic plays an important role in the debate. A national consensus around the rules of gender relations, which include a specifically French gift for the art of seduction, is said to have been temporarily under threat from feminists in the 1970s. Now, however, this threat is no longer seen to be particularly worrying in France. Feminism today is an American excess, which must be prevented from upsetting the understanding which French men and women have for each other.

Anti-feminism is not new in France and is a phenomenon which can be expected to accompany all manifestations of feminism, to the extent that effective challenges to existing power structures will always be resisted by those who benefit from these structures. However, a particular manifestation of anti-feminism has been seen in the media in recent years. This has often been expressed as postfeminism. Popular interpretations of masculinity which have appeared in the press and on the bestseller lists are situated within a postfeminist framework.

According to this perspective, feminism has brought to an end the unequal distribution of power between men and women. Feminism's gains are portrayed as so extensive that women are said to be at an advantage over men in many respects: in particular they control decisions about reproduction and invariably "win" conflicts over the custody of children after divorce and separation. The point of many of these postfeminist portrayals of masculinity is to argue that women need to be more reasonable and allow men to behave in more "masculine" ways. The blurring of the distinction between men and women is seen as a threat to French society, which has always valued sexual difference. The popularized version of the masculinity debate presents itself as part of a reaction to feminism. The effects of feminism on men are portrayed as damaging to French society and a postfeminist consensus is required to solve the problem of the male identity crisis.

This has many implications for the production of theories of masculinity and for the reception of feminist theories. The construction of postfeminism silences feminists. The reduction of feminism to one of its historical manifestations, the MLF of the 1970s, means that today's struggles against men's continuing domination of women on a structural level are not recognized as feminist struggles. Feminist debate in all its diversity is ignored. Instead, individuals such as Elisabeth Badinter are selected to represent feminist ideas, despite the fact that their analyses of changing masculinities are situated in the same postfeminist framework.

The refusal to engage with feminist debate is evident not only in interpretations of masculinity which have appeared in the press and popular books; it is also a problem in academic institutions. Women's studies has had to struggle for recognition as a legitimate area of teaching and research, and feminist epistemology and methodology have had little, if any, impact in the mainstream disciplines. While this is by no means unique to France, French feminist intellectuals, such as Marie-Victoire Louis (1996) and Christine Delphy (1991c), see the resistance to feminist theory as particularly pronounced among French male intellectuals and the institutions whose hierarchies they dominate. The production of French feminist theory has been severely affected by the lack of institutional support, funding and publishing outlets. That it has taken place at all is attributed by ANEF to the commitment of individual researchers and feminist organizations such as AVFT (ANEF, 1995: 702). While it is difficult to assess the relative impact of anti-feminism in different societies, it is clear that structural reasons prevent French feminist theory from being produced and published in the same quantities as Anglo-American feminist theory.

The reception of feminist theory

The representation of French feminism was affected by the appropriation of the name "mouvement de libération des femmes" by Psych et po in 1979. Antoinette Fouque's willingness and ability to use the media to disseminate her own views in the name of the MLF, while at the same time describing herself, her group and her publication, *des femmes en mouvement*, as "anti-feminist", was initially an effective way of silencing the rest of the movement. It broke an unspoken rule that no-one would speak in the name of the MLF and raised questions about the nature of a movement which resists organization and hierarchy, only to find that there is no control over who speaks in its name. The effectiveness of this practice was reduced when the media began to distinguish between Fouque's MLF and the broader women's movement. However, French feminists have reported that Fouque continues to feed the media with distorted accounts of feminist activity in which she claims a central role. With more limited resources and a certain reluctance towards such a use of the media, other feminists have remained relatively unable to counteract her influence.

The reception of French feminist theory abroad has been affected by several factors, some of which have their origin within French feminism and some of which are external. Firstly, French feminist engagement with European and international initiatives and debates has been influenced by the fact that many French feminists do not speak or read English and by an uneasiness about, or a resistance to, the perceived domination of international conferences and debates by Americans. As the links between national feminisms multiply, and as feminists increasingly target their demands on European and international organizations, this issue is gaining importance. Feminists have proposed a wide range of solutions, from establishing non-Anglophone networks (*Cahiers du CEDREF*, 1995) to overcoming what they describe as a masculine obsession with the importance of the French language and a refusal to accept that English is the international negotiating language (Louis, 1996).

The difficulties faced by French feminists who feel excluded from an international feminism whose language is English have been exacerbated by the distorted representation of French feminism abroad. The construction of "French feminism" exaggerated the influence of a very small number of French women theorists, some of whom would not describe themselves as feminists, nor would they be described as such by feminists in France. This has had the effect of rendering the rest of feminist theoretical production in France practically invisible. The recent publication in English of some of the most influential French materialist feminist texts of the past 25 years should go some way towards correcting the distorted image of French feminism which has dominated Anglo-American representations of it (Guillaumin, 1995; Adkins & Leonard, 1996).

Feminists and masculinity

For French feminists, the question of whether or not to theorize masculinity explicitly has been problematic. Feminist theory has always been indirectly concerned with the nature of masculinity and its role in producing and maintaining the power relations between men and women. However, during the 1970s many French feminists believed that, while there was much to be discovered about masculine identity, this should be done by men. It was only as they began to find it necessary to respond, often critically, to men's groups' attempts to do this that they were drawn into the debate. Their criticisms were often based on the fact that many of the men's groups' explorations of masculinity ignored feminist theory and could be interpreted as a way of absolving the authors of responsibility for a type of masculinity which they themselves had transcended. It thus showed few signs of challenging the existing structure of gender relations. This left feminists faced with a choice between accepting men's groups' critiques or producing their own versions. This was situated within a broader feminist debate on the role of men in feminism. While the women-only nature of the MLF was one of its essential characteristics, its preservation gradually came into question, especially in areas of feminist activity most directly concerned with men and masculinity. In recent years, a number of projects have been undertaken jointly by feminists and pro-feminist men. These include the establishment of centres for violent men, such as SOS-hommes et violences en privé in Paris and the publication of *Des hommes et du masculin* by CEFUP and the Centre de recherches et d'études anthropologiques. Many feminists resist such joint projects, however, and it remains to be seen whether the trend will continue to develop.

The arguments in favour of its development seem convincing. Having established that violence is not a biologically inherent characteristic of men, but is instead a product of social constructions of masculinity, feminists insist that for male violence to be brought to an end these constructions need to be challenged. It seems clear that men must participate in the redefinition of masculinity, but if this is to modify gender relations in a way which benefits women, it needs to be done on feminist terms. This change cannot be brought about while men are cast as incapable of contributing to the feminist project.

Difference and masculinity

Whether or not they support joint projects, some feminists have argued that the explicit study of masculinity is vital to a feminist understanding of gender relations and how they operate on a global and local level. Developments in the difference debate, which has played an important part in French feminist theory and strategy, have contributed to the trend towards examining masculinity as well as femininity and, in particular, the relation between them. The difference debate within French feminism has not been cut through by identity politics and poststructuralism in the same way as its Anglo-American counterparts. It thus continues to be constructed around a binary opposition between sameness and difference. This is often superimposed on the opposition between universalism and particularism which occupies an important position in the French republican tradition. Universalism is a means of guaranteeing equality, but this equality is guaranteed on the basis of sameness. Differences can lead to discrimination and must therefore be avoided. According to this view, "equality in difference" is impossible. So, if women's subordination by men is to be removed, this must be on the grounds that there are no significant differences between them. While anatomical differences undeniably exist, the importance attributed to these differences is seen as socially constructed and therefore not immutable. Particularism, on the other hand, focuses on difference, in this case the difference between men and women. Difference feminists value what is specific to women and femininity and demand an end to their inferior status. Since this position runs counter to the dominant tradition of universalism, it has been less popular in France than in the United States.

Among difference feminists there has been a greater interest in understanding femininity than masculinity. The project of difference feminism has been to unveil the feminine which has been obscured by masculine structures of thought and language posing as neutral. Irigaray, for example, offers a detailed critique of the masculinity of these structures and attempts to create the conditions in which femininity can express itself in terms other than those imposed on it by phallocentrism. Irigaray's work is an important challenge to Western thought and raises new questions for feminism. She contributes to an understanding of masculinity at the discursive level. However, her analyses do not relate to the material reality of men's lives, their experience of masculinity and its effect on gender relations. It is difficult to produce a satisfactory analysis of male violence towards women without taking these factors into account. It is for this reason that theories more directly concerned with masculinity as part of a gender relation feature more prominently in this book.

An examination of social constructionist interest in men and masculinity reveals a trend towards focusing more clearly on both sides of the gender relation. Initially, social constructionist feminists argued that masculinity and femininity were not biologically inherent. Sex role theory was popular with sociologists and early feminists as a way of explaining why individuals behaved in a way appropriate to their sex. However, its shortcomings meant that it was gradually replaced by the concept of gender. At first, this concept referred to the characteristics which were not biological, but which were different for women and men. Later, it developed into the concept of gender as a relation, both sides of which needed to be studied in order for an understanding of the power differential between them to be reached. One of the consequences of this development is that masculinity has been established as a legitimate area of research.

The theoretical contributions of Delphy, Mathieu and Guillaumin paved the way for the analysis of gender relations and, later, for the theorization of masculinity. By placing the emphasis on the power relation between men and women and its role in the construction of masculinity and femininity, these theorists were able to challenge the notion that there is an essential difference between the sexes. This "ideology of difference" is used, they argue, to justify the oppression of women and needs to be exposed if change is to be possible. An important aspect of their work, therefore, was the critique of naturalism, and this critique is still being developed by feminist biologists, sociologists and psychologists.

The work of feminist biologists has contributed to the exploration of the link between sex and gender and the idea that sex itself is a social construct. Feminist biologists have provided evidence to support their claims that sex is a continuum and that its division into two categories is artificial. This confirms the theories developed by Guillaumin, Delphy and Mathieu that sex is the *result* of the gendered power relation, not its cause.

The explanation of this relationship remains to be developed. This area of feminist thought opens up the possibility of explaining how masculinity is constructed within and by this power relation. Devreux has begun this project with her study of the construction of masculinity in the army, but further case studies are necessary in order to provide a more complete understanding of the way in which this construction takes place.

The systemic analyses of male dominance elaborated by feminists in the 1970s offered few possibilities for change, other than by destroying patriarchy. The sex class "men" dominated the sex class "women", and individual men and women could not escape this relation of oppression. These early theories did not attempt to account for differences in the experiences of individual men and women within the system, nor did they explain how gender identity is acquired or how gender interacts with other social relations. However, their construction of a framework for the analysis of gender has been particularly important in the emphasis it places on the *relation* between masculinity and femininity. The idea that femininity and masculinity exist only in relation to each other led to the recognition of the importance of studying both, in order to understand the power relation between them and its effects on men and women.

Attempts to explain how the system of gender relations is maintained and reproduced have found that it is very flexible. New models of masculinity can be incorporated into the system without the overall balance of power being affected. This raises fundamental questions about whether change is possible after all. It also raises once again the relation of the gendered individual to the structure of gender relations, which is a central question to feminists theorizing gender and those working on violence.

The similarities between Anglo-American and French feminist theories of gender are often ignored, but there are many. There are similarities in the trends from sex role theory to theories of gender; from structuralism to more flexible systems (whether accompanied by a rejection or adaptation of the concept of patriarchy); and from the optimistic belief that the social construction of masculinity could be changed to a re-examination of the mechanisms of social change and of the reproduction of existing relations. There has also been a growing interest in the re-introduction of biology into theories of gender. The maintenance of the binary division of the sexes is challenged by the work of biologists in France, as in Britain and the United States, who claim that biological sex is less rigidly divided into two categories than had previously been thought. Feminist biologists argue that the differences are much more indistinct, that difference is socially constructed and exaggerated into an opposition, but that individuals do not fit easily into this opposition, and are instead situated on a continuum. They attempt to demonstrate that, since there is no scientific basis for the binary division of the sexes, it is based on a social decision, which is responsible for the perpetuation of this division. Christine Delphy and Nicole-Claude Mathieu argue that sex and gender cannot be easily separated. Sex is defined through the framework of gendered power relations. Anglo-American feminists are similarly interested in this artificial division, and have challenged the opposition between natural fixed biology and socially constructed gender.

While I have emphasized the importance of resisting the construction of "French feminism" as exotically different to Anglo-American feminism, stressing the similarities between them in many areas, there are culturally specific characteristics which cannot be ignored. One of the most striking distinguishing features of French feminism, from a British feminist perspective, is the absence of considerations of multiple differences between women, and the interaction of gender, sexuality and ethnicity. The most plausible reason for this is the French republican tradition of universalism which thinks of equality in terms of sameness. Thus, "universalist" or "sameness" feminists who work within this tradition minimalize the differences between men and women in order to claim equality between them. While feminists such as Irigaray, who reject this tradition, claim that women and men can and should be different *and* equal, their interest in difference does not extend to differences *between* women. It is for this reason that they are sometimes seen as essentialist. The debate around sexual difference continues to take place within French feminism in terms of a binary opposition between sameness and difference, whereas in British and American feminisms the criticisms of black, third world and lesbian feminists shifted the terms of the debate at an early stage. There is evidence, however, that some French feminists are searching for ways to move beyond this dichotomy. Feminists on the extreme left have always been aware of the problems of conflicting identities among women involved in both feminist and class-struggle politics. Articles in *Cahiers du féminisme* on parity raise the question of identity-based claims for political representation, which could include not only women but other groups with a shared identity. However, many of the main actors in the parity debate stress that the difference between the sexes has nothing in common with other differences. It remains to be seen whether the deeply entrenched divisions around sameness and difference can be overcome.

Violence and masculinity

French feminists involved in projects around male violence towards women have also contributed to an understanding of men and masculinity. In contrast to theorists of gender who have largely examined the structure of gender relations and the oppression of women on a global scale, activists working with survivors of male violence initially gathered empirical evidence which they then analyzed to produce explanations of the interaction between violence and masculinity on a local scale. Patterns emerged from the individual cases which enabled them to draw broader conclusions.

My account of French feminist activism around male violence reveals several trends in its development, all of which lead to a greater emphasis on men as the perpetrators of violence towards women. This represents a significant shift, since early work in this area focused on women as the victims of male violence. This reflected the widely held view that the victims of rape and domestic violence were often themselves responsible for the attack. This attitude played an important role in the response of the police and the criminal justice system to these attacks and explained in large part why women survivors of male violence usually endured it in silence and isolation. It also reflected the urgent necessity for feminists to respond to the needs of survivors. Their work therefore concentrated on providing helplines for survivors of rape and, later, refuges for women escaping domestic violence. At the same time, they sought to raise public awareness of violence towards women, demonstrating the extent of the problem through the numbers of women who contacted them.

While support work was, and still is, important, it became increasingly clear that the common denominator in most acts of violence is the sex of the perpetrator. This led to the argument voiced by some feminists that if violence was to be prevented, then it was necessary to work with men, rather than focusing solely on the women they attacked. The debate around whether feminists should devote their energy to this type of action mirrors that which divides feminists involved in the production of theories of gender. Many claim that, while this is essential to the understanding of masculinity and male violence, it is a project which should be undertaken by men. Others argue that preventive measures need to target the construction of gender relations at an early age. Educating children in a way which encourages the development of respect and understanding between boys and girls would, they claim, do much to remove the causes of gendered violence.

On a theoretical, as well as a practical level, the focus has been shifted from asking why particular women are subjected to male violence to why particular men become violent. The connections between the construction of masculinity and violence are at the centre of this question. Many obstacles had to be cleared before this question could be addressed. The first was to destroy the myths surrounding violence which removed responsibility from men. These included the ideas that women enjoy being raped, that violent men are mentally ill or alcoholics, and that men are at the mercy of their uncontrollable sexual urges, rape being an expression of their need for sex.

The idea that violence is a natural characteristic of men also inhibited the exploration of the links between masculinity and violence. It offered no means of explaining why some men are violent and others not. It was also incapable of explaining why some women use violence. The analysis of cases of violence towards women contributed to the rejection of these ideas and to the insistence that men were responsible for the violence they perpetrated.

The role of the state is also important. Police attitudes towards violence affect the number of women who report violent attacks, the number who press charges and the likelihood of prosecution. Studies carried out by AVFT have demonstrated that, while there has been some improvement in the way the French police respond to survivors of male violence, there is also evidence that solidarity between male police officers and violent men can affect the efficiency of police action (Louis, 1990a: 154).

The criminal justice system can make it very difficult for women to pursue cases of violence. In particular, women who have been raped find their personal and sexual histories on trial in an attempt to prove consent. Until 1980 there was no legal definition of rape in France, leaving its interpretation to judges. Their interpretation was often narrow. Feminist campaigners for legal reform have attempted to produce change in these areas. In the 1970s they focused on the definition of rape. This resulted in the adoption of a relatively broad definition in the law passed in 1980. However, in practice, the courts continued to interpret the term "rape" far more narrowly.

The relation between feminism and the state has posed problems for French feminists, split over a rejection of a political and legal system which is dominated by men and operates in their interest, and a desire to reform politics and the law in order to make them more effective at guaranteeing women's rights. This debate raises a number of questions. For example, would the laws on violence towards women be different if debated, passed and applied by women politicians and judges? If so, then bringing the number of women in these sites of power to a critical mass should be a feminist priority. However, feminist opposition to this tactic is raised mainly by those on the extreme left, who argue that feminists should not concentrate on promoting a female elite which would join the existing male elite. Instead, they should be focusing on the material conditions which prevent the partners of violent men from leaving them.

Some of the earliest contributions to an understanding of the relation between violence and masculinity were provided by feminists working in refuges and on helplines. Through an analysis of the cases they dealt with, they established that violent men are not exceptional or marginalized in society, but "ordinary" men. They also discovered that in the majority of cases the attackers are known to the women they attack. This has meant that explanations of male violence have had to look beyond common "excuses", such as the perversion of a small number of social deviants.

As French feminists "discovered" more and more forms of male violence towards women, they began to situate them on a continuum, seeing each form as a manifestation of male power. The sexual abuse of children in the family is particularly revealing of the power relations at work in cases of male violence. It demonstrates the importance of the division between the public and the private domain. Violence committed within the family is seen as a private issue in which the state should not intervene. This is confirmed by the analysis of domestic violence and marital rape. It also raises the question of the central role played by the notion of consent in cases of sexual violence. The work of Nicole-Claude Mathieu has made an important contribution to the understanding of consent, exploring the question of the extent to which the oppressed can be said to consent to their oppression. Refuge and helpline reports have also stressed that women do not consent to domestic violence, and that financial dependence on a violent partner plays a much greater part in their inability to leave, along with a feeling of shame and the effects of long-term humiliation. In the case of children abused by someone in authority, usually their father, it is difficult to see how an assessment can be made of whether or not they consented to the abuse. French feminists argue that the abuse of power which features prominently in cases of incest is sanctioned by a society which refuses to intervene in familial affairs and refuses to hold men responsible, choosing instead to portray incest as a symptom of a dysfunctional family. Feminist action has played an important part in raising public awareness of incest and in challenging this interpretation of its origins.

The need for an analysis of the causes and functioning of male violence has become more pressing as feminist action around male violence moves towards a demand for preventive rather than punitive measures. Some of the most important aspects of French feminist attempts to analyze male violence are, firstly, that explanations which are based on the personality of the individual violent man are unable to account for the fact that male violence towards women occurs throughout society and is committed by men who are apparently perfectly "normal". Moreover, social tolerance of violence towards women seems to be very high, and this is reflected in the way the police and the courts respond to it. This suggests that the structural relations between men and women must be at the centre of any analysis of this violence.

Secondly, the premeditation involved in many of the attacks and the interpretation by violent men of their own acts of violence suggest that male violence does not occur in moments of madness. Instead, violence is used consciously as a means of dominating and controlling the behaviour of women. The links between the construction of masculinity and the desire to dominate and control are gradually being explored.

This work builds on early feminist analyses of violence as a form of the social control of women. These theories interpreted violence as an essential tool of the patriarchy. Rape, or the threat of rape, was seen to control women's behaviour, and all men were said to benefit from this, whether or not they ever use violence themselves. More recent analyses have adapted this structural view. Marie-Victoire Louis, for example, argues that while patriarchy as a whole benefits from the social control imposed on women by the reality and threat of violence, this does not mean that all men are rapists or even that all men benefit from the situation (interview, 1993). The systemic analyses of male dominance in the 1970s were unable to account for the variations in men's access to, and abuse of, power. More flexible frameworks of gender analysis which can explain the contradictions within an overall pattern of male domination are being developed by feminists involved in the theorization of both gender and male violence, and it is at the point where these analyses meet that we can expect to find the most exciting developments in this area of French feminist theory.

It is clear that the study of men and masculinity has aroused interest among some feminists in France. A growing interest has been demonstrated among feminists who produce theories of gender and among those active around the problem of male violence. However, the insular conditions in which much of the work examined in this research is undertaken may be limiting its development. Certainly, some of the most productive and interesting ideas about masculinity are emerging from groups and individuals who are involved in the cross-fertilization of ideas, whether this is between the movement and research; between men's groups and feminists; or between Anglo-American and French theories. Although in most cases this is only just beginning to happen, a growing number of feminists and pro-feminist men are stressing its importance, and, if the trend continues, significant contributions to the masculinity debate can be expected to result.

Notes

1   This is well documented. See, for example, the introductions to Duchen (1987) and Moi (1987). It is also often mentioned in books and articles which then go on to concentrate on only one aspect of French theory which has been constructed as "French feminism" outside France. See, for example, the introduction to Fraser and Bartky (1992).

2   For an overview of the main points of contention see Acker (1989).

3   One significant example is that Andrea Dworkin, one of the best-known and widely read American feminist writers, had never been published in France until 1993, when one of her articles appeared in *NQF* (Dworkin, 1993).

4   Maison des femmes de Paris, 8 cité Prost, 75011 Paris.

5   *Cahiers du féminisme*, 2 rue Richard-Lenoir, 93108 Montreuil.

6   Collectif féministe contre le viol, 4 square Saint-Irénée, 75011 Paris.

7   Maison des femmes, 31 rue du chemin de fer, 95800 Cergy-St-Christophe.

8   The review published by the Trotskyist Ligue communiste révolutionnaire, *Les cahiers du féminisme*, has also been appearing regularly since 1977. Despite the split in the *QF* collective which led to the creation of *NQF*, I am treating them as a theoretical continuum, since the editor (Christine Delphy) and the position of the journal as it was intended by Delphy and Simone de Beauvoir from the outset remained unchanged.

9   *La revue d'en face* could have been described as such during its existence between 1977 and 1984.

10 The only major feminist publishing house in France is des femmes, owned by Antoinette Fouque of Psych et po. See Chapter 2.

11 For example, Mathieu (1991) and Guillaumin (1992).

12 Feminists objected to the term "de la femme" and insisted on the use of the plural "des femmes". See Picq (1993, 17).

13 According to Anne Zelensky (interview with author, Paris, 1993), although labels are often given to feminists ("tendance lutte de classes", "féministes révolutionnaires", etc.), many activists do not recognize themselves in these categories.

14 See also Françoise Picq's (1993) reluctant use of the same divisions.

15 This led to the split of the *QF* collective in 1980.

16 For a hisitory of Psych et po's appropriation of the movement's name, see *Chroniques d'une imposture: du mouvement de libération des femmes à une marque commerciale*, Paris: Tierce, 1981.

17 See for example the article by Françoise Giroud, "Les voiles flasques du féminisme", *Le monde*, 8 April 1979 and the response to it – "Des féministes hystériques aux féministes historiques ou de la caricature à l'enterrement" – signed by numerous groups from the MLF which *Le monde* chose not to publish, and which appeared in *QF*, 6, September 1979, 102–4.

18 See *NQF* **13**, 4, which is devoted to abortion.

19 See any number of *Paris féministe* during 1992–3; for an account of the actions against and analyses of the rapes committed against these women, see Visser (1993).

20 See the special number on Aids of *Les cahiers du féminisme*, 65, summer 1993.

21 See, for example *Clara Magazine*, 33, March 1995 dossier and issues of *Cahiers du féminisme*.

22 Reynaud (1981) later expanded on the ideas in this article in his book.

23 The popularity in France of Robert Bly's *Iron John*, published in translation in 1992 (*L'homme sauvage et l'enfant: l'avenir du genre masculin*), suggests that this is not an uncommon view.

24 *La revue d'en face*, 9–10, 1981, *Spécial "hommes"*. For a recent historical review of this debate see Baudoux and Zaidman (1992).

25 For example, the publication of Sullerot (1992) was followed by a collection of articles in *L'événement du jeudi* on "Le mâle français", 13–19 August 1992, 52–89; Badinter (1992) was followed by a collection of articles entitled "Qu'est-ce qu'un homme, aujourd'hui?" in *Le nouvel observateur*, August 1992, 4–13, which featured an interview with Badinter. Both books became bestsellers.

26 For an account of the debate see Allwood (1995).

27 See for example Fuss (1989) and Grosz (1990).

28 The order of narrative poses certain problems, since feminist theories of gender did not develop in a strictly linear fashion, but rather in what the CNRS researcher Michèle Ferrand (1991: 224) describes as "a process which is chaotic and non-linear, from the initial consideration of the feminine condition to analytical approaches proposing the construction of social relations of sex, a recent name for a concept which was already being explored by feminist theorists in the 1970s". Although this section is arranged in a mainly chronological fashion, the continuity of theoretical trends takes precedence over chronological accuracy.

29 Their opposition to the term does not imply that they do not employ the concept of "social sex" (*sexe social*) which differs from "biological sex".

30 One of the first groups to undertake this task was APRE. In a collection of papers published by this group in 1985, Danièle Combes and Dominique Fougeyrollas (1985: 103) offered some definitions of "social relations of

sex", highlighting the difficulty of trying to unravel the diverse meanings which it has had in different contexts, and concentrating on those which refer more explicitly to a relation between two terms.

31 With the possible exception of Devreux (1992).

32 For examples of both of these positions, see Waters (1989) and Walby (1990).

33 In my search for the beginnings of an interest in men and masculinity, I do not intend to minimize the importance of all the feminist work on women as survivors of male violence, which not only had to precede any feminist analysis of men and masculinity, as will be shown below, but also still continues today.

34 For a selection of early examples of the growing interest in violence towards women, see Le Péron (1978); Des féministes révolutionnaires (1977); Collin (1976); and for a first-hand account of the period, see Halimi (1992).

35 Press reports concerning this opening are collected in Agence femmes information (1980).

36 See the account of the trial in Halimi (1978).

37 For further details of this debate, see Le Péron (1978).

38 The first was by Brigitte Gros and other senators: Proposition de loi no. 324, Sénat, annexe au procès-verbal de la séance du 20 avril 1978; the two other bills presented to the Senate were by Robert Schwint and the members of the Socialist group (Proposition no. 324, Sénat, annexe au procès-verbal de la séance du ler juin 1978) and Hélène Luc and the members of the Communist group (Proposition no. 445, Sénat, annexe au procès-verbal de la séance du 15 juin 1978). The first bill presented to the Assemblée nationale was by Florence d'Harcourt and 31 other deputies (Proposition no. 271, enregistrée à la présidence de l'Assemblée nationale le 17 mai 1978). The other two were presented by François Mitterrand and the members of the Socialist group, and Gisèle Moreau and the Communist group. These were both identical to the bills presented to the Senate by their respective groups. All cited by Mossuz-Lavau (1991: 217–19).

39 Law no. 80–1041 of 23 December 1980, which appeared in the *Journal officiel* on 24 December 1980.

40 Marie-Victoire Louis (1990a: 141), for instance, wrote, "On ne peut que se réjouir de cette campagne officielle. Elle a eu le grand mérite de poser ce difficile problème." ("We can only be delighted that this official campaign took place. It deserves credit for raising this difficult problem.")

41 The term "incest" has been rejected by some British feminists in favour of "child sexual abuse". In France, however, the term is widely used by feminists. It is used here for that reason, and because it is understood that when French feminists use the term "incest" they are referring to one kind of child sexual abuse – that which is perpetrated by a close relative, usually the father.

42 Art. 16 of the Loi sur la protection de l'enfance, passed on 14 July 1989.

43 Although incest is not mentioned as such in the Penal Code which was passed in July 1992 and came into force in March 1993, rape is aggravated if the victim is under 15 years old and the rapist is in a position of authority over the victim. (Code Pénal, *Journal officiel*, 23 July 1992, section 3, article 222–24). Thus, incestuous rape is now punishable by a sentence of 20 years' imprisonment.

44 "Divorce can be requested by one partner for acts attributable to the other when these acts constitute a serious or repeated violation of the duties and obligations of marriage and render the continuation of the partnership intolerable." Quoted in Devèze (1991: 215).

45 See also Collin (1990: 10).

46 There are currently two other centres open in France, one run by RIME in Lyons and one by Vivre sans violence in Marseilles (cf. Dhoquois, 1990: 12).

47 See Carole Pateman's influential contributions to this area of feminist theory, e.g. Pateman 1989.

48 In particular this has taken place in *Projets féministes*, the journal of AVFT.

References

Acker, J. 1989. The problem with patriarchy. *Sociology* **23**, 2, 235–40.

Adkins, L. & D. Leonard (eds). 1996. *Sex in question: French materialist feminism*. London: Taylor & Francis.

Agence femmes information. 1980. *Dossier femmes battues*. Paris: Agence femmes information.

Albistur, M. & D. Armogathe. 1977. *Histoire du féminisme français du moyen âge à nos jours*. Paris: des femmes.

Alia, J. 1991. Ça va, les hommes?: un sondage exclusif Sofrès – *Le nouvel observateur*, 1388, 13–19 June, 4–24.

Allwood, G. 1995. The campaign for parity in political institutions. In *Women and representation*, D. Knight & J. Still (eds), 7–20. Nottingham: WIF Publications.

ANEF (Association nationale des études féministes). 1995. Etudes féministes et études sur les femmes en France en 1995. In Ephesia (1995), 689–703.

Appignanesi, L. 1994. Liberté, égalité and fraternité: PC and the French. In *The war of the words: the political correctness debate*, S. Dunant (ed.). London: Virago, pp. 145–63.

Attallah, N. 1991. France's femme fatale, *Observer*, 16 June, p. 41.

Auger, C. 1982. Violeurs acquittés: viol légalisé. *Nouvelles questions féministes*, 4, Autumn, 97–100.

Auger, C. 1985. Le viol en justice. *Cahiers du féminisme*, 33, 11–13.

Badinter, E. 1986. *L'un est l'autre*. Paris: Odile Jacob.

Badinter, E. 1992. *XY: de l'identité masculine*. Paris: Odile Jacob.

Banner, L. 1989. Review article. *Signs*. spring, 703–8.

Basch, F. 1983. Nouvelles . . . de France et des colonies. *Nouvelles questions féministes*, 5, 87–92.

Battagliola, F., D. Combes, A.-M. Daune-Richard, A.-M. Devreux, M. Ferrand, A. Langevin (eds). 1986. *A propos des rapports sociaux de sexe; parcours épistémologiques*. Part 3. Paris: CNRS.

Baudoux, C. & C. Zaidman (eds). 1992. *Egalité entre les sexes: mixité et démocratie*. Paris: L'Harmattan.

Beauvoir, S. de. 1972. *The second sex* (tr. H.M. Parshley). London: Penguin.

Beauvoir, S. de. 1982. Témoignage. *Nouvelles questions féministes*, 3, 110–12.

Bly, Robert. 1992. *L'homme sauvage et l'enfant: l'avenir du genre masculin* (tr. Christian Cler & Maxime Loiseau). Paris: Seuil.

Bordeaux, M., B. Hazo, S. Lorvellec. 1989. Viol et violences contre les femmes. In Centre national de la recherche scientifique, *Recherches sur les femmes et recherches féministes: présentation des travaux 1984–7*. Nantes: CNRS, 69–76.

Bristow, J. 1990. Review article. *History Workshop Journal*, 29, 191–3.

Brun, O. (ed.). 1984. *Ruptures et féminismes en devenir*. Paris: Voix Off, Imprimerie de Femmes.

Cahiers du CEDREF: continuités et discontinuités du féminisme. 1995. 4/5. Paris: Université de Paris VII.

Canaan, J.E. 1991. Is "doing nothing" just boys' play?: integrating feminist and cultural studies perspectives on working-class young men's masculinity. In *Off-centre: feminism and cultural studies*, S. Franklin, C. Lury, J. Stacey (eds), 108–25. London: HarperCollins.

Carrigan, T., Connell, R.W., Lee, J. 1987. Hard and heavy: toward a new sociology of masculinity. In *Beyond patriarchy: essays by men on pleasure, power and change*, M. Kaufman (ed.), 139–92. Toronto and New York: Oxford University Press.

Casalis, M.-F. 1988. Viol. In *Le féminisme et ses enjeux: vingt-sept femmes parlent*, Centre fédéral FEN, 259–66. Paris: Edilig.

Casalis, M.-F. 1990. L'inceste. *Actes: les cahiers d'action juridique*, 70, spring. Special issue: Les violences faites aux femmes (produced in conjunction with *Hommes et libertés*), 12.

Castelain-Meunier, C. 1988. *Les hommes aujourd'hui: virilité et identité*. Paris: Acropole.

CEFUP (Centre d'études féminines de l'université de Provence) and Centre de recherches et d'études anthropologiques. 1992. *BIEF: des hommes et du masculin*. Lyons: Presses universitaires de Lyon.

Chapman, R. 1988. The great pretender: variations on the new man theme. In R. Chapman & J. Rutherford (eds) (1988), 225–48.

Chapman, R. & J. Rutherford (eds). 1988. *Male order: unwrapping masculinity*. London: Lawrence & Wishart.

CNRS. 1989. *Recherches sur les femmes et recherches féministes: présentation des travaux 1984–7*. Nantes: CNRS.

Collectif féministe contre le viol. 1987. Viol-femmes-informations. *Cette violence dont nous ne voulons plus*, 5, June, 25–9.

Collectif féministe contre le viol. 1991. *Viols, femmes, informations*. Paris: Collectif féministe contre le viol.

Collin, F. 1976. Entre le chien et le loup. *Cahiers du GRIF*, 14–15, Violence, 3–9.

Collin, F. 1989. Ringard ou ringuèle?: la question des stratégies. *BIEF: Bulletin d'information des études féminines*, 20–21, Le féminisme . . . RINGARD?, 163–7.

Collin, F. 1990. Le désir engage non un objet mais un autre désir. *Cahiers du féminisme*, 55, winter, 10.

Collin, F. 1992. Théories et praxis de la différence des sexes. *M*, 53–4, 5–9.

Collin, F. 1995. La raison polyglotte ou Pour sortir de la logique des contraires. In Ephesia (1995), 669–77.

Combes, D. & Fougeyrollas, D. 1985. Cadres théoriques d'analyse des rapports sociaux de sexe. In *Production/reproduction et rapports sociaux de sexe*, APRE, Cahiers no. 3. Paris: CNRS, September, 101–2.

Combes, D., Devreux, A.-M., Ferrand, M. 1988. Le corps support des rapports sociaux de sexe: nouvelles données, nouvelles lectures du biologique et construction des catégories de sexe. *Cahiers de l'APRE: les rapports sociaux de sexe: problématiques, méthodologies, champs d'analyses*, Actes de la table ronde internationale des 24–5 et 26 novembre 1987. Paris: CNRS, 1988, 3, 158–74.

Connell, R.W. 1987. *Gender and power: society, the person and sexual politics*. Cambridge: Polity.

Connell, R.W. 1995. *Masculinities*. Cambridge: Polity.

Daune-Richard, A.-M. & Devreux, A.-M. 1986. La reproduction des rapports sociaux de sexe. In Battagliola et al. (1986), part 3.

Daune-Richard, A.-M. & Hurtig, M.-C. 1995. Catégories et représentations de sexes: introduction: un débat loin d'être clos. In Ephesia (1995), 426–37.

Delphy, C. 1970. L'ennemi principal. *Partisans*, 54–5, July–October. numéro spécial: Libération des femmes, 157–72.

Delphy, C. 1977. Nos amis et nous: les fondements cachés de quelques discours pseudo-féministes. *Questions féministes*, 1, 21–49.

Delphy, C. 1980. Nouvelles du MLF: libération des femmes an dix. *Questions féministes*, 7, 3–13.

Delphy, C. 1981. Le patriarcat, le féminisme et leurs intellectuelles. *Nouvelles questions féministes*, 2, October, 59–74.

Delphy, C. 1984. *Close to home: a materialist analysis of women's oppression*, translated and edited by Diana Leonard. London: Hutchinson.

Delphy, C. 1985. Book review: La passion selon Wittig. *Nouvelles questions féministes*, 11–12, 151–6.

Delphy, C. 1991a. Les origines du mouvement de libération des femmes en France. *Nouvelles questions féministes*, 16–18, 137–48.

Delphy, C. 1991b. Penser le genre: quels problèmes? In Hurtig et al. (1991), 89–101.

Delphy, C. 1991c. Editorial. *Nouvelles questions féministes*, 16–18, 1–12.

Delphy, C. 1993. Rethinking sex and gender. *Women's Studies International Forum* **16**, 1, 1–9.

Delphy, C. 1995. Editorial. *Nouvelles questions féministes* **16**, 3, 1–6.

Delphy, C. 1996. The European Union and the future of feminism. In Elman, R. (1996), 147–58.

Des féministes de Collectif féministe contre le viol, Elles voient rouge, et al. 1979. Des féministes hystériques aux féministes historiques ou de la caricature à l'enterrement, *Questions féministes*, 6, 102–4.

Des féministes révolutionnaires. 1977. Justice patriarcale et peine de viol. *Alternatives*, 1. Paris: Editions Alternatives et Parallèles, 15–17.

Devèze, G. 1984. Femmes battues: brisons le mur du silence 1. *Paris féministe*, June–July, 19–24.

Devèze, G. 1985. Violences conjugales: des femmes ne s'avouent pas battues. *Cahiers du féminisme*, 33, Autumn, 18–20.

Devèze, G. 1988. Viol conjugal. In Centre fédéral FEN, *Le féminisme et ses enjeux: vingt-sept femmes parlent*. Paris: Edilig, 267–73.

Devèze, G. 1990. La violence conjugale. *Actes: les cahiers d'action juridique*, 70, spring. Special issue: Les violences faites aux femmes (produced in conjunction with *Hommes et libertés*), 6–8.

Devèze, G. 1991. Viol conjugal: comme tous les viols, un crime. *Nouvelles questions féministes*, 16–18, 214–16.

Devèze, G. & Le Breton-Viala, C.-M. 1988. Foyer Louise-Labbé: halte aide aux femmes battues. Entretien. *Cette violence dont nous ne voulons plus*. September, 25–9.

Devreux, A.-M. 1988. Les rapports de sexe constituent un rapport social et les hommes en sont l'un des termes: conséquences sur la construction des objets d'analyse. In *Cahiers de l'*APRE*: les rapports sociaux de sexe: problématiques, méthodologies, champs d'analyses*, Actes de la table ronde internationale des 24–5 et 26 novembre 1987. Paris: CNRS, 1988, 3, 150–57.

Devreux, A.-M. 1992. Etre du bon côté. In *BIEF: des hommes et du masculin*. CEFUP and Centre de recherches et d'études anthropologiques. Lyons: Presses universitaires de Lyon, 147–64.

Dhavernas, M.-J. & Kandel, L. 1983. Le sexisme comme réalité et comme représentation. *Les temps modernes*, 444, July, 3–27.

Dhavernas, O. 1990. La dénonciation, et au-delà. *Actes: les cahiers d'action juridique*, 70, spring. special issue: Les violences faites aux femmes (produced in conjunction with *Hommes et libertés*), 44–6.

Dhoquois, R. 1990. Entretien avec Marie-France Casalis. *Actes: les cahiers d'action juridique*, 70, spring. Special issue: Les violences faites aux femmes (produced in conjunction with *Hommes et libertés*), 10–13.

Dialogue: Revue trimestrielle éditée par l'association française des centres de consultation conjugale (1980), no. 69, Le malaise masculin.

Doaré, H. le. 1991. Note sur une notion: le rapport social de sexe. *Cahiers d'encrage*, numéro hors série, premier trimestre, 8–10.

Domenach, N. (ed.). 1992. Le mâle français. *L'événement du jeudi*, 13–19 August, 52–89.

Duchen, C. 1986. *Feminism in France: from May '68 to Mitterrand*. London and New York: Routledge.

Duchen, C. 1987. *French connections: voices from the women's movement in France*. London: Macmillan.

Duchen, C. 1995. Féminisme français et féminismes anglo-américains: spécificités et débats actuels. In Ephesia (1995), 352–7.

Durand-Delvigne, A. 1995. Pouvoir et genre. In Ephesia (1995), 453–5.

Dworkin, A. 1993. Israël: franchement, à qui appartient ce pays? *Nouvelles questions féministes* **14**, 2, 7–35.

Edley, N. & M. Wetherell. 1995. *Men in perspective: practice, power and identity*. London and New York: Prentice Hall/Harvester Wheatsheaf.

Eliane, D., Monique, D., Odette, B., Paula, B. 1984. Les hommes contre le sexisme. *Paris féministe*, 1–15 December, 26–7.

Elman, R.A. (ed.). 1996. *Sexual politics and the European Union: the new feminist challenge*. Providence and Oxford: Berghahn Books.

Ephesia, (ed.). 1995. *La place des femmes*. Paris: La Découverte.

Ezekiel, J. 1995. Anti-féminisme et anti-américanisme: un mariage politiquement réussi. *Nouvelles questions féministes* **17**, 1, 59–76.

Falconnet, G. & N. Lefaucheur. 1995. *La fabrication des mâles*. Paris: Editions du Seuil.

Faludi, S. 1991. *Backlash: the undeclared war against American women*. New York: Crown Publishers.

Fédération nationale "solidarité femmes", *Il vous bat. Battez-vous!* (pamphlet).

Ferrand, M. 1991. "Rapports sociaux de sexe: effets et questions épistémologiques. In Groupe d'études féministes de l'Université Paris VII (GEF), (eds) *Crises de la société: féminisme et changement*. Paris: Revue d'en face/Editions Tierce, 223–36.

Ferrand, M. & A. Langevin. 1986. De l'origine de l'oppression des femmes aux fondements des rapports sociaux de sexe. In Battagliola et al. (1986), part 1, 4–9.

Finkielkraut, A. 1984. La nostalgie de l'épreuve. *Le genre humain*, 10, Le masculin, 57–64.

Forest, I. 1990. Violences conjugales: il ne suffit pas d'en parler. *Cahiers du féminisme*, 52, spring, 7–9.

Forest, I. 1996. Demain, des assises nationales pour le droit des femmes. *Cahiers du féminisme*, 75/6, 39.

Fournier, G. & E. Reynaud. 1978. La sainte virilité. *Questions féministes*, 3, 30–62.

Fraser, N. & S.L. Bartky (eds). 1992. *Revaluing French feminism: critical essays on difference, agency and culture*. Bloomington and Indianapolis: Indiana University Press.

Fuss, D. 1989. *Essentially speaking: feminism, nature and difference*. London and New York: Routledge, 1989.

Gaspard, F. 1994. De la parité: génèse d'un concept, naissance d'un mouvement. *Nouvelles questions féministes* **15**, 4, 29–44.

Gaspard, F.C. Servan-Schreiber, A. Le Gall. 1992. *Au pouvoir citoyennes!* Paris: Editions du Seuil.

Gilles, F. 1981. D'étranges frères étrangers (à propos de la contraception masculine). *La revue d'en face*, 9–10, Spécial hommes, 35–42.

Granger, A.-M. 1987. Viol: solidarité. *Cahiers du féminisme*, 43, winter, 9–10.

Granger, A.-M. & J. Trat. 1990. Violences contre les femmes: une lutte de longue haleine. *Cahiers du féminisme*, 55, winter, 8–9.

Grosz, E. 1989. *Sexual subversions: three French feminists*. Sydney: Allen & Unwin.

Grosz, E. 1990. Conclusion: a note on essentialism and difference. In *Feminist knowledge: critique and construct*, S. Gunew (ed.), 332–44. London: Routledge.

Guerlais, M. 1991. Vers une nouvelle idéologie du droit statutaire: "Le temps de la différence de Luce Irigaray". *Nouvelles questions féministes*, 16–18, 63–92.

Guillaumin, C. 1978. Pratique du pouvoir et idée de nature (2): le discours de la nature. *Questions féministes*, 3, May, 5–28.

Guillaumin, C. 1979. Question de différence. *Questions féministes*, 6, September, 3–21.

Guillaumin, C. 1984. Masculin banal/masculin général. *Le genre humain*, 10, le masculin, 65–74.

Guillaumin, C. 1992. *Sexe, race et pratique du pouvoir*. Paris: Côté-Femmes.

Guillaumin, C. 1995. *Racism, sexism, power and ideology*. London and New York: Routledge.

Halimi, G. 1978. *Viol: le procès d'Aix-en-Provence*. Paris: Gallimard.

Halimi, G. 1992. *La cause des femmes* (new edn). Paris: Gallimard.

Halimi, G. 1994. Plaidoyer pour une démocratie paritaire. In *Femmes: moitié de la terre, moitié du pouvoir. Plaidoyer pour une démocratie paritaire*. Paris: Editions Gallimard, 11–22.

Hanmer, J. 1990. Men, power and the exploitation of women. In Hearn & Morgan (1990), 21–42.

Hanmer, J. 1996. The common market of violence. In Elman, R.A. (1996), 131–45.

Hearn, J. 1996. Is masculinity dead?: a critique of the concept of masculinity/masculinities. In *Understanding masculinities: social relations and cultural arenas*, Mac an Ghaill, Mártín (ed.), 202–17. Buckingham and Philadelphia: Open University Press.

Hearn, J. & D. Morgan (eds). 1990. *Men, masculinities and social theory*. London: Unwin Hyman.

Hester, M., L. Kelly, J. Radford (eds). 1996. *Women, violence and male power: feminist action, research and practice*. Buckingham and Philadelphia: Open University Press.

Hirata, H. & D. Kergoat. 1993. La classe ouvrière a deux sexes. *Politis: la revue*, 4, July–August–September, 55–8.

Hocquenghem, G. 1978. Subversion et décadence du mâle d'après mai 68. *Autrement*, 12, 158–63.

Hurtig, M.-C., M. Kaïl, H. Rouch (eds). 1991. *Sexe et genre: de la hiérarchie entre les sexes*. Paris: Editions du CNRS.

Hurtig, M.-C. & Pichevin, M.-F. 1995. Psychologie et essentialisme: un inquiétant renouveau. *Nouvelles questions féministes* **16**, 3, 7–32.

Iff, S. 1988. Notre corps nous appartient. In *Le féminisme et ses enjeux: vingt-sept femmes parlent*, Centre fédéral FEN (ed.). Paris: Edilig. 218–42.

Irigaray, L. 1984. *Ethique de la différence sexuelle*. Paris: Minuit.

Irigaray, L. 1994. L'identité féminine: biologie ou conditionnement social? In *Femmes: moitié de la terre, moitié du pouvoir*, G. Halimi (ed.). Paris: Gallimard. 101–8.

Jackson, S. 1996. *Christine Delphy*. London, Thousand Oaks, New Delhi: Sage Publications.

Jardine, A. 1985. *Gynesis: configurations of women and modernity*. New York: Cornell University Press.

Jenson, J. 1989. Ce n'est pas un hasard: the varieties of French feminism. In *Contemporary France: a review of interdisciplinary studies*, J. Howorth & G. Ross (eds). London: Pinter.

Jenson, J. 1990. Representations of difference: the varieties of French feminism. *New Left Review*, 180, 127–60.

Kandel, L. 1980. Post-scriptum: "une presse anti-féministe" aujourd'hui: "des femmes en mouvements". *Questions féministes*, 7, 37–44.

Kelly, L. 1994/5. Stuck in the middle. *Trouble and Strife*, 29/30, winter, 46–50.

Kennedy, M., Lubelska, C., Walsh, V. (eds). 1993. *Making counnections: women's studies, women's movements, women's lives*. London and Washington DC: Taylor & Francis.

Kergoat, D. 1992. A propos des rapports sociaux de sexe. *M*, 53–54, April/May, 16–19.

Lagrave, R.-M. 1990. Recherches féministes ou recherches sur les femmes? *Actes de la recherche en sciences sociales*, 83 masculin/féminin–1, 27–39.

Lapierre, C. 1981. A propos des groupes d'hommes. *La revue d'en face*, 9–10, Spécial hommes, 27–33.

Le Doeuff, M. 1989. Un père incestueux attaque sa fille en diffamation. *Cette violence dont nous ne voulons plus*, 9, October, 6–9.

Le Doeuff, M. 1992. Gens de science: essai sur le déni de mixité. *Nouvelles questions féministes* **13**, 1, 5–37.

Le Doeuff, M. 1993. Le chromosome du crime, à propos de XY. In Riot-Sarcey et al. (1993), 173–83.

Le nouvel observateur. 1991. Ça va, les hommes?: un sondage exclusif Sofrès – *Le nouvel observateur*. 1388, 13–19 June, 4–24.

Le Péron, M. 1978. Priorité aux violées. *Questions féministes*, 3, 83–92.

Lees, S. 1993. Judicial rape. *Women's Studies International Forum* **16**, 1, 11–36.

Les nouvelles féministes, no. 10 SOS femmes-alternatives in Agence femmes information, *Dossier femmes battues*. Paris: Agence femmes information.

Lesselier, C. 1992. Quelles perspectives pour le mouvement féministe? *M*, 53–4, 10–13.

Lesseps, E. de. 1980. Sexisme et racisme. *Questions féministes*, 7, February, 95–102.

Lévy-Willard, A. 1995. L'offensive conservatrice relance sa polémique sur les campus américains. *Le Figaro*, 19 April, 35–6.

Louis, M.-V. 1990a. Violences conjugales. *Les temps modernes*, April, 132–68.

Louis, M.-V. 1990b. Postface. In Association européenne contre les violences faites aux femmes au travail, *De l'abus de pouvoir sexuel: le harcèlement sexuel au travail*. Paris: La Découverte, pp. 231–51.

Louis, M.-V. 1992. Le harcèlement sexuel: quels enjeux pour les féministes? *Chronique féministe*, 44, June–July, 34–6.

Louis, M.-V. 1994. A propos des violences masculines sur les femmes: ébauche d'une analyse féministe du nouveau code pénal français. *Projets féministes*, 3, 40–69.

Louis, M.-V. 1996. Eléments pour une critique des rapports des féministes françaises au pouvoir. In *La démocratie "à la française" ou les femmes indésirables*, E. Viennot (ed.). Paris: CEDREF, 91–107.

Lovenduski, J. & Randall, V. 1993. *Contemporary feminist politics*. Oxford: Oxford University Press.

Macleod, L. 1990. Programmes à l'intention des agresseurs. *Cette violence dont nous ne voulons plus*, June, 37–49 (originally published as Pour de vraies amours . . . Prévenir la violence conjugale, Conseil consultatif canadien sur la situation de la femme, June 1987, 99–109).

Mamou, Y. (14 September 1980). Malaise chez les nouveaux hommes. *Le monde dimanche*, 1–7.

Marks, E. & de Courtivron, I. (eds). 1981. *New French feminisms*. Brighton: Harvester.

Mathieu, N.-C. 1973. Homme-culture et femme-nature? *L'Homme*, 13, 101–13.

Mathieu, N.-C. 1977. Masculinité/fémininité. *Questions féministes*, 1, November, 51–67.

Mathieu, N.-C. (ed.). 1985. *L'arraisonnement des femmes: essais en anthropologie des sexes*. Paris: Editions de l'Ecole des hautes études en sciences sociales, 169–245.

Mathieu, N.-C. 1991. *L'anatomie politique: catégorisations et idéologies du sexe*. Paris: Côté-femmes.

Maugue, A. 1987. *L'identité masculine en crise au tournant du siècle*. Paris: Rivages.

Maynard, M. 1993. Violence towards women. In *Introducing women's studies: feminist theory and practice*, D. Richardson & V. Robinson (eds). Basingstoke and London: Macmillan, 99–122.

Miles, R. 1991. *The rites of man: love, sex and death in the making of the male*. London: Grafton.

Moi, T. 1985. *Sexual/textual politics*. London and New York: Routledge.

Moi, T. 1987. *French feminist thought: a reader*. Oxford: Blackwell.

Mossuz-Lavau, J. 1991. *Les lois de l'amour: les politiques de la sexualité en France (1950–1990)*. Paris: Editions Payot.

Mossuz-Lavau, J. 1995. Les Françaises aux urnes. *Modern and Contemporary France*, NS3, 2, 149–57.

Nouvelles questions féministes. Editorial: "Féminisme: quelles politiques?", 2, October 1981, 3–8.

Pateman, C. 1989. *The disorder of women: democracy, feminism and political theory*. Cambridge: Polity Press.

Peyre, E. & Wiels, J. 1984. Différences biologiques des sexes et identité. In *Femmes, féminisme et recherches*. Toulouse: AFFER, 818–24.

Peyre, E., Wiels, J., Fonton, M. 1991. Sexe biologique et sexe social. In Hurtig et al. (1991), 27–50.

Pichevin, M.-F. 1995. De la discrimination sociale entre les sexes aux automatismes psychologiques: serions-nous tous sexistes? In Ephesia (1995), 457–61.

Picq, F. 1981. Sauve qui peut, le MLF. *La revue d'en face*, 11, 4e trimestre, 11–24.

Picq, F. 1984. Quelques réflexions à propos des études féministes. In *Femmes, féminisme et recherches*. Toulouse: AFFER, 914–19.

Picq, F. 1991. Si c'était à refaire... In *Crises de la société: féminisme et changement*, Groupe d'études féministes de l'Université Paris VII (GEF) (eds). Paris: Revue d'en face/Editions Tierce, 257–65.

Picq, F. 1993. *Libération des femmes: les années-mouvement*. Paris: Seuil.

Picq, F. 1996. L'ANEF, la manifestation du 25 novembre 1995 et après. *Bulletin de l'ANEF*, 20, 1–9.

Planté, C. 1993. Questions de différences. In Riot-Sarcey et al. (1993), 111–31.

Questions féministes. 1977. Variations sur des thèmes communs: une revue théorique féministe radicale, 1, 3–19.

Ramazanoglu, C. 1989. *Feminism and the contradictions of oppression*. London and New York: Routledge.

Ramazanoglu, C. 1992. What can you do with a man?: feminism and the critical appraisal of masculinity. *Women's Studies International Forum* **15**, 3, 339–50.

Rameau, J.-L. 1985. Evolution juridique. *Homophonies: mensuel homosexuel et lesbien du comité d'urgence anti-répression homosexuelle*, 54, April, special issue on "Viol et violences sexuelles", 30–31.

Remy, J., Dagouat, M., de Saint Pern, D. 1993. Qu'est-ce qu'un homme aujourd'hui? *L'express*, 2196, 12 August, 26–39.

Remy, M. 1990. *De l'utopie à l'intégration: histoire des mouvements de femmes*. Paris: L'Harmattan.

Reynaud, E. 1981. *La sainte virilité*. Paris: Syros.

Ridder, G. de. 1982. *Du côté des hommes: à la recherche de nouveaux rapports avec les femmes*. Paris: L'Harmattan.

Righini, M. 1979. Mâles d'aujourd'hui. *Le nouvel observateur*, 26 February, 52–3.

Riot-Sarcey, M., Planté, C., Varikas, E. (eds). 1993. *Féminismes au présent*. Paris: L'Harmattan (Supplement to *Futur/Anterieur*).

Rojtman, S. 1991. Le collectif féministe contre le viol: un lieu d'information, de solidarité et de lutte. *Nouvelles questions féministes*, 16–18, 217–23.

Roper, M. 1990. Introduction: recent books on masculinity. *History Workshop Journal*, 29, 184–7.

Roussier, M.-R. 1980. Malaise masculin face à l'évolution de la femme? *Dialogue: revue trimestrielle éditée par l'association française des centres de consultation conjugale*, 69 le malaise masculin, 7–18.

Sarde, M. 1983. *Regard sur les Françaises, XE–XXE siècle*. Paris: Editions Stock.

Scott, J.W. 1988. Deconstructing equality-versus-difference: or the uses of post-structuralist theory for feminism. *Feminist Studies* **14**, 1, 33–49.

Segal, L. 1990. *Slow motion: changing masculinities, changing men*. London: Virago.

Sert, J. 1989. Un homme sur deux est une femme. In *Mai '68 par eux-mêmes*, Chroniques syndicales, Femmes libres (Radio Libertaire) et le groupe Pierre-Besnard de la Fédération anarchiste (eds). Paris: Editions du monde libertaire.

Sineau, M. 1992. Pouvoir, modernité et monopole masculin de la politique: le cas français. *Nouvelles questions féministes* **13**, 1, 39–61.

Smart, C. 1989. *Feminism and the power of law*. London and New York: Routledge.

Stanley, L. & Wise, S. 1984. Sexual sexual politics: an editorial introduction. *Women's Studies International Forum*, special issue Men and sex, **7**, 1, 1–6.

Sturrock, J. (ed.). 1979. *Structuralism and since*. Oxford: Oxford University Press.

Sullerot, E. 1992. *Quels pères? Quels fils?*. Paris: Fayard.

Thébaud, F. 1992. Introduction. In G. Duby & M. Perrot (eds) *Histoire des femmes en Occident 5: le XXE siècle* (sous la direction de F. Thébaud). Paris: Plon, 13–23.

Théry, I. 1980. Divorce: les femmes et les enfants d'abord. *La revue d'en face*, 8, premier trimestre, 64–7.

Théry, I. 1981. Le mâle de vivre. *La revue d'en face*, 9–10 , Spécial hommes, 43–7.

Trat, J. 1990. Un centre d'acceuil pour hommes violents. *Cahiers du féminisme*, 55, winter, 22–5.

Trat, J. 1992/3. Book review: Elisabeth Badinter, "XY: de l'identité masculine". *Cahiers du féminisme*, 63/4, winter/spring, 52–3.

Trat, J. 1996. L'Alliance des femmes pour la démocratie: une suspicion légitime. *Cahiers du féminisme*, 77, 27–8.

Tristan (Zelensky), A. & de Pisan (Sugier), A. 1977. *Histoires du MLF*. Paris: Calmann-Lévy.

Varikas, E. 1993. Féminisme, modernité, postmodernisme: pour un dialogue des deux côtés de l'océan. In Riot-Sarcey et al. (1993), 59–84.

Varikas, E. 1995. Une représentation en tant que femme?: réflexions critiques sur la demande de la parité des sexes. *Nouvelles questions féministes* **16**, 2, 81–127.

Vinteuil, F. 1985. Ordre et violences. *Cahiers du féminisme*, 83, autumn, 8–10.

Viovy, J.-L. 1985. Nouvel homme et vieux sexisme. *Les temps modernes*, 462, 1330–45.

Visser, W. 1993. Viols contre les femmes de l'"'ex'–Yougoslavie". *Nouvelles Questions Féministes* **14**, 1, 43–76.

Walby, S. 1990. *Theorising patriarchy*. Oxford: Blackwell.

Walby, S. 1993. "Backlash" in historical context. In Kennedy et al. (1993), 79–89.

Waters, M. 1989. Patriarchy and viriarchy: an exploration and reconstruction of concepts of masculine domination. *Sociology*, 23, 193–211.

Weedon, C. 1987. *Feminist practice and poststructuralist theory*. Oxford: Blackwell.

Welzer-Lang, D. 1989. Mythe du viol et viol d'hommes. Cahiers gai-kitsch-camp, *Actes du colloque international: série imaginaires et représentations*. Sorbonne 1 and 2 December, 38–44.

Welzer-Lang, D. 1991. *Les hommes violents*. Paris: Lierre et Coudrier Editeur.

Welzer-Lang, D. 1992a. Les études ou écrits sur les hommes et le masculin en France. In BIEF: *des hommes et du masculin*. CEFUP and Centre de recherches et d'études anthropologiques. Lyons: Presses universitaires de Lyon, 13–23.

Welzer-Lang, D. 1992b. Le double standard asymétrique. In BIEF: *des hommes et du masculin*. CEFUP and Centre de recherches et d'études anthropologiques. Lyons: Presses universitaires de Lyon, 127–46.

Welzer-Lang, D. 1995. Les transgressions sociales des définitions de la masculinité. In Ephesia (1995), 447–52.

Welzer-Lang, D. & Pichevin, M.-F. 1992. Préambule. In BIEF: *des hommes et du masculin*. CEFUP and Centre de recherches et d'études anthropologiques. Lyons: Presses universitaires de Lyon, 7–11.

Wittig, M. 1980. On ne naît pas femme. *Questions féministes*, 8, May, 75–84.

Yale French Studies. 1981. no. 62.

Yuval-Davis, N. 1993. Beyond difference: women and coalition politics. In Kennedy et al. (1993), 3–10.

Zelensky, A. 1984. Projet de recherche sur femme-publicité-sexisme, proposé par une femme de la Ligue du droit des femmes au Ministère des droits de la femme et subventionné par celui-ci. In *Femmes, féminisme et recherches*. Toulouse: AFFER, 595–9.

Zelensky, A. 1988. Crie plus fort, les voisins sont sourd-muets. In *Le féminisme et ses enjeux: vingt-sept femmes parlent*. Centre fédéral FEN. Paris: Edilig, 274–86.

Zelensky, A. & Gaussot, M. 1986. *Le harcèlement sexuel: scandales et réalités*. Paris: Editions Garancières.

Index

abortion 101

academic institutions, feminism in 31, 32, 33, 138

Acker, J. 6–7

activism

  related to male violence 101–7, 110–11, 119, 123–4, 143–4

    incest 112–14, 146

    rape 102–7, 109, 116, 135

  relationship with theory 13–14, 25, 32, 37–8, 99, 100, 119, 135–6

  see also women's movement in France

Alia, J. 53

Alliance des femmes pour la démocratie 36

American feminism, French representations of 12, 39, 40

Anglo-American feminism

  definition of 9

  difference debate in 64, 65–6, 86

  selective representations of French feminism by 1–2, 41–2, 43–4, 139

  theories of gender 6–7, 93–4

    compared with French feminism 96–7, 142–3

  theories of masculinity 4–5, 7, 60–61, 64, 65–6, 93–4

anti-Americanism 12, 39, 40

anti-feminism 38–9, 47–8, 137–8

Appignanesi, L. 40

APRE (Atelier production/reproduction) 90, 92, 93

army, as site of gendered socialization 95

ATP (Actions thématiques programmées) 31, 32, 33

AVFT (Association européenne contre les violences faites aux femmes au travail) 15, 29

backlash, *see* anti-feminism

Badinter, E. 12, 40, 59–60, 128

Banner, L. 52

Bonnin, N. 112

Bulletin d'information des études féminines (BIFE) 15

Cahiers du féminisme 15, 71–2

capitalism, domestic mode of production in 82

Carrigan, T. 94

Casalis, M. 113–14

Castelain-Meunier, C. 55–7, 60, 128

CEFUP (Centre d'études féminines des l'université de Provence) 50

Cette Violence dont nous ne voulons plus 15

Chapman, R. 96–7

child sexual abuse, *see* incest

Cixous, H. 29, 42

Clarac, V. 112

class

  Delphy's work on 82–3

  and male violence 128

class struggle tendency in women's movement 27–8

CNRS (Centre nationale de la recherche scientifique) 31, 32, 33

Collectif féministe contre le viol 109, 112, 114, 124, 125–6, 129

Collin, F. 37, 72, 107, 120, 129

Combes, D. 89

Connell, B. 94
consent to violence 130–31, 145–6

de Lesseps, E. 129–30
de Ridder, G. 47
Delphy, C.
    analysis of women's oppression 79,
        82–4, 86, 87, 92
    on feminism 27, 35, 42, 50
    use of term 'gender' 89–90
Devèze, G. 110, 111, 116, 126, 127
Devreux, A. 89, 92–3, 95
Dhavernas, O. 117
difference, French theorization of 40
difference debate
    in Anglo-American feminism 64, 65–6,
        86
    challenges to 64, 65–6
    and continued research on gender 97–8
    difference and equality positions 63–4
    in French feminism 64–5, 67–9, 86,
        140–41, 143
        campaign for political parity 69–72,
            136–7
    importance for feminism 67
    nature of 12–13, 63–4
    QF position in 80–81
    and theories of masculinity 63, 73–5,
        140–43
domestic mode of production 82
domestic violence 102, 110–11, 130
Duchen, C. 2
Durand-Delvigne, A. 96

equality (sameness) feminism 63–4, 67,
    68, 143

Falconnet, G. 46
fatherhood, and discourses of masculinity
    57–9
Fédération nationale solidarité femmes
    110
feminine, Irigaray's theory of 73, 75, 141
feminism
    anti-feminism 38–9, 47–8, 137–8
    definitions of 8–9
    dialogue and work with men 46, 48–9,
        50, 123, 140

difference debate in, *see* difference
    debate
impact on men and masculinity 52–4,
    55, 56, 58, 60–61, 137–8
men's responses to 45–6, 55, 56
national differences and continuities 9,
    10, 39, 40, 96, 139, 142–3
responses to men's group's critiques of
    masculinity 49–52, 139–40
theories of gender, *see* gender
see also Anglo-American feminism;
    French feminism; materialist
    feminism; radical feminism;
    revolutionary feminism
feminist research
    increasing in 1980s 31–3
    relationship between theory and
        activism 13–14, 25, 32, 37–8, 99,
        100, 119, 135–6
    role in current French feminism 36–7
féministes révolutionnaires 28–9, 106,
    107
Ferrand, M. 89
Finkielkraut, A. 49
Fonton, M. 88–9
Forest, I. 111
Fouque, A. 29, 36, 136, 138–9
Fournier, G. 46–7
Fraser, N. 41
French feminism
    current state of 33–8, 136–7
    definitions and diversity of 9, 11, 42
    difference debate in 64–5, 67–9, 86,
        140–41, 143
        and campaign for political parity
            69–72, 136–7
    impact of poststructuralism on 66
    increasing research in the 1980s 31–3
    materialist feminism 79–80
    origins and development of 2, 26
    publications of 14–16
    reception of feminist theory 138–9
    relationship between theory and
        activism 13–14, 25, 32, 37–8, 99,
        100, 119, 135–6
    representations of 11, 38–41
        in France 42–3
        selective 1–2, 41–2, 43–4, 139

relation to institutions 30, 31–2, 33, 135–6
revolutionary feminism 28–9, 106, 107
study of 1–3
theories of gender compared with Anglo-American feminism 96–7, 142–3
theories of male violence, *see* male violence
theories of masculinity, *see* masculinity
see also women's movement in France

Gaspard, F. 70
Gaussot, M. 120
gay movement, critiques of masculinity by 48
gender
    compared with social relations of sex 89–91
    continued feminist research on 97–8
    feminist theories of 1970s 13, 78–9, 141, 142
        Delphy's work 82–4, 86, 87
        Guillaumin's work 85–6, 87
        Mathieu's work 85–6, 87
        role of *QF* 80–81, 86–7
    feminist theories of the 1980s and 1990s 87–91
    French compared with Anglo-American theories of 96–7, 142–3
    male violence and theories of 119, 121–2, 124, 132–3, 146
    masculinity and theories of 6–7, 92–6
    representations in France of 40
    themes of feminist theories of 92
Grosz, E. 43, 74
Guillaumin, C. 49, 85–6, 87

Halimi, G. 70, 105, 107
Hanmer, J. 4–5
Hearn, J. 6
hegemonic masculinity 7, 94
Hocquenghem, G. 48
human rights 132–3
Hurtig, M. 38

identity politics 64, 68
Iff, S. 51

incest 112–14, 146
institutions
    relation to French feminism 30, 31–2, 33, 135–6
    represented as masculine 97
    state responses to violence 116–18, 144–5
Irigaray, L. 43, 71, 73–5, 141

Jackson, S. 80
Jardine, A. 9
Jenson, J. 2

Kelly, L. 136
Kergoat, D. 90–91
Kristeva, J. 42

Lapierre, C. 50–51
law in France
    feminist involvement with legal reform 117, 145
    relating to incest 113, 114
    relating to rape 103–7, 115, 145
    state responses to violence 116, 117
Le Péron, M. 102–3, 107
Lee, J. 94
Lefaucheur, N. 46
Les petites marguerites 28
Ligue communiste révolutionaire (LCR) 27–8
Ligue du droit des femmes 29, 101
Louis, M.
    on feminism 37, 43
    on violence 111, 116, 120, 122–3, 124, 128, 132

McTighe Musil, C. 66–7
male sexuality
    myth of uncontrollable 102–3, 107, 125
    violence and social construction of 128–30
male violence
    domestic violence 102, 110–11, 130
    feminist action and thought on
        during the 1970s 101–8
        during the 1980s 108–16, 130, 135, 146

feminists' work with men on issues
of 123
identification of characteristics of
violent men 125–7
interest in violent men and causes
119, 120–23, 144, 145
link between theory and practice
100, 119, 135
social explanations 126–30
trends in 99–100, 117–18, 143–4
as form of control 107, 121, 123, 130,
131, 146
incest 112–14, 146
prevention of 119, 123–4
rape, *see* rape
state responses to 116–18, 144–5
survivors of
aid for 101–2, 109, 110, 112, 122,
144
use of term 100
and theories of gender 119, 121–2,
124, 132–3, 146
and theories of masculinity 13, 119,
125–30, 143, 145
women's consent to 130–31, 145–6
marital rape 115–16
masculinity
concepts and discourses of 3–4
and difference 12–13, 63, 73–5,
140–43
feminist interest in 4–5, 6–7, 10
gender/social relations of sex and
92–6
influences on 64, 65–6
links between male violence and 13,
119, 124, 125–30, 143–6
French debate and discourses of
books 12, 54–61, 128
dialogue between feminists and
men's groups 46, 48–9, 50, 140
feminist debates 12–14, 49–52,
139–40
media discourses 12, 52–4
men's groups 4, 11–12, 45–52
social and political climate of
137–8
hegemonic masculinity 7, 94
reality and representation of 97

reproduction of 94–6
study of 3–7
materialist feminism 79–80
Mathieu, N. 84–5, 87, 89, 130–31
Maugue, A. 51
media
discourses of masculinity 12, 52–4
representations of French feminism 38,
39
men, dialogue and work with feminists
46, 48–9, 50, 123, 140
Men Against Sexism conference 48, 51
men's groups
critiques of men and masculinity
45–9
feminist responses to 49–52
dialogue with feminists 46, 48–9, 50
emergence and nature of 11, 45–6
men's studies 4, 5, 49, 52
Miles, R. 61
Ministry for Women's Rights 30, 31–2
Moi, T. 42
Mossuz-Lavau, J. 136
mouvement de libération des femmes
(MLF), *see* women's movement in
France
Mouvement pour la condition masculine
et le soutien de l'enfance (MCM)
47–8
Mouvement pour la condition masculine
et paternelle (MCMP) 48

national connections and differences in
feminism 9, 10, 39, 40, 96, 139,
142–3
naturalism, feminist critiques of 79
new man, discourses of 52, 53, 57
Nouvelles questions féministes (NQF) 15,
29

parenthood, Sullerot's notion of 58–9
Paris féministe 15
particularism 68, 140
patriarchy, feminist theorizations of 6, 7
Peyre, E. 88–9
Pichevin, M. 38, 50, 96
Picq, F. 2–3, 27, 28, 34, 35, 52
political correctness 39

political parity, campaign for 69–72, 136–7

postfeminism 30–31, 38, 39, 54, 137–8

poststructuralism, impact on difference debate 65–6

power, feminist analyses of violence, gender and 132–3

Projets féministes 15

Psychanalyse et politique (Psych et po) 29, 36, 73

public awareness campaigns, relating to violence 102–3, 110–11

Questions féministes (QF) 15, 29, 80–81, 87

radical feminism
and materialism 80
see also revolutionary feminism

Ramazanoglu, C. 5, 8

rape
feminist thought and action of the 1980s on 108–9, 115–16
as form of social control 107, 130
French law relating to 103–7, 115, 145
gender relations and male rape 121–2
gendered perceptions of 129
marital rape 115–16
myths of 102–3, 125–6, 135
public awareness campaigns 102–3

reform, feminist involvement with 35
legal reform 103–7, 117, 145

Refuge Flora Tristan 102

Remy, M. 2–3, 35

research
increasing in the 1980s 31–3
relationship between theory and activism 13–14, 25, 32, 37–8, 99, 100, 119, 135–6
role in current French feminism 36–7

revolutionary feminism 28–9, 106, 107

Reynaud, E. 46–7

RIME (Recherches et interventions masculines) 121

role theory 77–8

Roper, M. 51–2

sameness (equality) feminism 63–4, 67, 68, 143

Sarde, M. 10

Scott, J. 66

Segal, L. 4, 5, 96

sex, theories of social construction of 88–9, 141, 142

sex class, Delphy's concept of 83

sex role theory 77–8

sexage, Guillaumin's concept of 85

sexual harassment 40

Smart, C. 117

social constructionist theories of gender 13, 77–9, 141
in the 1980s and 1990s 87–91
work of *QF* theorists 80–7

social relations of sex
compared with gender 89–91
masculinity and feminist theories of 92–6
themes of feminist theories of 91–2
see also gender

SOS femmes-alternative 101

Stanley, L. 5

state responses to violence 116–18, 144–5

Sullerot, E. 12, 57–9, 60, 128

survivors of violence
aid for 101–2, 109, 110, 112, 122, 144
incest survivors 112, 113, 114
use of term 100

telephone helpines, for survivors of violence 101, 109, 110–11

Thébaud, F. 34

theory, *see* feminist research

Théry, I. 58

Trat, J. 36

universalism 39–40, 68, 69–70, 71, 72, 140, 143

Varikas, E. 43–4, 71

victim, use of term 100

Viennot, E. 70

Vinteuil, F. 130

Viol-femmes-informations 109, 112

violence
  by men, *see* male violence
  forms of 100–1, 132

Welzer-Lang, D. 48, 50, 120–22
Wiels, J. 88–9
Wise, S. 5
Wittig, M. 81, 87
women's movement in France
  activism related to male violence 101,
    119, 123–4, 143–4
    domestic violence 102, 110–11
    incest 112–14, 146
    rape 102–7, 109, 135
  changes during 1978–81 30–33,
    135–6
  current state of French feminism 33–8,
    136–7

mouvement de libération des femmes
    (MLF)
  divisions within 27–9
  Fouque's appropriation of name 29,
    138–9
  origins and development of 26–7
  publications and studies of 2–3, 14–15
  relationship between theory and
    activism 13–14, 25, 32, 37–8, 99,
    100, 119, 135–6
  see also French feminism
women's refuges 102
women's rights 132–3
women's studies courses 32, 33, 138

Yuval-Davis, N. 66

Zelensky, A. 120, 123, 129